MW00438821

Advance Praise

"*This story gives readers hope, encouraging us to look back at childhood and what has gone wrong without our having any say or any control over it. It narrates the painful but rewarding path to let go of anger, resentment, and shame and move forward to become the best version of ourselves. Beautifully shown, we learn that it takes only one person who is supportive, caring, and has a stable presence in the life of a child to help them adapt and overcome childhood trauma. The power of the one adult, the author's great aunt Glad, is the key to a resilience born in John that was tested over and over in his life. His trust in Glad's wisdom on how to recognize and break the chains of generational trauma and destructive patterns seemingly led him on a quest to reduce the impact of generational trauma on future generations and focus on developing capacities to overcome it. This book was hard to put down, and often, I found myself wondering what else would happen to this guy and how a human deals with so much pain and adversity.*

"*His life story is full of male characters, like his father and the Marine Corps, that valued toughness and a certain warrior mindset. Yet, it is his trust in his aunt Glad that impacts him more than any of the cruel or frightening experiences he went through. Her gentle teachings that asked him as a young boy to believe in love, to keep his heart open, and to believe in the power of choice were ultimately the source that made him not only survive but also thrive and build a life worth living.*"

—SYLVIA B., LMHC, trauma and addiction therapist

"Be the Dawn in the Darkness *is a powerfully written journey focused on the multitude of challenges the author faces in coming of age that grippingly captivated and held my attention so deeply that I ended up reading it in one sitting. The author weaves a masterful tapestry of graphic, intense, and striking words and imagery that effectively pull us, the reader, into his story line, where we feel ourselves present in each situation, wondering how we will navigate and often survive the harsh realities that he so vividly walks us through, page by page. While the author reveals the often forceful and sometimes brutal moments he faces, he continually reveals and weaves in the underlying themes of love, caring, generosity, and gratitude that keep us, and him, moving forward in his journey through the varieties of human experience that form the tapestry of his life.* Be the Dawn in the Darkness *is a potent example of the hero's journey that he, you, and I are all on. The author presents us with a book that you won't forget, a must-read that will help you discover and recover, as he did, the love and tender heart that we all must nourish as we navigate our own hero's journey."*

—RICHARD MILLER, PhD, Founder of iRest Institute, author of *iRest Meditation: Restorative Practices for Health, Resiliency, and Well-Being* and *Awakening to Your Essential Nature*

"*I am amazed by how profound and beautiful this story of personal growth is. You certainly do not have to experience the type of trauma the author has had to endure to respect the sense of this work. Every human has their own cross to bear and story to live, but I am kindly reminded to start chipping away at my own Michael. I love this book and will treasure the gentle nudge it has given me."*

—JUDY M.

"Be the Dawn in the Darkness *was like reading a mirror image of my life in many ways. I rarely read a book cover to cover, but I could not put this book down. Not only was it relatable to my own personal experiences from my journey, but it was inspiring to see someone else with similar struggles. As a US Army Veteran of the Iraq and Afghanistan conflicts struggling with PTSD, anxiety, and depression, I had a hard time adjusting to life as a civilian and feeling anger and resentment toward the world. My relationship with my significant other wasn't where it needed to be, and I felt a sense of chronic dissatisfaction when one loses their sense of purpose. The chapters of this book helped me get back on my path and helped heal old unaddressed wounds by looking deep into myself and picking myself up. As a result, I can better connect with my partner and our son. The character Glad was the guardian angel many have in their lives that many may overlook, but reading this book helped me realize the people that impacted my life and appreciate them better. Like my grandfather teaching and mentoring me through life's struggles and helping set a tone for the path I would later follow,* Be the Dawn in the Darkness *enabled me to see my struggles and understand them better. This work has truly helped me to be a better father and a better person."*

—JARED, OEF/OIF US Army Combat Veteran

"Be the Dawn in the Darkness *speaks to anyone who has been through trauma in their life. The story takes the reader through the accumulation of trauma, adapting to life with trauma, and ultimately transcending the trauma through acceptance and transcendence. It is a powerful journey that sucks the reader in. I served in the military and had an extremely difficult transition out of the service. I shudder to think how my life would have turned out had it not been for some well-placed messengers and matriarchal/patriarchal guides who helped me along the way. The insights and lessons learned throughout this book have been instrumental in my life, and my family has benefited from a more present father/husband. I am the man I am today because of the personal work I have done. I encourage anyone who has experienced trauma to read this book and pass along to you the most powerful message I took away from this work for creating personal transformation in my life: progress, not perfection."*

—DENNIS T., OEF/OIF US Army Combat Veteran

"Be the Dawn in the Darkness *by J.H. Parker is an immersive page-turner, captivating until the last page and transcending genres. Part autobiography, part personal growth guide, and part inspirational literature, this narrative has universal appeal. Despite its size, it is a quick read, difficult to put down, and easily revisited again and again. Parker's story, a hero's journey from a scared young boy to actualization, is filled with fascinating heroes and villains, each of whom informs Parker's journey. Characters such as the warm, wise, and worldly female war correspondent, sadistic drill sergeants, as well as a myriad of healers impart wisdom and tools along his path to healing. The author shares intimate details of a troubled upbringing and the human 'guideposts' and experiences encountered along the way that led him through the darkness. Who will this book speak to? Certainly, anyone who appreciates a deeply personal autobiography, but more importantly, those of us on our own personal journeys of healing and recovery, will find solace and strength in this tome. I highly recommend this easily read and deeply meaningful book."*

—THOMAS JAMES HUNT, MD

"*This book is an important journey seen through the eyes of and lived by J.H. Parker. It is powerful, purposeful, and enlightening. The cycle of abuse devastates many people daily, and they see no way through it. By sharing his vulnerability and perseverance, the author shows there is hope because of the indomitable strength that lies within each of us and that God is love. It is an insightful and unique journey through the challenges life throws at all of us every day. A great read and a powerful message of self-learning and self-understanding. Well done.* Semper Fidelis!"

—CHRIS LEIGHTY

"*This is a gripping, powerful, heartbreaking, brutal, and funny story. It pulls you in and takes you on a journey of courage and vulnerability. It is amazing to see how the human spirit can experience so much trauma and abuse yet have the ability to survive, transform, and heal. It also demonstrates how the smallest acts of love and kindness can affect and change you forever.*

"I was deeply moved and inspired by how committed John is to letting go of his past and moving forward to be a balanced, kind, and loving human. This is a book I will read again and again."

—LESLIE MCKENNA

"This book rang close to home for me. It brought back a flood of buried memories that were tough to handle but also created a sense of peace and healing. Aunt Gladys is an angel whose influence brought light to a dark time and provided inspiration and direction. The life experiences of the boy becoming a man, as told by the author, are challenging, scary, and also entertaining. The drive to find inner peace and love, heal old wounds, and break the pattern of violence is admirable and relatable. Essential reading for anyone on their journey to self-discovery."

—RICK M.

"Because of the severity of the author's destructive upbringing and how he has risen above that upbringing, this story will appeal to many audiences. He was emotionally and physically abused by his father, not well protected by his mother, and bullied in the rough neighborhood he grew up in. He did not do well in school due to significant learning deficits but managed to enlist in the US Marine Corps. There he began to excel, but he nearly got discharged for misbehavior. His course in life begins to change in the Marine Corps because he is free of his father and his neighborhood. But many years of ongoing effort are needed before he feels full confidence in himself, how he wants to live, and who he is meant to be. Especially remarkable is his ability to gain and benefit from the support of those around him. As a child, he entered a profound relationship with an aunt. That relationship matured over decades. Several of his Marine Corps

leaders guided and watched out for him. In midlife, he started finding teachers of all types. They provided further insight, helping him grow to the emotional stature to live a healthy and normal life. This work is well worth reading by anyone interested in personal development. Parker's insights about how to view oneself, how to face seemingly insurmountable challenges, and how to live according to one's principles despite all the events that are 'not supposed to happen' are worth reading on their own merits. But his story is also written as a thriller! We know he turned out well in the end, but how does he overcome these potentially life-threatening experiences and gain the wisdom we now see manifested? He reveals his up-and-down, tumultuous process, providing further insight about how to throw oneself into life. If you are focused on becoming who you are meant to be, there is no better place to start than this book."

—TOM HORVATH, PhD, ABPP clinical psychologist, author of *Sex, Drugs, Gambling, Chocolate: A Workbook for Overcoming Addictions*, Co-founder of SMART Recovery

BE THE DAWN IN THE DARKNESS

The Relentless Pursuit of Becoming
Who We Are Meant To Be

J.H. PARKER

HARVESTING
WISDOM

Hardcover ISBN: 978-1-5445-3648-4
Paperback ISBN: 978-1-5445-3646-0
Ebook ISBN: 978-1-5445-3647-7
Audiobook ISBN: 978-1-5445-3965-2

*"The two most important days of your life
are when you are born, and when you find out why."*

—MARK TWAIN

*In childhood, it takes only a single person of
healthy character to influence our self-concepts and
nurture the possibilities of who we may become.
This book is dedicated to one such matriarch and mentor,*

Gladys.

*I pen this work as a message of hope
with no attachment to who finds it.
But secretly,
I hope this finds
you.*

Contents

Introduction

Michelangelo's Statue of David, Completed in 1504, Florence, Italy

Each year of my early childhood, I received three books for Christmas from my great-aunt Gladys. They were timeless chronicles of great adventures, like *Gulliver's Travels*, *The Iliad*, *The Trojan Horse*, and stories of exceptional leaders, artists, and sculptors from ancient times. Before I could read, I studied and dreamt about the powerful illustrations on their pages.

One Christmas, when I was seven, I found a handwritten note tucked into the pages of one of the books about Michelangelo. At the time, I didn't realize my hero's journey had already begun and that Glad was provisioning me for the odyssey that lay ahead.

Folded into a page next to an illustration of Michelangelo's Statue of David, her note read:

Remember the story of the sculpting of David;
through your most challenging experiences
you must chip away all that is not you
to discover your true self and your life's purpose.

David is a biblical hero who slew Goliath with a rock and sling. In 1464, artist Agostino was commissioned to create a statue of David from a massive block of Carrara marble. After beginning the project, Agostino discovered a significant crack in the stone and abandoned the endeavor. Several other master sculptors turned down the commission, as they, too, considered the crack a fatal flaw. As a result, the block of marble sat unfinished and exposed to the elements for decades.

But in 1501, a young Michelangelo saw what others could not. He viewed the stone's flaws as strengths and could clearly see David trapped within the marble and began the work of freeing him.

In 1504, when the statue was unveiled, Michelangelo was asked how he was able to create such a beautiful likeness of David.

His answer:

"David was always there in the marble;
I just chipped away everything that was not David."

The story of Michelangelo's David has stayed with me, forever etched into my mind, as has Aunt Gladys's gentle instruction. My marble was also weathered and imperfect. I have endured a life of trauma, depression, anxiety, grief, and loss. Some cracks ran so deep that they threatened everything.

"I must chip away all that is not me."

Like Michelangelo, I sought the story within the stone and sculpted until I found my true self and purpose. When I look back now, I see that the cracks and flaws of my past have fallen away, revealing wholeness, fulfillment, and joy.

CHAPTER 1

Gladys

In the early years of my childhood, my great-aunt Gladys would stay with our family for a month or so during the holidays to escape the harsh Canadian winters of Ottawa.

"Glad," as we affectionately called her, is the voice of wisdom I carry with me to this day. Of all the women in human history, she was my heroine. Now, she is the angel on my shoulder.

Glad and I shared a secret, and my sister and brother never caught on. Each morning just before dawn, I would sneak out of my room to the kitchen while she made her breakfast. I enjoyed her company and treasured this special time together. I remember one morning, at the first glimpse of the horizon's orange blush, Glad pointed and said, "You see, John. There it is; the dawn of a new day is being borne from the darkness. In my life, there have been times when I was not sure if I would survive the night. The only thing that gave me a hint of hope was the first glow of dawn."

I always found the way she spoke to be so interesting. It was different. She would often start or end her comments by saying my name. It was her way of getting me to look straight at her, though she always had my undivided attention whenever she spoke.

These were formative mornings during my early and impressionable years. They were my escape and my private time to be in Glad's angelic presence. I soaked up her love and wisdom like a flower responding to water and sunlight. Little did I know, she was equipping me for a great journey ahead, one that would last my entire lifetime.

Glad's life was full of perilous experiences. Many of the stories she shared with me in my early years I later read as historical facts captured in her book, *One Woman's War*. Many years later, I was even more astonished to see her book brought to life when she was depicted in a documentary, *Eyewitness to War*.

Glad had been a journalist during the time building up to the Nazi invasion of Europe and throughout World War II. During the rise of fascism and the occupation of Paris, Glad was Canada's only war correspondent stationed in France and England. For her journalism, support of the Free French, and steadfast reporting of Canada's war efforts, Glad was awarded a Legion of Honor medal by the French government. This was bestowed upon her a few decades after the end of the war.

I would often ask to see her medal, and she would let me hold the jewel box as we talked. It was beautiful lying against the black velvet cushion—gold, white, and green with a dark red ribbon—and when I held it in my hand, I was there, living her stories. It was magical.

I remember how, in fifth grade, I brought her to visit my class as a special guest. She showed my classmates her medal and talked about having the courage to follow our dreams, doing our part to make peace in the world, and why we should not bow down to bullies.

I had never seen our class so enthralled. Even the most rambunctious students sat still and silent, transfixed, with their mouths open and amazed. Glad allowed each of my classmates to hold the open jewel box containing her medal, and we passed it around the classroom with reverence as she spoke.

When she finished her talk, the teacher dismissed the class for recess. All of the boys immediately ran out to play, but nearly all the girls stayed to hear more and ask her questions. The girls remained with Glad all through recess until the teacher called the class to begin.

I beamed with pride and made a few new friends that day, mostly girls.

Coffee, Cream, and Maple Syrup

It had been a year since Glad's first visit. My six-year-old self agonized in anticipation of her arrival, counting down the final weeks, days, hours, and minutes before her return.

When the day finally came, I eagerly awoke at dawn and raced to the kitchen to help Glad prepare her breakfast, a ritual of cheddar cheese, thick-cut bacon, toast, and coffee. As she carried her tray of food, I glanced over at my father and back to Glad.

"Can I have a taste of your coffee?" I asked.

"Of course, John. I'll teach you how to have a proper tasting of coffee," she said, as she took another cup out of the cupboard. She poured it half full, added some cream, and smiled as she looked down. "Here's something we Canadians love in our tea and coffee: maple syrup." She stirred in a few drops while placing the cup on our food tray.

We settled into the living room. Glad occupied her favorite chair, a high-back Victorian with gold-stitched material. There were carved designs on the ends of the arms, and its dark, wooden legs curved into clawed feet. She looked so regal, like a queen presiding over her court. I positioned myself on a pillow at her feet in order to be close to her. All was right with the world whenever I was in her presence.

"May I show you how to appreciate coffee, John?" Glad asked.

"Sure," I replied, eager to learn.

She raised her cup and shared, "Before you take a sip, you must take in the aroma and the qualities of the coffee." She put her cup to her nose, closed her eyes, and began a long, slow inhale. She tilted her head back with a joyous smile as she paused, then she let out a long, luxurious sigh.

"Heaven," she said. She slowly opened her eyes and looked upward. "John, there is a god, and God must love coffee. It's as if He created this magical potion just for me."

She gazed down at me again. "The smell and taste of coffee has been my faithful friend and comforted me through the worst of times. Now, it's your turn." She gestured for me to put my cup to my nose. "Inhale slowly and deeply through your nose, allowing your senses to fill with the aroma and all of its qualities. Feel the warmth of the vapors filling your nose and lungs, then pause to take it all in. That's right. Good job, John. And now slowly exhale and relax."

She paused and asked gently, "What are you experiencing?"

I tilted my head back and closed my eyes. "I smell maple syrup."

"Good. What else are you smelling and experiencing?"

"Creamy…nutty…yummy," I said with a giggle.

"Now, open your eyes, and take a sip."

I smiled and let out a long "Mmmm" as we savored the moment together.

"And what are you experiencing now?" she asked, beaming. The promising light of morning spilled into our living room as if her smile alone had summoned it.

"Yum," I said, and then suddenly, "*Happy*. It tastes happy."

Glad chuckled. "You see, God must have created coffee to make us happy."

She handed me a piece of cheese and bacon and said, "Now, take another sip and savor it for a few seconds, and then take a bite of each and chew slowly. Take in all of the flavors."

I did as she directed and moaned as my senses filled with comfort and pleasure.

We sat almost in total silence, sipping and nibbling as we enjoyed our breakfast, chuckling and savoring the moment.

This was, by far, my fondest experience with Glad.

If God Is Love, Why Is This Happening to Me?

The second morning of Glad's visit, I woke to the smell of bacon, and a smile came over me, inside and out.

Glad! I quietly climbed down my bunk bed's ladder, tiptoeing to the door so as not to wake my brother.

As I approached the curtain separating the living room from the dining room and kitchen, I could hear Glad and my father having a conversation. I waited nervously for a lull between words and slipped through the curtain to find her holding her breakfast tray. My father was sitting at the kitchen table reading the newspaper.

"Hi, Aunt Glad," I said excitedly.

"Oh! Hello, John. How are you this morning?" she asked in her usual cheery way.

"I'm fine," I replied.

"Come with me. I was just going to the living room to have my breakfast."

I nodded as she passed by me and through the curtain. My father sent me a stern look of disapproval as I followed her; I think he was annoyed I had taken her attention off of him.

Glad took her seat on her throne, the high-backed Victorian chair, and again, I sat at her feet—her faithful subject.

Glad was beautiful and regal. She dressed every day as if she were preparing to meet foreign dignitaries at the French Embassy in Ottawa or to meet them for lunch at the Chateau Laurier Hotel.

I think what I enjoyed most about Glad was that she always saw the good within me. She convinced me early on that I would make something extraordinary of my life. She was the only person in my childhood who sat with me and asked how I was doing and feeling. I liked myself best when I was with her.

The quests and noble deeds that *I* fantasized about were all in my head, but *hers* were real. Glad's life had been full of danger. Once again, I would ask to see her medal, and she would let me hold the jewel box as we talked. I was there, living her stories.

I wanted to dive into her stories partially because I was suffering so badly in mine. Aside from spending time with my grandparents, the relief Glad's annual visits provided me were some of the only times of relative safety I can recall of my childhood years. My father's presence was terrifying, but he would not dare show his violent temper in the slightest degree around Aunt Glad.

Before Glad's arrival each year, my father would march my sister, brother, and me into the hallway and pin us against the wall at attention. He'd get down on one knee to tell us how we would be and act with Glad during her visit. As he spoke, he looked us in the eyes. The threat promised there punctuated his words, and they were delivered in a deep and terrifying tone. He would make a fist with his middle finger's knuckle sticking out to emphasize his point. As he spoke, he jabbed his protruding knuckle into our chests. You could hear a painful *thump* each time he poked us.

"Keep your mouths shut! Don't you say a *thing* to Gladys about what happens in our home. We don't talk about anything that happens here."

The pressure he applied to our chests sent us sliding down the wall to the floor, screaming in agony. Undeterred, he'd stand us back up and continue his unrelenting abuse.

"If I hear even a *whisper* to Glad about me, you will pay. I promise you this." He took a long, dangerous pause and scanned our terrified eyes. "Do you read me?"

"Yes, sir," we replied, trembling.

And from the moment Glad arrived at the airport, we felt the menacing presence of his surveillance.

To Glad, my father acted gallant and charming. To us, he was a violent prison guard, and we were frightened, helpless inmates. Whenever we were sitting with Glad in the living room, he would smile and give her wonderful greetings and compliments. He also made a habit of settling in at the kitchen table. It was behind a curtain he'd put up as a makeshift separator. The fabric provided a false sense that our conversations with Glad were private.

Every few minutes, he would ruffle his newspaper unnecessarily or smack his coffee cup on the saucer to send my siblings and me the unspoken threat that he could hear even a whisper.

One morning, Glad settled into her throne and said, "I have something to tell you, John, and I want you to listen closely." Her tone was wise and serious. "In my early years, religion was very confusing to me because I just couldn't understand why there were so many."

I stared at her, listening attentively.

Glad continued, "My advice to you is simple. If you find a faith that you want to devote yourself to, then do so, but *do not judge* or build barriers in your heart toward other faiths. Wars have been fought since the beginning of religion itself because of these barriers. I have made the choice to not be bound by the religious doctrine of any faith. Instead, I am a spiritual person who believes there is a universal force for good beyond our understanding. I am deeply spiritual and have found peace and forgiveness in my heart while appreciating and accepting people of all faiths."

My father cleared his throat from the kitchen, sending a spike of anxiety all the way through me. However, Aunt Glad registered no interruption.

"There is a universal truth I have discovered that I believe will serve you, John. Throughout my lifetime, I have learned many things about most of the world's great religions and found one absolute truth in all of them. It made all the difference to me. At the heart of all religious teachings throughout human history, there is a goodness and a truth that runs like a thread between them: God is love."

She smiled lovingly as she looked into my eyes. "Do you understand what I am saying, John?"

I paused and thought for a moment. "I think so," I responded, but I'm sure she noticed me squirm as my eyes darted toward my father behind the curtain.

"God is love?" I repeated, confused. Inside, my stomach went into a knot. I wanted to scream, *No!* The introduction of her worldview was at odds with my experiences and sent my mind racing with anxiety. *No, this isn't true!* I screamed inside. What I couldn't say out loud was, "You can't be right. This isn't real; I'm frightened all the time. Why does my father hurt us?" I was not permitted to give away any sign of trouble.

She patiently gazed at me, her face alight with a nurturing smile. Glad lived by her principles, and she was the embodiment of love.

This has to be true, replaced my previous internal dialogue and echoed in my mind. Still, I struggled to grasp the important message she was giving me. It was like an unsolvable riddle.

But I couldn't see it because I couldn't believe it. Outside of Glad's presence, my fear was too raw and too real to feel anything but sadness and suffering.

Puzzled, I silently stared off into space, pondering her question as she continued to nibble on her food. She shared some with me. It was incredibly delicious; the bacon and cheddar anchored me forever in gratitude for the safety and wisdom she provided.

My pain, suffering, and fear were like a three-headed dragon, standing sentinel and in direct opposition to my ability to know and believe this truth Aunt Glad wanted me to understand.

If God is love, why are these bad things happening to me? I wanted to scream the question out loud to Glad, but when a look of empathy came over my great-aunt's face, I realized we *both* felt my captor's silent and ominous presence.

Concerned, Glad put her hand on my shoulder, and she sent me a half-smile of encouragement.

I slumped and rested my head on her knee. I felt a deep sense of hopelessness as I ruminated, *If God is love, why is this happening to me?*

Glad, sensing my despair, seized the moment and asked, "John, would you get my coat and walk me to the park?"

That perked me up right away. "Sure!" I leapt to my feet in excitement, my focus shifted to our magical walks. I darted down the hallway to get changed, grabbing her coat as I returned to her. I didn't have to ask the monster for permission because if Glad wanted something, she didn't ask—she just nicely shared what she was going to do.

"We will be back in a while," she declared to my father as we departed through the door. A rustling of his newspaper was his only response.

The air outside was cold but refreshing. Walking with Great-Aunt Glad always presented me with an opportunity to show her I was a gentleman. My grandmother had taught me to take her by the arm and escort her on the left. In the old days—before paved streets, she would remind me—men always walked on the left side of a woman just in case a car would come by, threatening to splash water and mud.

When we rounded the corner from our home, Glad said, "John, I can see you're struggling with what I said—God is love—but don't worry. You will find this truth for yourself. I promise you this."

It was nice strolling with Glad. She walked as if she didn't have a care in the world. Even the bullies who routinely picked on me didn't dare say or do anything when they walked by or watched us from across the street. Being in Glad's presence was like having a force field of peace and tranquility.

As we walked, she shared, "John, I know it is difficult for you to speak freely when we are around your father; I can sense your fear of him. But these moments alone together, this is our time, and you must learn to trust that I am here to listen and to help you whenever I can."

We arrived at the park and found a bench in the sunlight for Glad to rest on. The wooden slats were ice cold at first. It was crisp but not freezing, and the sunshine was starting to warm the air, so it was bearable. As we sat for a few moments, I could tell she was studying me.

"What's on your mind, John?" she asked. "I can tell you have been deep in thought since breakfast."

"I can't talk about anything," I said cautiously.

"What do you mean? Talk about what? Did your father tell you this?"

"I can't talk about anything," I grumbled. Just thinking about my father was enough to make me anxious.

"I see," she replied slowly. "Anything? Well, we've talked about a lot of things since I arrived. What about what we talked about this morning? Your father was close by and didn't seem to mind."

I shook my head. "That's different."

"So, we can talk about some things but not other things. Is that what you mean?"

I let out a sigh of relief. "Yes, I guess so." That made sense to me.

"Alright then, let's continue with *God is love*. Earlier, you became very quiet for a long while. You seemed deep in thought. Troubled." She paused, but I remained silent. Eventually, she asked, "How did you feel?"

I couldn't find the words.

"It's alright, John. Just tell me what you think you can share. I promise this is just between us."

I wanted to trust Glad, but my father's terrifying warning—*Not a whisper to Glad, do you hear me?*—was still fresh in my mind. Finally, I said, "When you say, 'God is love,' I believe you." I looked up at the trees and the blue sky. "It must be true…but not for me. I'm sad and scared all the time."

Glad studied me and nodded. "These are certainly mysteries I've often wondered about, too," she answered. "Let's start with the feeling of love. Love is something you feel when you care deeply for someone. Do you care deeply for someone, John?"

"You…and my mom, I guess," I replied.

"Good. Does it make you happy to know we are safe and cared for?"

"Yes," I said.

"Is there anyone else you love?"

"Our cat, Tiny. She lies on my chest and purrs and squeezes her paws to wake me up every morning for school."

Glad chuckled. "Wonderful. See, you do understand love. Well, John, I'm sorry you feel sad and afraid."

"I'm afraid all the time," I lamented. "If God is love, why am I afraid all the time?"

"I have been afraid most all of my life," she said softly.

I gaped at her. "*You? Afraid?*" I replied, astonished.

"Yes. You see, we have more in common than you think. When I was a young girl, my father passed away. My mother had to go to nursing school far away to find a way to support your grandfather and me, so I was sent to live with relatives for many years. I was not much older than you, and I didn't know them very well. I was terrified I wouldn't fit in. And when I was in France during the war,

I spent a good part of my time being afraid of not having enough food, of freezing, or afraid of being captured or killed—these were very real dangers."

I was captivated by the thought of her being in danger. She was the bravest and most amazing person I knew.

She continued, "But if all I had done was focus on my fear, I would not have been able to do anything in my life; nothing would have ever changed for me, and I may not have survived. It is what we choose to do with our fear that matters most, John. Instead of being frozen in my fear, I was able to find a purpose greater than myself. That gave me the courage to do things I never thought possible. Finding courage is about finding something that means more to you than what you fear. Whenever you find yourself feeling fear, you must find your courage and act—even if that means simply taking one more step, one foot in front of the other. Sometimes, the courage to continue is all you have."

Several birds gathered near our feet, looking for food. Glad was focused on me, though, and she added, "My purpose, as I discovered, was to seek the truth and share what I found with others through my writing. For me, this meant going places all over the world to discover what was true and important that needed to be shared, and then I would write about it. My writing has provided my purpose, and it has carried me through my darkest and most fearful and even heartbreaking moments. Have you discovered your purpose yet, John?"

"No, not yet." I watched the birds hop around our shoes. "I think I'm too young to have a purpose."

"You're probably right," she agreed. "Now is the time to be a young boy. These are some big thoughts for you at your age, but remember this: you are never too young to dream big dreams and to have courage to follow them—no matter *what* your life feels like right now. You have lots of courage inside of you, and I know this is true already, John."

For the life of me, I couldn't see how she knew that. "How?" I asked.

"When you talk or think about your father," she explained, "you get very quiet and a little stubborn. You also frown a bit. I'll bet you imagine that, someday, you will be a grown-up and free from him. Do you ever think this?"

"Yes, a lot," I agreed.

Glad nodded. "It seems far away right now, but before you know it, you'll be a man, and you will live your own life. I want you to put your hand over your heart and promise me you'll always remember what I'm about to tell you. Can you do this, John?"

My heart swelled at the opportunity to do something for Glad. I placed my hand on my heart. "I promise," I vowed.

"Someday, you will have children, and you'll be a father. But *you* can choose to be a loving and gentle father. You will have the wisdom to know how afraid a little boy can be of his father. You will remember growing up in fear, you will remember how difficult this is for a child, and that wisdom will serve you. You have the power to choose to be a kinder, gentler father—this is your power, *the power to choose how you will be different.* You have goodness in your heart. I see who you really are, deep down. You are playful and gentle, and part of you is also afraid of your father. Your fear is not who you are, John. Always, always, remember that. *You are not your fear.* We feel fear, but this must never be confused with who we *are* deep down. Don't reproduce how your father has made you feel with your own children someday."

She paused, finally giving the birds at our feet a glance before returning her attention to me. "Here is the promise I want you to keep: promise you will be a kind, gentle, and loving father to your children. Promise you will never strike your children in anger, and you will never cause your children to live in fear of you. You have the power to see and understand how your father raised you and how your grandfather raised your father."

She had my full and undivided attention. Glad put her hand on her chest, smiled, and gazed into my eyes. "Will you promise me this?"

It felt as though I had been knighted by the queen and entrusted to safeguard an extraordinary treasure. I knew she could see the future.

"I promise," I responded, nodding.

My great-aunt glowed with approval. "John, this is our sacred promise to each other. You may choose to share this with your father someday, but not until you are fully grown. For now, you must hold this promise between us. Can you promise me this as well?"

"Yes, Glad."

"Someday, you will pass this promise on to your children, and the cycle of violence of your father—and his father before him—will be broken. And this, John, is the secret to creating your future. You hold the power to choose how you will live your life, regardless of the fear you have experienced in these early years."

For the first time I could recall, I felt calm and still. I had no fear and no anxiety.

"So, what do you see when you think about being a grown-up?" she asked.

I replied excitedly, "Someday, I will leave home on a great adventure, and all of this will go away."

"That will require a lot of courage," she responded. "As I said, I think you possess a great deal of courage inside of you already. What do you think about this?"

I stared back, puzzled. "Courage? You mean like the lion in *The Wizard of Oz*?"

Glad chuckled. "Exactly, just like the lion."

I thought about it for a moment. "I don't know," I responded.

"Would you like me to show you how to find your courage, John? Just like the lion in *The Wizard of Oz*?"

Astonished, I broke into a grin. "You can do that?"

"Absolutely," she replied. "Let me show you. Have you ever had an experience when you felt strong or courageous?"

I thought for a moment, tracing the lines of the wooden bench with my finger. "No."

"Surely, there must be something you've done or accomplished where you felt strength or courage?"

A picture popped into my head. "The circus!" I shouted. Some of the birds squawked in protest, startled. "I got to ride in the

Ringling Brothers Circus parade for winning a drawing contest on *The Wallace and Ladmo Show*."

"Oh, that sounds exciting," she told me. "Tell me more about that!"

"My father helped me draw a tiger with a top hat, and I colored it all in. I got to go on *The Wallace and Ladmo* kids show and got a bunch of prizes and a Ladmo bag of toys. But the best part was I got to ride in the big circus wagon in the parade at the start of the show. We were all clapping, and I waved at the people sitting down."

Glad smiled. "That's amazing, John, and a very important example of when you weren't afraid. You stepped into your courage. It took a lot to do that, don't you think?"

"It did, and I wasn't afraid," I said proudly, remembering how powerful I felt standing and waving to the crowd.

"Would you like to play a game with me?" Glad asked.

"Sure!"

"We're going to play a game where you imagine you can go back to that powerful experience you had in the circus wagon. Close your eyes and stand up. Imagine you are back in that powerful moment right now and stand with your hands up, waving, just the way you did, John."

I hopped off the bench, sending the birds flapping away. I stood tall, waving my hands wildly over my head.

"Try to see the people waving and smiling at you. Hear the sounds again, the ones you remember, just exactly the way it happened at the circus. Now, John, what are you experiencing?"

I felt elation swelling in my chest. I excitedly replied, "Power."

"Good, John. Now open your eyes."

I opened my eyes to see Glad's angelic face smiling back at me. "You see, this is the game I wanted to play with you. Even though you weren't really back in the circus parade, you are able to experience being powerful right now. You were here, but your imagination was there, making you feel powerful right now. Is this true for you?"

"Wow," I said, surprised. "It works! I am!"

"You have just learned a little magic for when you need to find courage or power. Now, let's do it again. Close your eyes, but don't stand up. Just imagine you are standing and waving at the crowd, seeing what you were seeing, hearing what you were hearing, and feeling what you were feeling. Go back, and float back into yourself and into that moment. Imagine all the powerful feelings at that moment. What are you experiencing right now, John?"

Just as before, a joyous sensation bloomed within me. "I feel powerful! Wow!" I said in amazement.

"That's right. You can feel powerful and courageous just by imagining or remembering a moment when you felt powerful, like when you were in the circus parade. This is important, John. Whenever you need to find your courage, it is right *here*." She placed one hand over my heart and the other cradled the side of my face. "It's right here, deep inside of you already, waiting to come to your aid. And it can happen in a blink of an eye if you simply use your imagination. As you grow throughout your life, you will collect more powerful and courageous memories that will come to your aid. How are you feeling right now, John?"

"Powerful...and hungry," I added with a grin.

"Good, John. Well done! You are a very fast learner," she praised me with a smile. Then, "An Army travels on its stomach. Let's go get something to eat."

CHAPTER 2

The Roots of Suffering

My early years read like the warning sign on the edge of the haunted forest in *The Wizard of Oz*: "I'd turn back if I were you."

My earliest childhood memory was seared into my being around age five. I was playing with my mother in my room, and the safety of the moment felt impenetrable. Together, we would escape into a magical world of play and adventures. She loved stories about heroes and knights and would tell me about them while showing me illustrations, pictures, and movies. I can see this is where my love for film and art took root. Her curious nature cultivated my imagination.

My mother was tall, blond, and slender. She was good-natured and friendly with a slightly crooked smile. I think because of her natural nervousness—and the Parkinson's that later developed—she didn't have many close friends.

As we were playing and laughing, suddenly, there came a loud, explosive voice from the other side of my bedroom door—it was my father. As his voice came closer, my mother's sweet smile evaporated. Her hand began to tremble as she slowly stood and turned toward the door. Though she glanced back at me with a reassuring smile, I will never forget the way fearful tears flooded her eyes and made them shine.

My father was a monster, and we were terrified of him. He was heavyset, with tattoos up and down both arms, and his face held a mean, scowling look most of the time. As a family, we were especially afraid of him when he was drunk—a nightly occurrence my mother, brother, sister, and I collectively dreaded.

He tore the door open, slamming it into the wall as he stormed into the room. His eyes were big, and his face was full of rage. His teeth were clenched in a drunken fury, and he clawed for my mother with his large hands.

Once he got her, he threw her against the wall, clutching her throat and pinning her in the corner. I could see her toes barely touching the ground as she frantically tried to peel away his fingers. She screamed and squirmed in desperation, but there was no escaping his wrath. He repeatedly jabbed her in the chest with his vicious finger as he snarled hateful threats in her ear.

I couldn't protect her. At five years old, this marked the first time I can recall feeling a deep sense of rage welling up within me. My hands tightened into fists as I screamed, "No!"

Undeterred, my father squeezed my mother's neck and growled more in her ear, lifting her entirely off the ground. Her feet dangled as she gasped and gurgled, begging him to stop as her face turned purple and red.

"No!" I screamed again, louder, at the monster. This time, he turned to look at me. He lowered my mother's feet to the floor as amusement twisted its way across his face. He raised an eyebrow at me and half-smiled.

He released my mother's throat. She slid down the wall and landed on the floor, then curled into a ball, helpless and sobbing. I was relieved my father had finally let her go, but now he staggered toward me. The monster knelt next to my bed, amused by my protective nature. His breath stank, and his voice grew perplexingly soft and quiet. It felt soothing but couldn't penetrate the confusion and terror pent up inside of me.

I didn't know what he was thinking, but at least he had stopped hurting my mother. He smiled even bigger and slurred, "Look, honey. Look at his little fists. He's a little fighter." My father laughed as he picked me up. Then, he clenched his fist in front of my face with the proud acknowledgment of a Spartan warrior. Terrified,

I looked over at my mother and saw her teary face. She was still reeling from panic. Fighting for composure, she drew herself up from the floor and came closer to me, smiling through pain that rattled her inside and out. She cleared her throat softly and stroked my head to appease the monster.

Escapes to Nogales

Though my mother was unable to drive due to suffering the early stages of Parkinson's, whenever my father went on a particularly atrocious drunken bender, her solution was to send us to my grandparents' house—herself included. She'd put my siblings and me on a bus traveling from our home in Phoenix to the border town where they lived, Nogales, Arizona.

My Canadian grandparents owned a thriving produce brokerage. Each harvesting season, they would carefully select the finest quality produce from the best growers and send trucks of provisions to their customers, the elite restaurants and resorts across Canada. And each year, as the produce season came to a close, they would lease a new Cadillac and drive up the West Coast to Victoria, British Columbia. They'd zigzag all across Canada to visit their customers. From what I could tell, they had the best life.

The armored cocoon of my grandparents' protection reminded me of Glad's loving forcefield. As with my great-aunt, I experienced an entirely different existence when I was with my grandparents. Visiting them was the most crucial part of pulling me out of the state of hopelessness my father often beat me into. Being in their presence helped shape the possibility that someday I could be happy and successful. They had nice cars, nice homes, beautiful clothes, and ate at excellent restaurants—I begged to stay longer every time we visited. My grandparents were peaceful and loving, and I always felt safe whenever they were close.

They would parade us around their favorite restaurants, and the chefs and owners would surround our table and converse while my sister, brother, and I had all the desserts we could eat. Being treated like royalty was something I never experienced at home. The way people showed respect to and spoke with my grandparents felt like something right out of a movie. My grandmother was always regal, beautiful, and graceful. My grandfather always wore nice suits and pressed ties and would never be caught without one of his many favorite pipes. Even the Michelob beer lining the doors of their refrigerator looked elegant, with their gold labels neatly facing out. Absolutely everything about my grandparents and their surroundings reflected class and affluence.

Eventually, my father would come down from Phoenix and ruin everything by forcing us to come home. I remember my grandfather meeting him at the door with his hunting rifle several times, threatening to kill him for abusing us. That was otherwise totally out of character for my grandfather. He only had one lung and was fairly thin and nonthreatening. My father—a Korean War and Vietnam Marine Combat Veteran—just stared blankly through him, waiting for the lecture to conclude. To my disappointment, we would eventually pack up in the car and head home. These return trips took place in total silence. We were being sent back to prison, and our abusive warden had us back in custody.

I just hibernated into my mind for the four-hour drive home.

I remember one of our escapes to Nogales in particular because I got in a lot of trouble. It was a couple of hours into the boring bus ride. We had just left Stuckey's, a rest area with a store and restaurant outside of Tucson situated next to a large, jagged rock formation. We called it "Cat Mountain" because it looked just like a pair of cat ears.

Still a child, I was restless and bored. A large, older man wearing overalls was sitting next to me, and he smelled awful. His sweaty arm was touching mine and taking up part of my seat. I decided to go to the bathroom at the back of the bus to escape for a few moments. As I opened the door, the god-awful smell from within physically pushed me back. The scent was so revolting that it almost made me close the door and go back to my seat.

I decided to fight my way into the stench and pulled the window open to let some air in. A car full of people was passing by. Some kids were in the back looking straight at me, pointing excitedly. I half-waved as they pulled ahead. As I moved closer to the window, another car came up behind them, and I poked my head out the window to look. The instant I looked away from the fierce wind, it grabbed my glasses and swept them off my face. It was surreal watching them flutter downward, disappearing under the tire of a car in the next lane.

After I heard the dull *thump-thump* of their distant shattering, I panicked.

Immediately, I pulled the window closed, sat down on the toilet, and hyperventilated. I stood and began frantically pacing back and forth—all of two steps the tiny space would afford me. Eventually, my mother pounded on the door.

"John, open the door right now!"

I opened the door with my stomach in knots, my face turned away from her. I came out and walked under her arm and down the aisle to my seat. When my siblings caught a look at my face, they looked away in pity. My mother sat down in the aisle seat across from me and snapped her finger next to my ear to get my attention.

"Where are your glasses?" she asked.

"I don't know," I replied sheepishly.

"What do you mean, you *don't know?*" she demanded. The people around us began to take notice. I could see the driver's eyes darting back at me through his large rearview mirror.

"Show them to me!" she demanded louder. "Where are they?"

"I don't know," I repeated. Inside, I was in a panic about what my father was going to do to me when he found out.

"Come with me," she said sternly, pulling me up and out of my seat by my ear. My mother pulled me down the aisle, bumping people's shoulders until we arrived at the reeking bathroom. She pushed me through the door and sat on the toilet to get eye-to-eye with me.

"You better tell me the truth, boy. Where are they?" She was fed up. I rarely saw my mother get this angry, and I knew there was no getting out of this. The smell was strong enough to make my eyes water. Still, I could not bring myself to tell her what had happened.

"I don't know," came out of my mouth again. I also didn't know why I couldn't manage to say anything else.

She stood up and started pacing back and forth. Then she looked at me and pointed to the toilet. "Are they in there? Tell me, did they fall in there?" She grabbed me by the arm and shoved me over the open toilet. It stunk of human waste and formaldehyde.

"I don't know," I whispered.

Like only a mother would do, she pulled her sleeve up over her shoulder and stuck her entire arm down into the clumpy, deep waste. Gagging, she swooshed the liquid around to all four corners, shouting, "This is disgusting!" She heaved a lot and almost threw up.

When she couldn't find my glasses, she pulled her arm out and went to the sink to wash. It was a tiny sink, and she contorted herself in all directions trying to clean all the way up to her shoulder. When she finally stood up and looked at me, the angry expression on her face was frightening.

She grabbed me by the hair on the side of my head and yanked as she put her face close to mine and screamed, "Where are they?"

I stared through her, frozen in panic.

She looked over my shoulder to the window and yelled, "Are they out there?" She grabbed the window lock and yanked it open, pointing her hand out the window. "Are they out there?" she screamed.

Still frozen and dazed, I stared out the window with glassy eyes, saying nothing.

"Wait until your father hears about this," she said as she led me back through the door, my shirt collar clenched in her fist. This was the only time in my life I ever pushed her this far. I didn't realize she had a terrifying side too, and I never wanted to see it again.

Luckily, my mother had my old glasses in her bag. They were taped together in the middle from when I'd broken them just a few weeks prior. She fished them out and thrust them at me, totally perplexed and enraged.

Feeling All-Powerful

The morning after reaching Nogales, my mother went to the store and left me with my grandparents. My grandfather had a big chair with a footrest, and I would crawl up beside him, so we could watch TV together. We were watching a police show, and there was a bank robbery with shooting and crowds of people running. A policeman ran out into a busy street full of cars and put up his hands. All the vehicles in both directions stopped instantly. No one dared disobey him.

That's power, I thought.

"Wow!" I exclaimed. I looked up at my grandfather. "I want to be a policeman."

I had no power, and I was always afraid of my father. But now I knew someday I could be a policeman, and then he wouldn't hurt our family—or me—ever again. I felt something inside me stir, flooding me with confidence. I thought, *That's it. I need to become a policeman.*

I hatched an idea to see if I was powerful enough to do what the policeman on TV had done. I needed to know how it felt. Eagerly, I crawled off the chair and snuck by the kitchen where my grandmother was doing dishes. When she turned away from me, I crept through the screen door into the carport. From there, I could see her through the kitchen window. When she looked away again, I darted around the wall and ran to the end of the driveway. It faced a busy street with two lanes of cars going both ways.

With a lump in my throat and my heart pounding, I stood tall and serious, put my hands in the air, and stepped off the curb. A car whizzed by, and its driver honked a warning. The man behind the wheel shouted something angry at me. His car had sped so close to me that I could have easily touched it.

Undeterred, I continued to walk into the street. The car behind the one that had just passed me skidded to a stop. A lady driving a car in the next lane slammed on her brakes and honked her horn, screaming at me out of her window. Even the cars going the other way stopped to see the spectacle.

Through the cacophony of alarm, I heard my grandmother screaming, "John! What are you doing?" She ran into the street, snatched me up into her arms, and ran back up the driveway.

Squeezing me tight, she scolded, "What were you thinking?"

My grandfather walked out of the kitchen door into the carport to learn what the commotion was about. My grandmother put me down and knelt on one knee to look me in the eyes.

She squeezed both of my arms and yelled, "What in the world were you thinking? You scared me half to death! Don't *ever* do that again! That was very dangerous!" She stood up and looked down at me angrily. "I want you to go to your room and stay there until your mother comes home."

I knew why my grandparents were worried, yet as I walked to my room, I couldn't shake the experience of stopping the traffic like the policeman on TV.

I was as powerful as him, and that made me feel ten feet tall.

After only a few minutes of sitting in my room, I had an over-whelming sense that I had to feel my power again. I made the decision to sneak back through the door and out to the street. This time, I ran straight into the road with my arms up and hands outstretched.

"Stop!" I yelled. Instantly, traffic in all directions screeched to a halt, and everyone was honking their horns.

"Yes, I am all-powerful!" I shouted in triumph.

I stood there victorious for only a few seconds. At once, I was snatched into the air. This time, though, it wasn't my grandmother. Instead, it was a large man who had been walking on the sidewalk. He'd watched me run into the street.

"Are you crazy or stupid, son?" he yelled, bewildered.

My grandmother was back outside in an instant. She yanked me from the man's arms and bolted back up the driveway. When we reached the carport, Grandma screamed, "Oh, my God! *What is the matter with you?* Don't you know that is dangerous? Didn't you hear anything I said?" She was in a panic and started walking in a circle, clearly unsure of what to do next. When she noticed me watching her, she ordered me to stand with my nose to the nearby corner.

My grandfather rejoined my grandmother. Perplexed by my behavior, they whispered to each other. Suddenly, my grandfather grabbed me by my belt loops, lifting me off the ground. My grandmother grabbed a flyswatter hanging next to the screen door and started swatting me across my backside.

I could tell by the looks on their faces this was hurting them more than it was me. Truly. They weren't swatting me very hard but didn't know what else to do to discipline me. It was kind of funny compared to my father's whippings.

I could take this all day long, I thought, but I wasn't an idiot, so I screamed convincingly. But then, my grandmother said something that hit me ten times harder than the fly swatter:

"I'm going to tell your father!"

My heart sank into my stomach. "No! Please don't tell him! No, no!" I cried, begged, and pleaded. The instant she saw my terror, my grandmother knew she'd found the perfect thing to say to get her point across.

My grandparents sent me to my room, and I sat there panicking until my mother came home. I didn't go back out in the street, and thank God, neither she nor my grandmother ever said anything to my father.

CHAPTER 3

Normal Chaos

My early years were spent feeling numb and detached—a hopeless existence, but it all seemed normal since I knew nothing else.

The very knowledge that my father would be home soon would send me into a panic attack every afternoon after school. At 4:45 p.m., I would crawl under my bed and scramble into the darkest corner, waiting for and fretting over his arrival.

The instant I heard the purr of his car's engine pulling into the driveway, my heart began to pound. I would pull my knees tightly to my chest, nervously rocking back and forth. As my throat tightened, I hummed monotone sounds and focused on the vibrations I created in my vocal cords and chest.

Next came the angry stomp of my father setting the brake, followed by the *click, click, click* of the engine dying. That sound tormented me like a sickening countdown before the telltale *thump* signaling my father had released the inside door handle. My anxiety skyrocketed every time I heard the solid *clunk* of the closing door, followed by his heavy footsteps as he walked from the driveway to the door. My mind raced in a panic, and I hummed louder.

The front screen door rattled as he opened it. It always slammed back into his heel as he opened the thick, oak door behind the screen. At the sound of the front door slamming shut behind him, I cringed, repeating in whispers, "Please don't. Please don't call me. *Please.*" Then, like clockwork, my father would yell for me, his voice loud and booming, "John!" When my terror caught my voice in my throat, he would demand, "*John!* Come out here!" Dread mounting, as I crawled out from under my bed, I could hear him yell, "Can't you come out and say hi to your dad?"

I felt sick to my stomach and hated him.

Each time, I would walk down the darkened hallway to the living room, where I would stand at attention in front of him. He lectured me and barked orders and always instructed me to get him a beer—usually the first of at least a twelve-pack every night. He treated our entire family like his personal slaves, and the only time he was nice to any of us was during the brief period between his sixth and twelfth beer.

We were always waiting for him to snap. The drunker he became, the more demeaning his insults and nicknames. For me, his favorites were titles like *Dumbass*, *Stupo*, or *Doofus*. When he felt humorous, he would call me *Doofus McClod* in a stupid, Irish accent.

In public, we were to always walk in front of him. If my feet were not exactly straight or if they pointed outward, my father would give me a kick in the ass so hard it would launch me off of my feet and into the air before I would crumble to the ground in pain.

"Walk with your feet straight!" he would yell.

He was the oldest of nine children, and no one in the family would dare challenge him. Once, he kicked me up and off my feet in front of everyone at a family reunion. "Walk with your feet straight!" he admonished. Everyone froze in horror. I could feel their pity and their shared, silent admission that nobody felt capable of helping me.

When I was in trouble for almost any reason, the drunken monster would chase me down the dark hall leading to my bedroom, whipping me with his thick, black leather belt. The edges left welts with straight lines and sharp corners across my hips and all down my legs. The pain of each lashing was intense at the moment of impact, but the agony I experienced the following morning when I tried to move and get dressed was worse. The swollen welts would harden under my skin, and the scrapes and abrasions would just be starting to scab.

Needless to say, getting my clothes on for school was a delicate and painful process.

By day three, the welts would harden into a thick, ripening mass of yellows, browns, and purples. I developed an odd fascination with how my wounds became numb to the touch. In school, I repeatedly pressed on them through my jeans to feel the thickest parts of the welts and their edges. They would vanish within a week or so. Sometimes, I would have a fresh welt right over the top of an older one. Observing the various stages of healing my wounded body went through became something of an ongoing, personal science project.

Each night, when my father finished his second six-pack, he would decide it was time to wrestle, signaled by the way he would start prodding and grabbing me. Eventually, he would ensnare me and roll off the couch with his arms locked around me. It wasn't really wrestling. I squirmed and evaded his attacks until he would eventually pin my arms and straddle me, his body smothering mine. I was helpless under his weight and could feel the rumble of his drunken laughter. Then, he would grind his razor stubble along my arm and down to my neck and chin, scraping me until my skin was raw. When I couldn't take it anymore, I would scream for my mother, and she would plead with him to stop. Eventually, he would let me up, but only to get him another beer.

He would often stagger into my room late at night after I went to bed. He would fall onto my bed with his elbows on each side of me, keeping us face to face. His weight and positioning tightened the blanket around me and trapped my arms to my sides. All I could do was stare back. Only inches from his face, the stench of alcohol and cigarettes on his breath was nauseating.

"I love you, son," he would slur. "No matter what you do, son—I don't care if you kill someone and go to prison—I will always love you, and I'll always be there for you."

I stared back in silence, stunned and unsure of what to say. Eventually, he would go from staring at me to staring through me with dead eyes. Then, he would stagger to his feet and trudge back through the door.

For most of my upbringing, I was confused and conflicted. I believed that deep down, he loved me, because he often told me this. So, when he beat me, I knew he still loved me.

It wasn't until I was in my mid-thirties that I realized the only time he ever said kind things to me was just before he passed out from being totally shit-faced drunk.

All these years later, looking back, it's clear my father was in pain, and he was suffering. I get this now, but he knew what he was doing to all of us was more than just wrong—it was criminal. It was abuse and domestic violence of the worst kind, and he should have gone to prison.

Every weekday morning, like clockwork, he would wake up, pissed off and hungover from his drunken stupor of the night before. He never remembered anything. Rinse and repeat; the cycle would start over. He would stomp off to the Air Force base for his daily grind.

All of us would peek through the curtains, anxiously awaiting his departure. The entire house breathed a sigh of relief when we watched his car pull away from the driveway.

The instant I knew he was gone, it was as if I entered a different world. I would lose myself in picture books, and when I was in school, I would daydream and draw. The welts on my legs were my only reminders.

Of course, as the day reached early afternoon, my feelings of doom and melancholy would return. I knew my father would be coming home again, and my cycle of panic would refresh.

I remember often asking my mom if she would ever get a divorce from my father. I always hoped she would say yes, but she would tell me they were married, and so divorce would never happen. In a tone of resignation, she would tell me that she married my father in their faith, and we were a family. To her, that meant we needed to be raised by a mother and a father. They would never divorce.

My only escape was to retreat to the depths of my inner self, checking out and going numb whenever possible. I lived in a fantasy world of movies, picture books, and television, learning about heroes and villains, good and evil, and generally absorbing myself into anything to avoid being present.

Like most abused children, *there must be something wrong with me* was my prevailing belief, and it felt lower than shame.

A real father was supposed to protect us, but instead, he abused us.

I remember the day he stopped whipping me with his belt and began using his fists. Over time, I had learned how to anticipate his belt strikes and was able to evade direct hits. When he realized what I was doing, it infuriated him even further. He threw the belt across the room and slugged me in the stomach. I went down instantly, unsure if I'd ever breathe again. Once I was sprawled on my back, he crouched over me. I kicked him in the stomach with both my feet. I was trying to get him off of me, and that made him even more violent.

He needed to dominate me. I was getting older and a little bigger, so I think he believed he needed to demonstrate that he would always be the alpha. He started slapping, punching, and kicking around my defenses at will. He was a sweaty giant, reeking of alcohol and cigarettes, and I was cornered with no way to retreat.

Eventually, my helplessness turned to resignation. There was nothing I could do and nowhere to run. I dissociated and gave no response at all. If he looked at my face, all he could see was a numbness in my eyes as I stared through him. After noticing my lack of response, he would stop and look at me, perplexed. Eventually, he would shrug his shoulders and walk away to find something—or someone—else to smash.

My numbness followed me to school. My eyes were glazed, but my mind was so full of racing thoughts I couldn't concentrate on anything. When the teacher told the class to read, I often sat in a daze, staring into space. Eventually, she would snap her fingers in front of my face to get my attention, making the entire classroom burst out in hysterical laughter. It was humiliating.

I couldn't focus on anything for very long. I couldn't read, spell, or count, and even the simplest math problems left me baffled, usually resulting in headaches. Whenever I read even a few pages, my mind would begin to shut down. I couldn't comprehend what I was reading, and as a result, I would get sleepy and doze off. I fell asleep in band class several times, right in the middle of a set while trying to read sheet music. The teacher would quiet the class until the silence woke me. When I opened my eyes, the entire room would be staring at me, waiting to burst into laughter. The teacher was always amused with himself over this and got a lot of laughs at my expense.

I thank my mother for her curiosity and imagination. She showed me how she escaped through the pictures and stories she shared with me. My mind's movie theater became so vivid that I could time travel for long periods and lose myself in a deep trance. It was there in my mind where I began to find a sense of safety, and I fortified my emotional perimeter with heroes and archetypes as my protectors.

The most consistent theme in my fantasy world was to imagine myself as the Hulk, surprising my father and all the other bullies who tormented me. One at a time, I imagined their terrified reaction when they figured out who I *really* was. I mostly pictured their eyes and the looks on their faces, fantasizing over their feelings of terror because it was the same emotion they had inflicted upon me.

CHAPTER 4

Discovering My Sense of Knowing

M y time with Glad created within me a sense of knowing that my life was being purposefully guided in ways I could not consciously understand.

My first awareness of this inner sense came to me in a dream when I was about the age of ten. I had a clear vision of myself pulling up in front of my parents' home in a gold Rolls-Royce. It was so real and vivid, and I drew from this vision a sense of conviction that my life was somehow predestined. Having a Rolls-Royce has never been important to me, but the dream was so powerful, it inspired me to pay more attention to the images and visions that appeared in my waking thoughts and dreams thereafter. For years, the Rolls-Royce was a recurring symbol in my dreams and always left me with a sense of assurance to continue on my path.

My dream of the luxurious, golden vehicle stood in stark contrast to the physical danger present all around me—a danger that intensified as I grew older. The dangers were not relegated to the inside of our home. We lived in a very menacing neighborhood, and real threats lurked outside our front door.

Escaping to the depths of my imagination continued to be a protective form of self-care that shielded me from the suffering that darkened my daily reality.

I imagined myself as the lethal embodiment of John Wayne, Bruce Lee, and the Incredible Hulk all wrapped up into one, beating and throwing people around effortlessly. My enemies would find themselves cowering and begging me to stop. The instant my mother asked me to go to the store to get groceries, I would snap out of my trance and fall straight into paralyzing fear. She made this request almost every night of the week. She didn't understand the danger she was putting me in, and it took all the courage I could muster to set foot outside our front door.

Many years later, I learned that when I went to the store, the neighborhood bullies living close by would telephone each other with the code phrase, "The rabbit's loose." They would descend upon me by the time I rounded the corner just a few houses away, and all of them took great pleasure in terrorizing me.

We lived near a shopping center. The grocery store was on the far side, about half a mile away. In an effort to preempt their attacks, I developed a set of waypoints along my route to scout ahead for danger. There were vast acres of parking lots I would have to traverse, fully exposed, to get to safety. Unfortunately, the bullies were like a pack of wolves, hiding and working together to coordinate their efforts. Most of the time, I rode my bike and would have to dodge, weave, fight, or outrun them.

The only time I can recall being relieved to go to the store was when my mother felt well enough to ride her bike there with me. By the time I was in my mid-teens, her Parkinson's had moved into an advanced stage, making it much more difficult to predict when her body would cooperate with her plans. Several times a day, her entire body would shrink into a frozen contortion with her spine and neck twisting, hands wrenched in different directions on her chest. She was completely awake and fully aware but physically suspended in a catatonic state. Sometimes, I would move her hands away and lay my head on her chest to listen to her heartbeat, hoping to comfort us both.

She usually went into a frozen state when her medicine was at a low point, and she was waiting for a fresh dose to kick in. Within twenty minutes or so of the episode's start, her body would start to wake up, and she would begin to move and untwist like a soaked towel being unwound. Suddenly, she would bolt upright with her legs and arms moving in all directions. She'd fall into things as she headed through her bedroom door and bounced down the hallway, knocking pictures off the walls everywhere.

About once a week, she felt stable enough to want to ride her bicycle to the store. It was a large tricycle with a basket in the back for groceries. She was never allowed to go to the store alone, so I rode my bike or jogged alongside her, and we would talk as she peddled along.

When we passed the hangouts where the predators gathered, they waved and smiled as they greeted my mother. Once she turned her head away, they sent me threatening, silent gestures.

I remember one incident when my mother and I were in the checkout line at the store. The clerk, who knew her well, reached into my mother's change purse to help her pay. Her medication was causing her to shake and gyrate uncontrollably, and she was struggling to complete the transaction on her own. She leaned against the register, holding herself up.

I was looking at a magazine and observed two men standing behind her, shaking and gyrating, mimicking her body movements, snickering as they entertained themselves. These were grown men at least in their late twenties. My rage boiled as I helped my mother out the door to put the groceries in her basket. I noticed the men walking toward the exit, so I told my mother I would catch up to her shortly and pushed her off on her way.

I confronted both of them, blocking their path, and yelled at the top of my lungs, "Remember that lady at the checkout stand you were making fun of? That was my *mother*, you idiots! What's wrong with you? Do you feel better, making fun of her?"

The men were shocked by my defiance, and people were stopping to stare. The clerk who had just helped my mother had also seen them making fun of her. He made eye contact with me as he fast-walked to get between me and the two idiots. He rested his hands on my shoulders and began to pull me back. I shrugged him off and yelled again.

"You're lucky I don't kick the shit out of both of you right now! You deserve it!"

Whatever their thoughts on the matter, the clerk asked them to please go.

I took a shortcut through the mall and caught up with my mother just as she was rounding the corner. She smiled as she saw me jogging toward her.

The Carnival

Every year, the park next to the shopping center hosted a carnival. For fear of the same neighborhood bullies, I usually resisted the temptation to venture into the park area—much less the carnival itself—unless I was with my parents. But for some reason, one year, around age fourteen, I decided to do it anyway. It was risky, but I had to get a look.

It was getting dark, and I nervously peered into the crowds of people from behind some large bushes. I had hoped I wouldn't be spotted, but it was already too late. I felt my attackers' eyes upon me, and as I looked around, a few of the bullies had already begun to encircle me. They started shoving, punching, and taunting me. They went back and forth, arguing about which one of them would fight me this time. One of the tougher bullies won out and said he wouldn't fight me—rather, his younger brother would because he was more my match.

Eventually, a couple of parents intervened and broke us up. I was able to fade into the crowd quickly and dodge through the bushes to escape. But instead of going home as I should have, I went to a friend's house not far from the park. I was in the beginning stages of taking karate lessons there—and that's overstating it. I was a white belt, the lowest level student, and I knew next to nothing. The teacher's name was Ron. He was one grade ahead of me and had a reputation as one of the neighborhood's toughest guys. My friend Frank, also one of Ron's students, was a wiry, muscular guy who was a wizard with nunchucks. He and I were huge Bruce Lee fans, and he vouched for me to Ron. And there were Greg and Larry, two other students who were also Bruce Lee fanatics.

When I got to Ron's house, I was nervous and upset. Even so, it took a while for the guys to finally pry out of me what had just happened at the carnival. Before I knew it, all of them declared we were going to the park to find the bullies.

This was not the response I expected, and I was immediately terrified. *Are they crazy?* I thought. But before I could talk them out of it, they shoved me into the station wagon Ron borrowed from his mother, and we hauled ass back to the carnival. I was so anxious, it made me nauseous.

We arrived within minutes and cruised by several kids who were hanging out by some cars.

"Is that them?" Ron barked.

"No," I replied. I was trapped, and this was happening whether I liked it or not.

We parked, and they escorted me through the crowd, telling me to point out who was bullying me. It only took a matter of minutes because the bullies spotted me first and came right to us. The tougher guys on both sides were instantly nose-to-nose; we almost got into it right then. After putting each other in check, the alphas on the bullying side declared for the second time that day that they wanted to pick one of their friends to fight me. To my surprise, my friends immediately agreed on my behalf.

An image of Glad suddenly flashed through my mind, striking me like a lightning bolt. At the same time, *Why is this happening to me?* reverberated through my body, strong and loud, like thunder.

I was going into a panic attack.

My reaction amused my tormentors. The bullies snickered as they mocked my visible fear and nervousness. I could tell that my sensei, Ron, expected me to demonstrate what I had been learning from him, and this was a test. I looked over and saw an adult carny taking a break by a trailer, smoking a cigarette. When my eyes met his, I felt a flicker of hope that he would intervene.

The carny shook his head and said, "I don't see nothin'."

My knees began to shake, and it was all I could do to control them enough not to be noticed. Before another word, the excitement took over, and the crowd moved us from the small, grassy circle we were standing in out into the light of the vast, asphalt parking lot. Word spread about a fight, and the small crowd immediately grew to well over a hundred people, most of whom were laughing and taunting us to get on with it.

"Fight! Fight! Fight!"

There was no one coming to rescue me, and I was almost blacking out from panic.

One of the alphas from the other side started backing the crowd up to expand the circle until it was about twenty feet across. Then, he shoved the guy in front of me, indicating it was this person I was going to fight. His name was Mike, and I knew him well from growing up in the neighborhood, but we had never fought for real. Mike looked pretty nervous, and after we both paused to size each other up, his brother shoved him toward me and said, "Kick his ass!"

We put up our hands, and he came at me. I backed up a couple of paces and glanced over his shoulder to see my sensei and other martial arts students. They were standing together with their arms crossed, nodding at me in silence to attack.

I returned my focus to Mike, scanning him for openings until I found one. I popped him in the chin with a quick left jab and followed through with a hard-straight right, flattening his nose and exploding it like a tomato across his face. The sudden action and loud *thud* from my punch hushed the crowd. I took another step in and kicked him full force in the groin, doubling him over. He groaned in agony, holding himself. I couldn't believe how much blood was streaming down the front of his face. But instead of going down and tapping out, as I had anticipated, Mike screamed and lunged toward me. I stepped aside and threw him to the ground, but he got up—still screaming—and came at me again. He swung wildly and grabbed me with a bear hug in order to tackle me.

I reached around both of his arms above the elbow, and I trapped him against my chest as we went down to the ground. He was on top of me with his forearms flat on the ground beneath me, unable to move or do any damage. His forehead pressed against the side of my face as a continuous flow of his blood ran directly into my ear. As we struggled, blood smeared across my cheeks and down my neck and chest, soaking my shirt. I locked my legs behind his waist, and there was nothing he could do to escape. Suddenly, hands were grabbing everywhere to pull us apart and get us back on our feet to keep fighting.

As we rose up, I looked over Mike's shoulder and saw his older brother lunging toward us to take over. *He's stepping in*, flashed in my mind, and my danger alarms went off the charts. I looked back at my bloody opponent and saw an opening in the circle of people behind him in the direction of the grocery store. Could I make it all the way across the parking lot?

Without thinking, I ran toward him and gave him a slug, knocking him to the ground, then broke into a full sprint, blasting through the opening in the crowd.

Though I had caught everyone by surprise, within moments, a thunderous sound of many feet drew close to me, and the boys were yelling, "Get him!" They were right on my ass, but I could tell without looking back that I was pulling away. A group of three or four on bikes caught the corner of my eye and veered right in front of me to block my path and slow me down. I dodged around one and clotheslined another. I heard a hard *slap* as the kid and his bike bit it hard, toppling to the asphalt. I hurdled over his bike and kept sprinting. The wreck slowed the crowd chasing me just a little as they stutter-stepped in all directions trying to avoid tripping over him.

I made it as far as the grocery store's electric doors before the group on bikes caught up again and grabbed me from behind. They pulled me by the hair and shirt, keeping me pinned just outside. I grabbed onto the edge of the opening door, screaming for help.

One of the clerks came to my rescue. He grabbed my arm and the belt around my waist. A few others arrived to help and eventually tugged me through the doors and into the store. The crowd chasing on foot arrived and completely blocked the entrance as they threatened and taunted with obscenities.

The manager yelled, "The police are coming!"

I was dragged across the floor to safety, breathlessly thanking the clerks. They were all looking at my face in shock, and many of them asked if I was okay.

I suddenly realized my shirt was soaked in Mike's blood. I could feel it caked in my ear and plastered down my face and neck.

"Oh, my God! You're bleeding!" one of the clerks yelled.

"It's not mine," I gasped, trying to catch my breath.

They walked me to the restroom in the back of the store to wash up. I was still in shock. After taking some time to recover, I came out cautiously and made my way back to the front of the store. I didn't see anyone waiting for me who looked threatening—the manager calling the police must've been enough to scare them away. I stood near the door and peered through the windows and still didn't see anyone, so I crept over and stepped onto the electric door pad to get a look outside.

Still no sign.

Before I could step back in, a few bullies grabbed me and shoved me through the doors. They had been lying in wait inside the store. As we wrestled in the doorway, a group of others hiding outside ran toward us to join in. Fortunately, the clerks were able to intervene again and pulled me back inside.

The police arrived within minutes, and the crowd scattered in all directions. I was relieved when the policeman gave me a ride home to safety.

CHAPTER 5

Chipping Away
All That Is Not Me

Glad was aging, and it had become too challenging for her to travel and visit my family during winters. I was in my early teens, and we kept in touch over the phone from time to time, but it wasn't the same. I missed her presence dearly. Mostly, I would call her when I was feeling overwhelmed by my father or trying to survive my neighborhood. Just the sound of her voice brought me relief.

I had not yet lost hope that Glad's belief—*God is love*—would someday ring true for me, but this had not been my experience so far. In fact, Glad's existence was my only evidence. Meanwhile, I remained puzzled over the prevailing question that left me armored up from too many traumatic moments to count: *why is this happening to me?*

One afternoon during summer break, I sat in my room feeling anxious and overwhelmed, unable to venture out into the neighborhood; it was just too dangerous. I came across the book Glad had sent me many years before about Michelangelo sculpting the statue of David and took this as a sign that she wanted me to pull it off the shelf.

As I placed the book in my lap, I could see the edge of her note protruding between the pages. I opened the book where her note was placed, revealing an illustration of the statue of David. Seeing her handwritten note took me back to the moment I first saw it many years before. At the time, I was too young to understand its meaning, but as I read her message, I knew Glad did everything with profound intention, and this was the exact moment I was supposed to find it.

I needed to talk to Glad immediately, but instead of calling from the living room where my mother was close by, cooking in the kitchen, I went to my parents' bedroom and closed the door. There would be more privacy if I used their phone. It was risky, and I knew it. I was forbidden by Father to ever be in their room, but I had to discover why she wrote this to me so many years ago and what it meant.

When Glad picked up, we exchanged greetings, and I said, "When I was a young boy, you gave me a book about the Statue of David for Christmas. Between the pages, you left me this note."

"Ah, you found my note," she replied warmly. "We never talked about that. I wondered if you had found it. It was sort of a test to see if you were paying attention and interested in these sorts of things."

"I didn't understand your note then, but it seems more important to me now," I said. "The last line reads, 'You must chip away all that is not you to discover your true self and your life's purpose.' What is my true self?"

"Well, John," she replied, "your true self is the deepest part of who you really are. It is much deeper than any of the experiences you've had in your life."

"Is my true self deeper than fear?" I asked.

"Yes," she continued. "Your true self is deeper than your fears and your experiences. Even though you feel fear, there is a part of you that is deeper than what you fear."

The gravity of her words kept me quiet for a moment, and Glad let me think it over.

Suddenly, a memory flashed in my mind. "I remember sitting with you on our favorite bench in the park when I was younger, talking about fear. You said I needed to find a purpose bigger than my fear?"

"Very good, that's right," she replied. "And that your purpose was already deep within you even then, waiting to be discovered. Do you remember that too?

"Yes! Yes, I do," I said excitedly.

"Now it is time for you to understand why I wrote this note to you." I could feel her approving smile through the phone. "Have you discovered what your purpose is yet, John?"

I didn't answer straight away. When I was ready, however, I replied, "I think that is why I'm calling you, Glad. No, I haven't found my purpose yet."

"This is why the story of Michelangelo creating the Statue of David is so powerful for you." She paused. "Are you ready to hear this, John?"

"Yes, absolutely," I replied. I pressed the phone even closer to my ear.

"You are not your fears, and you are not your worries—not about your father or anything else. Deep down, you are *you*, not your fear. Soon, you will be a man. You will be much older and will think for yourself. You will decide who you want to be in the world. As sure as we are talking right now, this day will come. The magical choice you have before you, John, is to choose between living a life of courage or a life of fear and regret. And this is why the story of *David* will serve you in learning how to free yourself from your fears. Just like you may be feeling right now, David was trapped in the stone, and Michelangelo could see him frozen within, waiting to be freed. So, he chipped away all the pieces of stone that were not David until David was revealed to the world."

She punctuated her point, saying, "You are not your fears, but your fears will hold you frozen unless you liberate yourself from them. You will still feel fear, but no longer will you feel trapped from a place of fear."

"This is what you meant by 'chipping away all that's not me,'" I said with certainty.

"Yes, exactly," she replied. "You see, this is what we all must do. We must look for the parts of ourselves that are not true for us, that no longer serve us, or that we want to change. We must then chip away the false self-images and stories we tell ourselves and let them fall away from us. What is left is our true self that is free to become the person we were meant to be."

She paused, and then: "What are you experiencing as I share this with you?"

"I'm relieved," I replied.

"You are old enough to take these matters seriously," Glad said in a motherly tone. "I am speaking to you as a young man, not as a boy. I will leave you with this until we speak again: your fears and experiences contribute to who you are becoming, but they do not define who you are. You must always remember that your fears and experiences are not here to master you; they do not define who we really are. Your fears present themselves to serve as lessons and teachers; they are messengers on your journey that greatly contribute to who you are becoming."

"So, I am not my fear, but I still feel fear?" I replied, considering her words carefully.

"Exactly, John. But you must stay awake to this. Don't go back into the numbness that fear creates. The opposite of fear is courage, and you are now ready to understand how to wield courage like a sword and a shield."

"I'm ready," I told her. My curiosity was building with the hope of someday conquering my fears.

"As you continue to discover who you really are, you'll find courage," she said. "The courage to learn from your fears and to carry on despite them will make you stronger and wiser and more ready to face your journey ahead. And the courage you seek is within the deepest part of you already. It is at the core of your being. We are all born with courage, but it is up to us to discover this for ourselves. Do you have something to write with?" she asked.

"Hold on," I replied and darted to my room to get paper and pen.

I checked on my mother, still in the kitchen, unsuspecting, and I raced back to the phone. "I'm ready"

"Good, I want you to write this down exactly: *courage is already within me at the core of my being.*"

I wrote it out on paper as she spoke. "Got it," I said.

"I want you to put this in a place where you can see it every day. Commit it to memory," she explained. "When I chose to leave Canada as a young woman and found my way to France, I was terrified. Still, my convictions and my purpose of finding the truths I sought were far more important than my fears and insecurities. I didn't speak a word of French, and in those times, young women did not go on adventures and travel the world alone. Women were cast in roles as teachers, homemakers, and secretaries, and I was just not going to stay and be who others thought I should be. I had a burning desire and a purpose to fulfill, and nothing was going to keep me from it. I soon found I was naive and idealistic in those initial few years of my journey. Still, I needed to go through my experiences to discover these truths for myself. I would not allow anyone to tell me who I should be or what I should think, and I knew I had to learn these things on my own.

"When I was escaping Paris during the Nazi invasion of France, I was often freezing, without food, or in extreme danger of being captured or killed. But because my convictions tethered me to a deeper purpose, I found I could endure intense fear and hardships. The atrocities I witnessed, I needed to see. The hardships and traumatic experiences I suffered—I needed to experience them all, so I could convey them in my writing. And through my writing, I began to discover my deeper purpose, which was to share my first-hand accounts with the world so that justice would someday be served. I didn't lose my faith in humanity, but my conviction for justice served its purpose by helping me survive.

"This is what I mean when I say, 'The courage you seek is already in the deepest part of you.' All you need do is discover for yourself what is bigger than what you fear."

Glad's wisdom and intention had pierced my armor, and I instinctively straightened up on the bed. Once again, she was provisioning me for my journey ahead.

I repeated slowly back, "Courage is already within me at the core of my being."

"Good, John. I'm proud of you for writing that down."

It was time for me to deepen my faith in her guidance. I still wasn't sure how to find the courage within me, but at least she had planted the seed.

At least I knew the possibility existed.

"I no longer have to be the victim," I declared.

"You see," Glad responded, pleased. "You're discovering the courage within you. This takes time, but this is progress. You've got a lot to think about from this conversation, John. Much more than you expected, I imagine. Is there anything else you would like to talk about?"

My head spun with all of the possibilities. "I'd like to think about all of this and call you back sometime soon. Thank you, Glad. I love you."

"I love you too, John."

CHAPTER 6

Surviving the Neighborhood

PeeJon and Porky

My older brother, Russ, had a knack for fixing things. I never told him, but I always admired that about him, I think because I'm not naturally mechanically inclined. He made fun of me, saying my motto was to measure once and cut twice, meaning I could make things fit, but it never looked as clean and proper. He was the definition of a shade tree mechanic, always working on his car in our front yard under the tree. Rain or shine, summer or winter, I was volun-told to be his assistant. As his younger brother, I was really there to bench press starters and transmissions into place while he bolted them in.

Russ and I had a contentious relationship. By age sixteen, Russ was already six-five with a full beard, and he towered over me by a foot. When my parents weren't around, the tormenting would start. He would ambush me in front of his friends and stand on my foot with his size thirteen-and-a-half shoe, so I couldn't get free. He enjoyed humiliating me while jabbing me in the face, doubling me over with body shots while I tried in vain to get away.

At the same time, he was my brother. There were parts of him I always admired and loved. He was creative, passionate, and great at fixing things. We were also bonded through trauma—two prisoners living under our father's violent, critical eye.

I grew to hate working on cars thanks to the extreme summer heat of Phoenix. On a typical Arizona day, it hit 110 degrees even in the shade. Grass wouldn't grow in our front yard, just patches of burnt yellow weeds. These experiences cured me of ever wanting to be a mechanic.

I remember one Saturday morning: We were working on Russ's pickup, and two kids from a few houses down, Brett and Bart, positioned themselves across the street with our neighbor, Joey, to taunt us. As their insults got more personal, we shouted back and made fun of the nicknames Brett and Bart's mother had for them: PeeJon and Porky. We started mocking their mother's funny voice as we imitated the way she'd often call them in for dinner at sunset.

"Peeeeeejonnn! Pooooorrrkyyy! PeeJon and Porky! Come for dinner!"

We knew they hated this, and it made them angrier, so they took it up a notch themselves. Their cruelty turned toward our mother and her illness.

It's one thing to make fun of each other, but that was a low blow. Russ became furious and decided to put an end to it.

Russ looked across at them and said, "Either shut up or get your ass kicked. What are you gonna do?"

Russ towered over all of us. I thought his threat would be the end of the situation, yet after a few more jabs from PeeJon, my brother looked at me and growled, "Come on." He grabbed me by the back of the neck, walked me across the street, and shoved me in front of them.

"I'm not gonna fightcha," Russ said, giving me another shove. "*He* is." Before I could run, the older brother, PeeJon, lunged forward and tried to tackle me. Fortunately, I turned and took him off balance, and we slammed down on the blistering asphalt. I was on top of him in full mount. He shrieked from the hot street as it burned his back, and in response, I slugged him in the face.

Then, he did something I'll never forget: PeeJon looked straight at me and grabbed my testicles with both hands, squeezed hard, and screamed up at me. I went crazy from the sudden jolt of pain and let out a primal scream. I beat down on him like a gorilla, my arms raising above my head and slamming down on him with all the force I could muster. After four or five serious wallops, he let go and started crying. His lips were bleeding, and his eyes were beginning to swell. "You give up?" I demanded. "*Say it!*"

"I give up," PeeJon mumbled, defeated.

Breathing hard, I turned to size up Porky and Joey. They were silent and watching me nervously.

Russ told them to keep their mouths shut, or next time he'd do it for them. PeeJon and Porky walked home in total silence and didn't look back. PeeJon was a year older than me, and word of our fight got out immediately. He was mocked to no end for being beaten up by a younger kid. In my neighborhood, that was a big deal.

I may not have won many neighborhood fights in my youth, but this was a true victory. It felt good to win a fight.

Gentleman Jim's

It took a while, but I made peace with Mike, the guy I fought at the carnival. Before the fight, we'd been friends, but I still hated his brother for making him attack me. One cold winter evening, Mike came to my house and told me his mom needed some things from the store. He asked if I wanted to go with him.

Though I was nervous I was being set up, I agreed, and off we went into the cover of darkness.

As we neared the store, he suggested we take the back way to see if we needed to avoid anyone standing out front.

I agreed, but the route took us through a dark alley with no light whatsoever. We were behind a BBQ restaurant called Gentleman Jim's, and it had just closed for the evening. The smell of Indian fry bread lingered in the air and made my mouth water. As we crossed through the parking lot into the alley, my anxiety tripled. I shoved my hands into the pockets of my baseball jacket and tried to be friendly with Mike despite my nerves.

Suddenly, I felt Mike's presence slow and fall back, and I sensed movement in the darkness all around me. Before I could react, a dark shadow jumped right up to me, and a pair of hands gripped both my upper arms tightly, pulling me up and nose to nose.

A deep voice growled, "Remember me?" in an unmistakable, sinister tone. I instantly knew it was Kelly, a guy who had been trying to run me over with his car for weeks. He'd undergone a growth spurt the summer before and was suddenly taller and larger than most of the guys my age. He was one of only a few in our neighborhood who had a car.

Often, as I would walk to the store, Kelly would cruise by with a car full of bullies and then go around the block to sneak up on me. He almost clipped me a couple of times and would even drive up into people's yards trying to run me down.

Mike had set me up.

I stood frozen as five or six others closed in all around me. Evidently, for them, this was a gut-busting laughter fest—including Mike.

Before I could react, I was shoved to the grimy asphalt as each teenager took a turn kicking, jumping, and stomping up and down on top of me, howling and laughing all the while. My learned response from my father's beatings was to curl into a silent ball and take it. They began to dance around me in a circle continuing to kick and stomp.

After a couple of final kicks and punches from Kelly, their laughter faded into the darkness. For a good while, I stayed in a ball, trying to assess my injuries.

Beaten, bloodied, but unbroken, I laid on the dirty asphalt, trying to make sense of what had just happened. My eye began swelling shut, and I could taste blood from my split lip.

My conversation with Glad was still fresh in my mind. I heard her wise voice echoing, "Courage is already within me at the core of my being."

It was hard not to see myself as a victim because I had literally just been assaulted. At that point, a sense of desperation seized me. This wasn't going to stop. I was going to have to do something.

I was going to have to be courageous.

I went home and pleaded with my father to let me take karate lessons. My friend Ron, the neighborhood karate instructor, was no longer teaching us for free.

"No!" he said. His tone was blunt and dismissive. "They don't know what they're doing, and you'll just end up getting hurt."

"Look at me," I yelled, frustrated. "I'm already getting the shit beat out of me. How much worse can it be than this?"

He roared, "*I said no!* We don't have the money! That's the end of it!"

I stood there shaking and bleeding, feeling the rage grow inside of me. I resented how my father hadn't even asked who had done this to me.

At that moment, I knew he wasn't ever going to protect me. He would always be the monster from my childhood. I was now aware I needed to protect myself. As a kid, I felt my only option was to start carrying a knife with me at all times. At least I would have something to reach for when I needed protection. One thing I knew for sure: I was no longer willing to be a victim.

I thought of the weathered, marble block that eventually became the Statue of David. This was a strike I could make with my chisel. I would have to learn to protect myself.

Salon Mexico

For a few of my teenage years, every Friday and Saturday night, my father worked as a door guard and bouncer at the largest Mexican nightclub in South Phoenix, Salon Mexico. Since he was a Combat Veteran, violence and dealing with dangerous situations came naturally to him. In fact, he thrived on it. Saturday and Sunday mornings became his personal "Show and Tell" time, where he would drink beer and proudly tell me about the previous night's events. Frequently, he would have a swollen and blackened eye, busted lip, or some stitches on his face he could point to in an effort to emphasize his stories. A few times, he had stitches on his hands and arms from being attacked with knives. However, he wore his wounds with pride and bragged about how he was injured and the people he pummeled. This was a confusing time for me, and I wondered how many of my friends' fathers shared these kinds of crazy experiences with their sons.

One Saturday morning in particular, while at the breakfast table, he recounted his evening from the night before and gave me a stone-cold look across the table as he pulled his billy club from his utility belt. He held it up to my face, slapped it hard into his open hand, and then thumped me on the knuckles with a loud *whack*. "If you ever get in a fight with a Mexican, break their hands first because they all carry knives."

At first, I was shocked. Why was he telling me this? Then, I realized that all my Mexican friends and enemies *did* indeed carry knives—and they knew how to use them. Of course, I had begun collecting them too, but I certainly wasn't going to tell my father that. In fact, my friends and I often traded and collected knives between us. I wouldn't leave home without at least two in my pocket—one for protection and one to trade or sell.

My father stood up and grabbed a butter knife sitting on the counter and tossed it to me. "Come at me and try to stab me," he ordered in a threatening voice.

I froze, petrified. *He wants me to stab him?* I wondered. And part of me wanted to.

"Do it!" he yelled, as he thrust his club into my chest.

I lunged toward him, and he whacked me on the wrist, causing the knife to fly across the room.

"That's how you do it," he said confidently. "Pick it up, and do it again. This time, come at me a different way."

I reluctantly bent down, picked up the knife off the floor, and slowly crept toward him. Then, I lunged, threshing—a slicing motion from left to right and back again. When I was in mid-swing, he brought his club upward and struck my forearm hard. I screamed in pain, and the knife was instantly knocked from my hand, clattering to the floor.

He darted toward me, close to my face. "You see, that's how you do it! If someone is coming at you with a knife, don't fight against the knife! If you have a stick, hit their hands or wrist. If you have a knife, slice their hand or wrist. If they try to kick you, slice their leg. They won't try to attack you more than a couple of times when they feel enough pain and see their own blood. They'll give up and run."

Throughout the day, this memory haunted me, and I kept re-playing this fucked-up situation. When I went to bed that evening, I had a nightmare where I dreamt I entered the public bathroom in Encanto Park, the largest park in Phoenix, and I knew it well. It had a man-made lake where I worked one summer renting out canoes. In my dream, as I entered the public bathroom, it was dark, and all of the stalls were closed except the one at the very end. As I reached the last stall, all of the stall doors flew open, and a well-known gang called the Wedgewood Chicanos stepped out to face me. They were all grinning from ear to ear and held straight razors in their hands, chanting in unison, "You got to show respect for the blade, ese!"

Although this was a dream, the whole thing felt so real. I pan-icked and made a run for the exit, and each gang member scored a few slices as I dashed past. I could see my own blood and felt the stinging pain of each razor's cut, but I never made it to the door. I awoke in a sweat, hyperventilating, and my heart was pounding out of my chest. This nightmare would haunt me for years and became a recurring dream with no ending.

The traumatizing lesson my father was trying to give me was confusing and weird to me. He wouldn't let me take karate lessons because I would get hurt, but he was willing to teach me how to fight with knives and weapons?

These were the kind of weird situations I didn't—and still don't—know how to process.

I recall one Saturday morning: my father stormed into my room and shook me awake, practically pulling me out of bed.

"John!" he yelled. "Get up, and get dressed. We've got to go now! You're going to work with me today. Move it!" he commanded, towering over me.

I barely had time to throw on some clothes and a ball cap. He grabbed and shoved me down the hall and through the front door to the car. As we sped away, I wondered what this was all about.

As we drove, he blurted, "Victor just fired his janitor, and I told him I would do the work," as if that was all he needed to say.

Victor was the owner of Salon Mexico, and I had heard about him for years from my father.

Little did I know, at that moment, I was being volun-told to give up my weekends for the foreseeable future.

It was the first time I'd been to any nightclub. As we pulled into the parking lot, my jaw dropped. It was a huge, grimy building with graffiti everywhere. The shabby roof was incomplete. Large patches of material were strewn on the ground from where the wind had clearly blown them to the earth. The building sat a few hundred feet from the road, and the vast parking lot looked more like a garbage dump. At least twenty trash cans overflowed into piles of trash stacked everywhere.

When my father unlocked the large double doors and pulled them open, a stench so foul billowed out toward us that I had to step back to keep from throwing up. We ventured into the darkness of the building, and my father told me to wait by the door. The pungent smell of beer-soaked carpets and cigarettes was nauseating.

The lights burst on, and I was taken aback by the size of the hall. There was a dance floor twice the size of a basketball court, and it was surrounded by elevated levels full of tables and chairs. There was a large stage at the other end, full of speakers and drums. As far as I could see, there was an ocean of tabletops filled with empty glasses and garbage from the night before. Styrofoam food containers and cups were strewn everywhere.

My father took me to the maintenance room and began to pull out mops, brooms, and cleaning supplies. "Let's get started picking up the trash. You get the parking lot, and I'll start in here," he commanded. It was not lost on me that he'd assigned the air-conditioned portion of the task to himself. He handed me a box of garbage bags and pointed toward the dumpsters outside. It took almost two hours to get all the garbage collected and dragged to the dumpsters.

My father often popped out the door to make sure I wasn't slacking. "Hurry up, goddammit!"

When I had finished and reported back, he told me to follow him. I couldn't imagine my situation getting any more disgusting, but it did. We entered the women's restroom, and the stench multiplied tenfold. It was so thick and oppressive that I was surprised I couldn't see it form a physical cloud.

As he propped the doors open with the full garbage can, he said, "You're in charge of cleaning the bathrooms while I mop and buff the dance floor. Let's move. The club staff gets here in a few hours, and we need to be wrapping this up."

I leaned against the filthy wall. I was nauseous and unable to breathe in through my nose. After a few seconds, I turned and heaved into a trash can.

I could hear my father howling with laughter as he made his way back down the hall.

The women's bathroom was a horrendous sight. I guessed it had endured at least fifteen hundred uses the prior night for it to be left in such a condition. It was an assault on my senses that left a scar in my mind. Overwhelmed by such a large project—there were at least fifteen stalls in both the women's and the men's bathrooms—I went out into the hall to collect myself.

Once again, I was trapped by my father with absolutely no say. All I could think of was when Glad told me I would be an adult someday, and I could make my own choices. At that moment, I vowed to get away from this uncaring idiot as soon as I possibly could.

I grabbed the box of trash bags and filled at least six of them with the god-awful piles of wet, soaked garbage using a dustpan and broom.

Though I was working as fast as I could, it took a good ninety minutes to finish. My father continually checked on me to tell me to hurry up.

Then came the next "fun" part. I was handed a sharp-edged paint scraper and a bucket and was instructed to patrol the entire dance floor and bar area in search of flattened gum to scrape up.

Once finished, he took me behind the bar to a long production line of dishwashing machines and showed me how to load glasses into racks. The smell was slightly more tolerable but still reeked of cigarette butts dunked in drink glasses of liquor.

After taking me through the entire process, he said, "We have about an hour to get everything done before Victor arrives. I'll finish waxing and buffing the dance floor, and you get this done, got it?"

"Got it!" I replied.

I wondered what Victor looked like because I had not yet met him. My father didn't respect many people, but it was obvious that Victor was an exception.

All of the Mexican families I grew up around were working families, but Victor was known to be in a wealthy class, and I imagined him to be much like my grandfather.

As I looked around and took in the sheer magnitude of the task before me, an overwhelming wave of dread came over me. On one side, the entire room was full of long, steel-topped tables crammed with thousands of dirty glasses. The other side was full of large, empty racks needing to be filled to hold them while in the dishwasher.

I took a deep breath, threw some racks on the conveyor, and began to fill them with dirty glasses. Sliding them forward on the conveyor and into the washer, I set the production line into motion. Oddly enough, within a few minutes, I fell into a rhythm. All said and done, I found the production line moved much faster than I thought it would.

Compared to the other disgusting tasks, I found loading the dishwasher strangely satisfying because I saw progress instantly. It also allowed me to fall into a sense of solitude when things started humming along. *I could do this all day*, I thought. Within forty-five minutes, all the glasses were washed and stacked near the bar, clean and orderly.

As I returned to the dance floor area, I noticed a few bartenders had arrived. They were unloading delivery trucks while laughing and joking in Spanish about the new kid—me. They were friendly and appeared to be impressed with everything I'd done to make the place so neat and tidy.

"Good muchacho," they repeated with a smile.

One thing I also noticed right away was that they all seemed to love my father. They would greet each other with authenticity and warmth. I had never met anyone who liked my father, and it was a side of him I had not seen.

I was surprised to learn he could be an entirely different person. Their fondness for him perplexed me, and though I hated to admit it, I was impressed.

I quickly discovered *this* was his second family. His job was as much about belonging and being accepted as it was about satisfying his needs for adrenaline and danger. I began to see another side of him that was genuinely warm and sincere as I watched him interact with his coworkers and their families.

Why is he so mean to us but so nice to them? I thought.

At Salon Mexico, every night was a celebration. Food trucks lined the parking lot to feed the intoxicated masses. My father learned how to cook everything imaginable from all the best chefs of the most popular trucks. They all saw him as their protector and treated him with great respect. They would not let him leave his shift without sending him home with a load of food for our family the next morning.

While he worked at Salon Mexico, Saturday and Sunday morning breakfasts were always delicious.

There was a high percentage of Spanish-speaking families in my neighborhood, so I grew very comfortable with their sincere and friendly ways. To them, family was everything, and they were close and fiercely loyal to one another. I have always admired this about their culture, and no matter where I have traveled, I count my Spanish-speaking friends as my most trusted and loyal. If they like you, it's for life; if they don't, you know it.

Being in the bar with the pungent stench of rotting beer and liquor reminded me of the first time I got drunk on Southern Comfort with my next-door neighbor, Rick. Even now, the sweet, syrupy smell of Southern Comfort still turns my stomach. He and I were the same age and inseparable for many years. I especially liked the delicious, authentic Hispanic food his family shared with me almost every time I visited their house. To this day, I still compare Mexican food to his mother's.

As my father and I stood in front of the bar waiting for his boss, Victor, to arrive, I daydreamed about being at Rick's house. I would arrive, and without saying a word, his mother would come from the kitchen with a smile, bringing me a plate or a bowl of whatever she was preparing for their family meal: fresh, homemade tortillas, tamales, chili verde, posole, and a soup called *menudo* that I thought was delicious. It was years before I understood from some friends that there was tripe in the soup, but I didn't care. I felt accepted. I had worked hard, and just thinking about it was making me hungry.

Victor and his entourage arrived. It was quite the spectacle. A long, gold Cadillac with a small motorcade of lowriders ahead and behind it pulled up in front of the entrance. A driver wearing a dark suit leapt from his seat and quickly circled around to open the rear door. Out stepped an impressive, middle-aged man in a cream-colored, double-breasted suit and hat. He had a matching dark brown tie and a hatband, a thin mustache, and oval aviator sunglasses.

Victor was probably one of the most successful Hispanic businessmen in South Phoenix at the time. He reminded me very much of my grandfather in his classy suit and Cadillac and with the way he sauntered casually about without a care in the world.

When he saw my father, he beamed and approached him with outstretched arms. My father and I had no such friendly relationship, and I watched them in silence. "Dell," he said, laughing. They bear-hugged, and he put his hands on my father's shoulders as a sincere gesture of their friendship.

Victor looked over at me.

"John," he said, shaking my hand with a smile. "Nice to meet you. Thank you for helping your father today. He is a good man who came to my rescue this morning."

Seeing my father so well thought of and respected completely baffled me. He was two different people. To them, he was nice and sincere, and they loved him, but to our family? He was a violent, abusive monster who terrorized us.

As we toured the building, Victor repeated, "Yes, yes! Very nice, Dell," with approval and enthusiasm. When he completed his in-spection, he palmed my father a wad of cash and said, "It would be a great favor to me if you would consider doing this for me on the weekends."

"Of course," my father replied with a smile.

My heart sank, and for me, the moment instantly soured. I real-ized what had just happened. I had made it through the gauntlet of the day's disgustingness and now would be expected to do it again, two days a week.

To add insult to injury, my father worked out a deal with Victor to pay me with the thousands of Coors Light beer cans left over from the night before. At the end of each day, after cleaning that miserable shithole, I would have the privilege of loading up hundreds of cases of empty cans onto a trailer. When we got home, I stacked them on the side of our house until I accumulated a wall of two rows that were about twenty cases high and thirty feet long. We would make the great haul to the recycling plant about once a month, where I would finally get paid. By the time recycling day rolled around, the neighbors were up in arms. The endless cases of putrid beer cans sat in the hot summer sun and stank horribly. The neighbors began to confront my father, and they almost came to blows.

To this day, when people tell me a job or task is beneath them, it always makes me chuckle.

Ditching School

During my second year of high school, the neighborhood became too dangerous for me to walk to and from school. The constant anxiety of being attacked and terrorized convinced me to detach and hide out as much as possible.

About this time, I stumbled upon my brother's stash of pot in his room, and I was curious. He had never let me roll anything, much less smoke it. I grabbed a couple of buds and some rolling papers but didn't know what to do next. I went to my neighbor Rick's house. Fortunately, he knew exactly what to do and quickly rolled us a couple of joints.

Upon my first toke, I was immediately transported to another world outside of my terror. It was my first experience of escaping, and it was astonishing. I'd seen Russ get high a hundred times, and now I could understand his drastic mood changes from anger to numb detachment. Within just a few minutes, my mind spaced out, and the anxiety melted away. I rested my head against the wall, feeling free as I gazed into the sky.

"Damn, dude! You're wasted!" Rick giggled. His eyes were drooping and bloodshot, and his jaw was so relaxed his mouth was hanging open. I pointed back at him and giggled.

I wanted to experience being stoned again, so I decided to find a way to buy some pot of my own. Within a week, I mowed enough lawns to buy a quarter-ounce bag and started self-medicating from morning till late at night. The downside of smoking too much pot was that, when I wasn't high, I had severe anxiety, and when I was high, I grew more and more paranoid—two sides of the same coin.

While my father was at work, I usually ditched school and went to friends' houses where I was safe to get high with them for hours. When I was high, I felt numb, and considering the trauma in my life so far, it felt like a welcome improvement.

For the most part, I went to school to meet and party with my friends and was absent far more than I attended my classes. I figured that if my father was going to beat me no matter what I did, I might as well do whatever the hell I wanted.

One morning, halfway through my junior year, I got high with a friend while ditching school. We got the munchies and went to a grocery store nearby to get some snacks. Everything came to a head when I was leaving the store. I almost ran straight into my father, who was waiting for me outside the door. He grabbed me so violently that it terrified my friend, and he ran away.

When the store manager saw what was happening, he rushed toward the door to help me. But my father locked eyes with him and made it clear his interference was dangerously unwelcome.

The manager slunk back behind the closing electric door and didn't look back. My stomach knotted in anxiety, and then things got much worse.

My father's signature move was to pick me up off the ground and slam me into the wall with only his one hand around my neck. He thumped me hard on the chest with the middle knuckle of his other hand.

"Ditching school again, you little bastard?" he growled into my ear, grinding his knuckle deeper into the muscle of my chest. I shrieked in pain. "Shut your mouth," he snarled through clenched teeth. At the time, I was too shocked to understand what was happening. Looking back, the school must have contacted him about my lack of attendance.

With hands like vice grips, my father grabbed me around the back of my neck and walked me to the parking lot. By the time we got to the car, several people had stopped to watch.

"What are you looking at? Mind your own business!" my father barked at them. He opened the door and shoved me in the driver's side, so he could keep a hold of me. "If you reach for that goddamn door, I'll break your *fucking* arm!" he said in a sinister voice. "Don't even think about trying to get away!"

I believed him. My terror, amplified by the weed, caused me to hyperventilate as I stared at my feet on the floorboard.

As we raced to the high school, he gripped the steering wheel and rocked forward and backward with rage, yelling, "Goddammit! Goddammit!" His massive forearms flexed, and his upper arms and shoulders stretched the sleeves of his shirt like the Incredible Hulk. It was terrifying. As he continued to curse and shout, he simultaneously slammed his fist deep into my thigh, instantly paralyzing it. I screamed in agony and wanted to jump out the door as we sped along, thinking I would at least go to the hospital and away from him. But instead, I was frozen.

Once we arrived at the high school, he ripped me out of the car through the driver's side. His anger seemed to have fortified his concrete grip. It felt as if his fingers were going to break the bones of my neck as he held me out in front of him, fast-walking toward the principal's office. Just as we reached the double doors, he stopped to slam me against the wall and knuckled me in the chest, growling, "When I let go, *don't you fucking run from me!* Do you read me?"

I nodded, mute with pain and fear. We turned to the door, and four staff members who had pressed their faces against the window to watch the spectacle scattered in all directions like scared cats. When we walked into the building, I could tell by the looks on their faces they were visibly shaken. All of them backed away from the counter.

In a stern voice, my father demanded, "I need to see the principal!" Instantly, the school secretary turned to sprint in the opposite direction through an office door. Quickly, the principal was power walking toward us with the panicked secretary close behind. He nervously gestured for us to come behind the counter into his office, and once there, my father forcibly launched me toward a chair and told me to sit down and shut up.

My father glared at the principal, gave my name, and demanded to see my attendance records.

"J-just a moment," the principal stammered. My stress meter went off the charts when he stepped out of the office and made his way to a massive wall of filing cabinets just outside. I knew what my attendance record was about to disclose. I watched him through the window, wondering if this would be the end of me. I saw him quickly pluck a folder out and lay it open, then he began flipping through the pages. He then closed the folder, looked out at the staff, made a hand gesture, and whispered something. They all turned away in unison, and the one closest to us picked up the phone.

I hope she is calling the police, I thought.

Instantly, two security guards appeared and nodded at the principal. They assumed visible positions just outside the door, staring directly at my father, who sat unfazed.

The principal walked back in and stood with his hands on his desk, looking stern. "I'm afraid you're going to be upset when I tell you about your son's attendance. If you become abusive to your son or to me, you will give us no choice but to call the police to have you arrested."

Because it was a work day, my father was in his military uniform, so I think the threat of calling the police really got his attention.

The principal then said, "You have every reason to be angry, but I can't allow you to be violent or abusive. May I have your word that you will calm down and be more reasonable?"

"Yes," my father replied sternly.

The principal continued, "Your son has been absent twenty-four days this semester."

"How many days are there in a semester?" my father asked.

"Fifty school days," the principal replied. "We contacted you earlier today to inform you that your son is being suspended for his lack of attendance and because he lags far behind in credits. He won't be graduating with his class next year. It's now the middle of his junior year, and he needs twenty-one credits to graduate, but John has accumulated only seven."

My father looked down at the floor, clenching his fists, and growled, "That's all I need to know." He gave me the death stare and said, "Let's go."

He reluctantly thanked the principal as we left, and the instant we got past the security guards, his hand snatched me around the neck to steer me toward the exit.

We stormed through the door and made it about twenty feet outside of the office before he threw me against the wall again, thumping me in the chest with his knuckle. As he let me down for a second, I thought about trying to escape, but it was futile. I looked around to see if the security guards were nearby, and the entire administrative staff were glaring at us through the window. Within seconds the security guards rushed through the doors coming toward us, and my father snatched me up and shoved me in the direction of the car. They followed us to the parking lot and watched us as we drove away.

I can't say I recall all of the details of what happened after we got home that afternoon, but based on the extent of my bruises and welts—not to mention the huge fist-size hole in the bathroom wall—I know it was far more violent than usual.

After about three days of solitary confinement in my room, my father ordered me to the kitchen table, where he placed a piece of paper and a pen in front of me. It was some sort of application.

After a stare down in awkward silence, he announced, "You are going into the Job Corps, you little shit. You're obviously not smart enough to stay in school, but you're not going to sit around here and eat my food and sleep in my house unless you have a job and are paying rent!" He thumped his knuckle on the table.

Reluctant to speak, I asked, "What's the Job Corps?"

"It's a trade school for teenagers getting in trouble where they teach you how to be a bricklayer or how to mix and pour concrete, and you're going! You will live there until you graduate, and then you'll go to work."

All I heard was, "You will live there." I had to hold back a smile. This was my ticket out from under his control and abuse. Without speaking, I nodded at him to signal my understanding.

By the end of the month, I'd been shipped off to the South Phoenix Job Corps. I was one of only three white guys in a dorm; the other two were older, bigger, and pretty intimidating. The rest of the guys—and there were about a hundred—were all Hispanic. Everyone looked tough except me. They had divided themselves into cliques in the outer perimeter of the squad bay of bunk beds and wall lockers. My top bunk was located near the center of the room. Within hours, it became clear I didn't belong here either, and the verbal insults began. Within a week, I was written up for fighting, even though I didn't start it. I couldn't let my guard down to sleep and would often find myself staring up at the ceiling all night, holding my knife. I was scared, and to cope, I began chain-smoking Marlboros and escaping with weed day and night.

Once again, I ruminated on the familiar question: *Why is this happening to me?* I shook my head in disbelief of Glad's conviction. *God is love? Where is God for me right now?*

I only lasted a few weeks. Afterward, I reluctantly moved back in with my parents. My father had completely withdrawn from almost all communication and wouldn't make eye contact. I was worthless, and he let me know it.

CHAPTER 7

Finding My Internal Compass

Not long after returning from the Job Corps, just before my seventeenth birthday, my girlfriend, whom I'd been seeing for about six months, announced she was pregnant.

We were both just kids and unprepared for what was happening. We sat in silence for a few moments, trying to collect ourselves and make sense of our situation.

The announcement hit me like a freight train. My knees went weak, and my life flashed before my eyes. We got along really well, I thought, and I couldn't remember a time we ever argued, so I concluded in that moment that I needed to do the right thing, and we should get married.

Excited, I said, "In a few months, I can get my father to sign the papers for the military's early entry program. I only have to be seventeen and a half. I know a guy who did this already. If we got married, they would give us a place to live and raise our child."

She looked at me and seemed sad. "I can't. I'm leaving for Oregon next week to live with some friends, and Dennis agreed to give me a ride." It all sounded so strange and transactional.

Dennis was a grimy biker dude who lived a few houses from my parents. He was a serious drug dealer with ties to some of the larger motorcycle clubs in the area. One time, he showed me his hall closet.

It was full of hundreds of little cubes of hash wrapped in tin foil, a massive pile of four-finger bags of pot, and large Ziploc bags full of speed and quaaludes. He had one of his motorcycles parked in the middle of his living room and parts were scattered everywhere. The place was filthy. We didn't like each other much from the start, but I could tell he took a liking to my girlfriend immediately.

I could do nothing and had nothing to offer to make her want to stay. When her stepfather heard she was pregnant, he threw her out, and she immediately moved in with Dennis.

Within a week, she and I said our goodbyes.

It didn't take long after she left for me to realize my life was going nowhere. Due to my inability to concentrate in class or to read and study, and due to my numerous absences, I had almost straight Fs in most of my classes and incompletes in the rest. After the principal told me I didn't have enough credits to graduate the following year, it was clear I had no choice but to drop out.

My brief attempt at becoming a bricklayer in the Job Corps had evaporated, and I had nowhere to go if my father kicked me out—an outcome that seemed imminent. When he was home, I was either gone or hiding in my room. We both avoided all contact.

By a stroke of good luck, I soon bumped into a guy I'd grown up with. He had just arrived home from the Army Reserves, looking like a completely different person. He was the older brother of one of my friends, and he told me about how the military put him through school to become an air conditioning technician. When he completed his training and came home, he immediately landed a job with a local company, and he was making great money. I was awestruck by his tailored uniform and envisioned myself wearing one someday. Thinking back, aside from my childhood fantasy of being a policeman, joining the military to escape my upbringing was the first real aspirational goal I can remember.

He had my complete attention. I needed job skills, and the military could provide me with them while also solving my immediate problem: getting away from my father. I looked up the closest recruiting office in the Yellow Pages and spoke with a stern man who insisted I address him as Sergeant Bagley. He told me what to bring and quickly set a time to see me.

When I arrived, Sergeant Bagley greeted me with a friendly hello and a vigorous handshake. His crisp uniform was mesmerizing, and I immediately felt that same jolt of motivation that told me signing up was precisely what I needed to do.

I shared what I'd heard from my friend and that I wanted to become an air conditioning and heating technician. Without hesitation, we sat down, and he started going through the paperwork to explain everything. The first thing he asked halted the entire process. "When do you graduate high school?"

I sheepishly replied with my pathetic story about not having enough credits to graduate.

He put his pen down and leaned back in his chair. "Since you will not be getting your high school diploma, you'll need to get a GED. There's nothing I can do to get you further along until you accomplish that first objective." His tone was firm, and he stared directly at me. "How bad do you want this?"

"I need this!" I insisted.

"Why?" He replied.

"A lot of reasons, but I need to get a job and to get away from my father. Almost all of my friends are going to jail and getting into trouble. I'm the only one of us without a felony. A guy I grew up with was just convicted of a felony for armed robbery and is going to prison. If I don't get out of here, I'm going to end up in jail just like them."

"Alright," Sergeant Bagley said. "I get what you're saying, son." He leaned back and grabbed a picture from his shelf. "This is my son—he just graduated from boot camp. He wanted to make me proud by doing something with his life. We had some big problems between us before joining up, but he's his own man now, and I respect him for enlisting. Respect—is this what you want from your father?"

"Yes, sir," I replied. "He was in the Marines and the Air Force. I think he'd respect me if I joined the military. I'm not going to college, that's for sure, and I'm not working construction in the summer heat ever again. The military seems like my only option."

"Nothing worth doing is easy, son," Sergeant Bagley warned. "Before I invest one more minute with you, I need to know you're serious. I get a hundred kids a month walking through that door just like you: wild-eyed and wanting to know more—but they never follow through on anything. I'd say only about five out of the hundred ever come back through that door again." He paused to size me up. "Which group are you in? The 95 percent who flake out or the 5 percent who show up and do what they say they're gonna do?"

Knowing this was my only chance, I said, "The 5 percent, sir. I want this, and I'll do what I need to do to get in!"

"I am a sergeant, not an officer," he informed me sternly. "Do not address me as *sir*; address me as *sergeant*."

"Yes, Sergeant," I said.

Sergeant Bagley continued, "I hear your words, but I only believe in actions. I've seen this movie before. Most people mean well, but they're full of shit. Here's your chance to prove me wrong. Focus on getting your GED—it's the exam you need to take in replacement of your high school diploma. Without your GED, I won't even fill out the application." He handed me a folder full of information. "Here are the instructions and the places you can go for testing. It's all there."

I accepted the folder as if it contained a treasure map. The sergeant stood. "One more thing, before we get ahead of ourselves. You're under eighteen, so I need to know your parents will give their permission and sign some paperwork. Here's some information to give them."

I left the recruiting office with a newfound sense of purpose. I needed to tell my father I wanted to join the Army and get him to sign my paperwork.

I studied his mood nervously that evening to determine when I would approach him. When I could see he was neither angry, drunk, nor happy, I decided this was the time to broach the subject. In a firm and direct tone, I blurted, "I've decided to join the Army, and

I need you to sign my paperwork for the early entry program that will allow me to join before my eighteenth birthday."

He sat in silence, studying me.

After a while, he sneered back and replied, "I'd be happy if you just did *anything*. Call the recruiter and find out what time they open tomorrow. We'll be there waiting."

"Okay," I replied.

Not long after our conversation, I left to go to a friend's house to avoid any further contact with my father. All I needed was his signature to get him out of my life, and I didn't want to take a chance of having another confrontation.

The next morning, we arrived fifteen minutes early and waited for Sergeant Bagley. He arrived early as well. He and my father locked eyes and greeted each other with a firm handshake.

After sharing a bit about their branches, units, and the conflicts they had been in, the Veterans got straight to business.

Sergeant Bagley began by saying, "Your son has decided he wants to join the Army Reserves to become an air conditioning and re-frigeration technician. How do you feel about this?"

My father crossed his arms over his chest. "Where do I sign?"

They both chuckled, and Sergeant Bagley handed my father the paper. He signed it without even reading it.

"John," Sergeant Bagley began, "you have made it clear to me that you are willing to do what it takes to get your GED, and it is your responsibility to do so. Everything stops right here until you bring me your certificate of completion for your GED. Is this clear, John?"

"Yes, Sergeant," I replied with as much conviction as I could muster.

Sergeant Bagley punctuated the moment by pulling the picture of his son off the shelf. He waved it in front of my father, beaming. "This is my son; he just graduated from boot camp, and I can already see significant improvements in him. He's his own man now."

My father's gaze drilled into me. "Take a good look at that, son," he advised. "This could be you in a few months."

Sergeant Bagley concluded, "I've given you all the instructions. Let's see how serious you are about this."

My father told me to wait outside Sergeant Bagley's office, and I caught a little of their conversation. It was evident my father hoped this would turn me around. There was a fair amount of laughter in their discussion, and as we were heading for the exit, my father thanked Sergeant Bagley for getting rid of me before he killed me. Although he said it in a joking manner, to me, him killing me seemed like a real possibility.

I needed to take the test a few times, and within a few months, I completed my GED. I immediately raced back to the recruiting office to present Sergeant Bagley with my certificate. I beamed with pride, and for the first time I could recall, I had a sense of certainty that my life was going somewhere. Getting my GED was the first real thing I had actually accomplished.

"Well done," Sergeant Bagley commented as he stood and shook my hand. "I'm sure your father is very proud of you."

"Yes, he is," I replied, but it was Glad who flashed across my mind's eye as I smiled.

The sergeant pulled out my file and his calendar and began to plan my next steps.

When I went for my physical, I was able to pass all the requirements. However, I had a significant injury to my lower left arm from two years prior that I needed to downplay. I had an accident with a broken window, and a shard of glass had cut almost all the way through the inside of my forearm, severing all the muscles, nerves, and tendons. I could move all my fingers for the most part, and everything appeared to be okay, but it wasn't. I had almost no feeling in my thumb and very little strength and feeling in my index and middle finger. Although I got through the physical, I couldn't flatten my hand out to do push-ups. Pull-ups were a problem as well because my index and middle finger wouldn't close all the way around the bar, leaving me with only my thumb and smaller fingers to work with. I could still do the required pull-ups, but if they looked close, it was easy to see I had a problem.

Fortunately, I was among hundreds of other young men being hurried along through the numerous lines of physical fitness testing. When I got to the push-up and pull-up stations, they were barely paying attention. They just wanted to hear me count off the required number of repetitions and only glanced up once or twice to check the boxes. I couldn't bend my hand back in the push-up position on the floor, so instead, I did them on my knuckles. When I stood up after my set, the physician evaluator looked at my chart, stamped it *passed*, and handed me back my folder.

That was a life-changing moment—I knew I made it.

All I could picture was me coming home from the military and impressing everyone who doubted me. I made a beeline to my neighborhood to tell my friends I was leaving for the Army. When they heard the news, I felt their envy; they could never join because of their criminal records. No one in my life had ever envied me, especially the guys I ran with, and it felt good. It made me stand taller.

Everything seemed to happen quickly, and a few weeks later, at dawn, I left for boot camp. It was a cold winter morning. Sergeant Bagley came to pick me up, and as we backed out of the driveway, my parents happily waved goodbye. It felt strange to see my father smiling at me from ear to ear—he was obviously happy to have me gone. My mother had an odd smile, one that said she loved me but that she was concerned for me. My German Shepherd, Buck, was eagerly wagging his tail, looking puzzled and probably wondering why he wasn't coming with me.

I felt a knot in my stomach. Everything familiar to me shifted, and I suddenly realized the magnitude of the decision I had made. All at once, I became disoriented and terrified.

As we waited in line at my gate in the Phoenix airport, Sergeant Bagley tried to provide me with insights into what was about to happen.

"You're going to feel awkward and out of place the first week, but so does every other recruit around you. Suck it up, keep your mouth shut, keep your eyes and ears open, and you will do just fine." We locked eyes, shook hands, and I bolted through the gate out to the plane.

I never saw Sergeant Bagley again.

Everything about the experience of traveling and flying for the first time was exhilarating. It was my first opportunity to be away from my father. I knew I'd broken his stranglehold, and I wasn't looking back.

I arrived at Fort Dix, New Jersey, at 1:00 a.m. to report in. I was relieved to see hundreds of other recruits milling along with me, and some were visibly terrified. Sergeant Bagley's words echoed in my head: all of us were awkward, and everyone was scared. Some of us just hid it better than others. I knew how to keep my composure and faded into the crowd so as not to bring attention to myself. About 30 percent of the recruits were women, and they stood in a separate line. I soon discovered we would be going through boot camp together. This realization made my nervousness subside. Maybe this wouldn't be as bad as I thought.

The physical challenges of boot camp started immediately at dawn, the instant we met our Drill Sergeants. They began to thrash us with push-ups, pull-ups, and leg lifts in the dark as if our efforts were what would make the sun rise. The ground was frozen, and the pull-up bars had ice on them from the rainy night before.

My old arm injury hindered me from the start, but I camouflaged my movements from direct observation of the Drill Sergeants by hiding in the blur of motion all around me. Everywhere and at all times—whenever possible—I made sure to stay out of direct observation. My knuckles were bleeding and scabbed all the time, but it wasn't the Drill Sergeants' job to care.

As far as carrying big, heavy packs, marching for twenty miles, and qualifying at the rifle range, I was good to go. I had motivation in spades. Interestingly, we were losing recruits left and right because they couldn't do what was required, and more men dropped out than women.

I found several creative ways to conceal my limitations during our physical fitness testing. I continued to do massive amounts of push-ups on my knuckles, and the Drill Sergeants thought it was hardcore. For pull-ups, I placed my thumb over my index finger to keep my two fingers from sticking up above the bar.

Unfortunately, a week or so before graduation, I was called out by the Senior Drill Sergeant. He had been giving me the stink eye off and on during our regular physical training.

He walked right up to me and put his face into mine. "Stand at ease! Eyes front, Private."

He stepped away and quickly gathered a few other Drill Sergeants into a circle while he spoke to them. Suddenly, they marched in my direction and formed a circle around me.

For the next five minutes, they took me through the familiar drill. "Get on your back, on your feet, on your back, on your feet, on your back, on your feet, mountain climbers, mountain climbers, mountain climbers, bend and thrust, bend and thrust, bend and thrust, faster, faster, *faster*."

The Senior Drill Sergeant ordered me to do pull-ups. I jumped and snatched the bar and counted out six reps when one of them yelled, "Hey, hero! What's wrong with your fingers?"

The Senior Drill Sergeant yelled out to the rest of them, "You see? This is what I'm talkin' about!"

He then glared back at me and yelled, "Get in the front leaning rest position—ready! Do push-ups."

After the count of ten, he yelled, "Get off your knuckles and outstretch your hands, Private!"

I outstretched my hand and kept cranking out reps, but my elbow stayed bent, and my shoulder lowered to compensate. I couldn't straighten my arm in the fully upright push-up position.

I was busted.

"Get on your feet, and lock it up, Private," the Senior Drill Sergeant yelled. The Sergeants then closed in all around me.

Nose to nose, the Senior Drill Sergeant studied me. "I'm going to ask you one more time, and one time only, Private Fuck-Up: what is wrong with your hand and your fingers?"

I snapped to attention, "Senior Drill Sergeant, sir, I injured my arm, sir!"

"Did you go to sick call?"

"No, sir!" I yelled back at him while staring straight ahead.

"Private Fuck-Up, show me your injury!"

I rolled up my sleeve. When he saw my scar, his eyes got big, and he went ballistic.

"What is that nasty-ass scar?" he yelled less than an inch from my nose, peppering my face with his spit. "You mean to tell me this is a preexisting injury? Before you joined my beloved Army, *you piece of shit?*"

"Uh, yes! Drill Sergeant!" I replied.

He looked around at the other Drill Sergeants. "I got this."

As they turned away, each barked a different insult, but all were in unison.

"Get him out of here!"

"Piece of shit!"

"Weak-ass non-hacker!"

The Senior Drill Sergeant grabbed me by the scruff and said, "Your ass is coming with me!"

We marched straight over to a nearby medic. The Senior Drill Sergeant yelled to all within earshot, "Process this lowlife piece of shit out of my sight and out of my beloved Army. This Private had a preexisting injury before he joined, and he's all kinds of fucked up."

He returned his attention to me and resumed yelling directly at my face. "My job is to take civilians and turn them into professional warfighters by the time they graduate. I don't give a *damn* if you are one week from graduation. You're broken and unreliable to your fellow soldiers in a combat situation. You ain't graduating with the platoon. Goodbye, Private Asshole. Go home to your momma—we can't use your broke ass." He then made a sharp about-face and marched away back to the platoon.

My mind raced with images of my father, disgusted with me again, and I envisioned my friends laughing at me. The idea of returning to my neighborhood like this was devastating. This disaster reinforced everything I knew was wrong with me.

I'm broken, thundered louder and louder in my head.

The thought of facing my father was unbearable, but I had nowhere else to go.

Later that evening, I called Glad in desperation. It took only a call with her to provision myself for the journey I was about to take from boyhood to manhood. A simple reminder from my Glad nudged me forward.

"When you were a young boy, and you were afraid all the time, we talked about how someday you would be a man and free from your father's abuse. Do you remember this, John?" she asked.

"Yes," I responded miserably.

Glad continued. "You may be afraid to face your father, *but you are not your fear*, and you are no longer the scared little boy you once were. You are now a man, and the time has come for you to live your own life. If you cannot reconcile with your father over this, then you must leave and make your own life. There is no third option. Either you must reconcile and allow him to see you as a man, or you must leave and build your own life—also as a man. He has no control any longer over you or your life choices. Do you understand?"

"You're right, Glad," I responded. "You're right. Thank you."

"I want you to focus your courage toward how you will choose to respond to your father if he becomes aggressive or abusive. This includes how he may want to judge you unfairly or belittle you.

"In your infancy and childhood, your father held you as his prisoner. His need to control you comes from a place of his own limitations, his own pain, and his own upbringing by his father—this is the only map he knows. Someday, perhaps you will find it in your heart to forgive him, but now is the time for you to take your sovereignty back. It is time to reclaim what is rightfully yours: you, the whole you, and all that comes with it. You will heal with time as you evolve and grow. But remember, all of your life experiences, no matter how traumatic, have made you ready. You can wish that you had an idealistic childhood, but this will blind you from opening the gifts of adversity that have been imparted to you through your pain. Each and every one of your experiences has come with a lesson—this is a gift to you in some way, shape, or form. Seek the lessons, and set yourself free from your attachments to those experiences."

Glad paused. "What are you experiencing as I share these things?"

A continuous flow of recollections of bad experiences cascaded across the screen of my mind. "I'm nodding my head and taking in what you have said."

"And how will you respond when your father attempts to intimidate you?"

I took a deep breath. "I will not face him or match his aggression. I will turn away and leave, no matter what he says or how aggressive he becomes."

"Exactly, John," Glad emphasized. "*Exactly*."

It took about thirty days of out-processing before I got my plane ticket home, and it was the longest month of my life.

When I arrived at the Phoenix airport, I dreaded calling my father to ask for a ride. That route struck me as a sure way to invite his abuse. So, instead, I took the bus. It was a depressing ride through my old neighborhood. My mind raced as I wondered what would happen when I met my father. As the bus rumbled down street after street, the reality sunk in that, once again, I would be stuck in this crime-infested, dangerous, godforsaken place with very few options. In theory, my father could no longer abuse me, but I had nowhere else to go. Glad's inspiring words and my newfound sovereignty had settled in, but the reality of where I would live was weighing heavy.

When I arrived at my parents' home, I decided not to walk through the door as I had done all of my life. Instead, I knocked, stood back, and waited on the porch.

My stomach soured when my father answered. He just stood in the doorway, silent and angry, blocking the entrance and glaring at me. He wouldn't shake my hand and stood sentinel as if to say with his crossed arms, *You will not pass.*

"Couldn't even make it through *Army* boot camp," he spat in disgust.

He was a Marine Combat Veteran in the Korean War and an Air Force Combat Veteran of Vietnam—old school, judgmental, and hard. He hadn't really thought much of me choosing the Army in the first place. My mother stood behind him. She was ecstatic to see me, but she was crying. I soon realized it was because she was unable to shove my father aside to let me in. After a long and awkward silence, I threw my duffle bag over my shoulder, turned, and walked away, just as I had told Glad I would do.

Once again, I faced the familiar feeling of being less than worthless to my father, but this time, something else had been triggered. I had taken my sovereignty back, and for the first time in my existence, the tethering of the control my father held over me had been irreparably severed. Forever.

A tribute to Glad, I thought. I was transformed and galvanized into a man the instant I took my power back from my father, and it didn't matter if he realized it or not.

I went next door to my friend Rick's house, and his mother let me sleep on the couch to give me time to figure things out.

The next day after my father left for work, I snuck over to see my mother.

"Your father will not allow you to live here," she cried. "There is nothing I can say or do to change his mind. Believe me, I've tried."

"It's okay, Mom," I assured her. She looked frazzled and tired, weakened in her advanced Parkinson's state. I tried to send her a confident smile. "Don't worry, I'll figure something out."

She gave me some money to get by and put some food in a paper bag. "Come by the house to eat and clean up when your father has gone to work. He'll change his mind."

He didn't. And when my mother forced him to allow me over for holidays, we didn't speak.

For the next ten months, I slept in the front yard next door or crashed at different friends' houses. When I thought I could get away with it, I slept in an old camping trailer on the side of my father's house. I think he found out eventually but didn't say anything about it.

After a few months of being completely miserable yet determined to get out of my neighborhood, I decided to see if it would ever be possible to rejoin the military. It seemed hopeless, but since I wasn't even on speaking terms with my father, I thought I had to give it a shot. Somehow, I needed to find a way to heal my forearm and hand enough to prove I was fit to rejoin.

When I went back to the recruiter's office, I discovered Sergeant Bagley had been assigned to a new duty station a few weeks prior. The recruiter who took his place was nowhere near as impressive. After telling him my story and that I wanted to find a way to rejoin, he chuckled and said, "Good luck with that. Ain't gonna happen."

His dismissive tone made my blood boil, so I asked to be bumped up the chain of command to the officer in charge.

Reluctantly, he stood and said, "Okay, hero. Wait here."

Within a few minutes, a Major appeared in the doorway.

"I understand you were separated during boot camp and given a medical discharge." He said, as he looked me up and down. "What was the nature of your injury?"

Pulling up my sleeve, I showed him my scar. "I had a severe laceration to my lower arm, and it wasn't completely healed before I enlisted, sir. I was about one week from graduation. Once it's fully healed, how do I reenlist, sir?"

The Major's voice took on a dismissive tone. "A medical waiver would be highly unlikely since you have already been separated once on a medical discharge."

All I heard was "highly unlikely" and seized the moment.

"*Highly unlikely*, sir? So, it's possible but highly unlikely?"

"*Very* unlikely," he emphasized.

"Sir, how do I find out what I need to do to try?"

The corners of the Major's mouth twitched though his expression remained otherwise unchanged. "There's a medical board once a month to review cases, and you would have to have a passing physical to get your file in front of them. But that doesn't guarantee anything. They don't approve many."

"Thank you, sir," I replied. "I will be back when my arm has healed up enough to take my physical."

The Major shook my hand and wished me luck.

I departed in a frenzy of excitement and anticipation for what the future held. I had hope, and that was all I needed.

If there was even a slim chance, it was all I had.

I found a sports medicine doctor willing to examine my arm. He indicated I had a good chance of regaining some of the range of motion in my hand, but I would need a number of sessions with his physical therapy team. I didn't have insurance and couldn't afford to pay for sessions, so he showed me a series of stretching exercises to begin and told me to come back in six weeks.

Within a few weeks, I had a small but increasing improvement in my range of motion, and my optimism began to grow. I decided it was time to reach out to the medical board office to prepare my paperwork to schedule my physical sometime in the coming months. When I got to my exam, I wanted to be ready.

By the time I returned to the doctor for my follow-up appointment, I could stretch and use my hand and wrist well enough to have a decent range of motion. Not quite good enough for a perfect push-up, but I knew I could get by in the boot camp exam and physical fitness tests. I still lacked a fair amount of strength and feeling in my two fingers and thumb, but the doctor said, if I was lucky, it might come back gradually over time.

About a month later, my mother gave me a letter that had arrived from the review board. My medical exam had finally been approved and scheduled. My persistence with anyone and everyone involved in the review board process had paid off. I had gotten to know several people there pretty well, and they were rooting for me. Two of them even had a fair amount of sway with some of the review board members.

When the day finally arrived for my physical, I was ready, physically and mentally. When I met the doctor, the building was full of recruits, and I figured this could work in my favor.

I decided to take the initiative in the first few moments with the doctor as he took my folder.

"Good morning, doctor. I'm here for a re-exam. I made it to a week before graduating boot camp, but an injury I had before joining hadn't healed up fully. I was separated on a medical discharge and told to try back when it was fully healed. That was about nine months ago, and now I'm good to go, sir."

I shut up and waited while he reviewed my charts and medical records. I figured being relaxed and sure of myself was my best shot, and it worked.

The doc simply looked up and said, "Okay, let's see how you do." He walked to the pull-up bar. "Get to it," he said.

I snatched the bar and cranked out twenty dead hang pull-ups, keeping my weakest fingers down on the bar. I still had significantly less strength and feeling in them, but I got them to rest on the bar alongside my other fingers. He then had me do a couple of sets of twenty push-ups along with other various flexibility exercises.

When we were done, he simply looked me in the eye and said he'd let me know in a couple of weeks after the next review board.

Those few weeks felt like the longest of my life. I didn't sleep and lost my appetite, hanging everything I had on hope.

A month later, I received an envelope from the medical board and was nervous to open it. As I held it in my hand, I knew that what was inside would determine my future. I decided to go to a park near my parents' house to read it, my thoughts racing as I walked. *Did I do all I could do? What will become of me if I don't get my waiver? I shouldn't have gotten my hopes up; this was a stupid idea.*

Preparing for the worst, I hoped for the best as I tore the end of the envelope and pulled out the folded letter. Closing my eyes while unfolding it, I paused for a moment before opening it.

As the letter came into focus, it contained only a single brief paragraph stating that my medical waiver had been issued, and I was eligible for reenlistment.

Remembering the Major's comment from the recruiting office, "highly unlikely," made me chuckle as I read the paragraph, over and over, feeling I was reissued a license to live.

I sat on the news for a couple of weeks, unsure whether I should reenlist without telling my father. The alternative was informing him and expecting him to be an ass about it.

While I was considering my options, I ran into a guy who was the older brother of one of my friends growing up.

Holy shit! What the hell happened to him? I asked myself as we shook hands. He was bigger, much more muscular than I had remembered. He had a super short, buzzed haircut, his skin held a dark tan, and he was wearing a cool-looking, collared shirt with a map of an island across the front with "PHILIPPINES" emblazoned in big, bold letters. He was on leave from the Marines, and man, he looked tough as nails—no shit!

While we caught up, he rolled up his sleeve to show me his tattoo of an eagle, globe, and anchor—the Marine Corps emblem—with the letters "USMC" underneath.

A vision of my father as a Marine at my age came to me, and an energetic charge hit me like a bolt of lightning. *Holy shit! I've got my waiver; I could do this!* Yeah, sure, it would make my father proud, but it would be something more challenging than anyone would ever expect me to do. I envisioned myself being in this guy's place: a Marine home on leave. No one messed with him.

I decided right then and there that there was no way I would be returning to the Army.

Excitement and purpose pulsed through my veins. *I'm joining the Marines!*

CHAPTER 8

Retribution Is Far Beyond Rage

Medical waiver in hand, I marched straight to the Marine Corps recruiter's office. The staff Sergeant I met with was skeptical at first, but once he understood my paperwork was legit, he joked, "So, you couldn't make it through Army boot camp, and now you want to go through something ten times tougher? This will definitely pull your head out of your ass."

Once I signed the enlistment paperwork, my gut told me to keep quiet, go to boot camp, and come home a Marine to show my father I had it in me. But after telling my close circle of friends the news, the excitement got to me, and I decided to tell him I had reenlisted. That evening I bought him a twelve-pack of beer as a peace offering to break the ice.

I stood in front of my parents' house, nervously pacing back and forth, conflicted. I wondered if telling him was a good idea, but the other part of me was sick of him looking right through me in disgust. All my life, it seemed my father didn't know what to think of me or what to do with me. I was sure every time he looked at me, I reminded him of his own failure as a father—by his metrics, anyway.

I guess this was why I hated calling him *Dad*. Whether or not I had failed *him* as a son, he had—by nearly every standard imaginable—failed me as a father. Our perspectives sort of canceled each other out.

I walked to the door and gave it a solid knock and within a few seconds, saw the light of the peephole darken, letting me know he could see me. First, the security chain clacked against the door, followed by two deadbolts unlocking. The door cautiously opened just a crack. As expected, when he looked at me, he telegraphed a sentiment of deep disappointment. As usual, he positioned himself on the threshold, sending me the familiar unspoken message: *You will not pass.*

"What do you want?" he asked. His voice was deep and condescending.

As I handed him the beer, I said, "I need to tell you something important. Can I come inside?"

I was astonished that, without a word, he stepped aside for me to enter.

My mother was surprised he let me in. Mom was elated and stood up from her chair, almost falling to greet me with a long hug and a kiss on the cheek. A silent nervousness radiated from both of us.

"What is it you want to tell me?" My father pointed to Glad's throne, the Victorian chair closest to the door, and commanded me to sit.

As I sat, memories of all the mornings I had spent with Glad sharing breakfast and soaking up her words swelled within me and settled my nerves.

"I'm leaving for Marine Corps boot camp in a few weeks," I informed him firmly.

My father's stern look deepened into a scowl.

"I went through the process of getting my medical waiver," I continued. "They cleared me to reenlist. I had a choice of branches and decided to join the Marines."

As he studied me in silence, I gripped the armrests of Glad's throne. My father was the monster I hated; he was a man who failed me and abused not only me but my mother and my siblings, yet, here I was, seeking his approval. I felt a sense of rage beginning to boil within me, and I wondered if my father and I were going to collide.

Finally, my father folded his arms across his chest and spoke. "You sure about this? I don't think you have any idea what you're getting yourself into."

I looked him straight in the eye, confident despite all my many feelings. "I'm sure."

He slowly pulled a beer from the twelve-pack and sneered. "Okay, let's see where this goes." To my surprise, he popped the top of the beer and handed it to me, then got himself another.

Sensing a moment of reconciliation, my mother tried to further break the tension by asking me if I was hungry.

"Sure," I answered. She slipped her hand into mine and hurried me away into the kitchen.

Within a few short weeks, it was time for me to go. It felt like déjà vu: my parents once again stood in the driveway while the recruiter and I pulled away, waving goodbye while my dog wagged his tail.

As we drove away, I felt the weight of a pit developing in my stomach. I was screaming to myself, *What the hell have I done?* And then the pit began to exude panic. I was leaving for thirteen weeks of pure hell to become a Marine.

All the way to the airport, the recruiter tried to fill me in on what to expect, but I knew he could tell—like all the other kids he recruited—I was scared and nervous.

When we got inside the terminal, he kept close to me, like a guard. He walked just behind me through security and beside me as we fast-walked to my gate. I could feel his unspoken message: *Don't run, kid.*

When it was time for me to board, I glanced back at him. He was impeccable in his uniform, staring at me with an iron jaw and a stone face, without a smile or a wave. He had accomplished his mission, and I'm sure this was a solemn moment he prepared for and executed a thousand times.

The plane ride from Phoenix to San Diego was just over an hour. All along the San Diego runway was a tall fence separating the airport from the Marine Corps Recruit Depot. I could see platoons of recruits in both clusters and in single file all over the obstacle courses. Knowing what I was about to go through was exhilarating and depressing all at the same time.

Stepping off the bus at the Recruit Depot was a shock. The instant I set foot on the asphalt, the drill instructors commanded, "Get on the yellow footprints, shitbags!" The same, panicked thought began flashing at the forefront of my mind like a warning sign: *What in the hell have I done?* My mind raced as I realized I was locked into the base with no other option but to deal with what came next.

Unbidden, Glad's advice returned to me like a cool breeze, and I repeated it as my mantra: *Courage is at the core of my being.*

I accurately anticipated some of what the first week was like thanks to my experience in the Army's boot camp—mostly orientation, dental work, and the issuing of all our gear. However, this was the only similarity between the two branches.

Army boot camp was a mix of about 70 percent men and 30 percent women. Boot camp there lasted only six weeks, and more men washed out than women. The Drill Sergeants were professional for all their incredible intensity.

Marine boot camp lasted thirteen weeks and was hell on earth. There was an extreme increase in the frequency and intensity of physical exertion. "Pain is weakness leaving your body!" was shouted at us like a merciless mantra until we could be made to believe it. Training began every day before sunrise and didn't end until well into nightfall.

The Army has Drill Sergeants; the Marines have Drill *Instructors*. I was made to quickly appreciate the difference, whether I liked it or not. Unlike the Army's Drill Sergeants, the Marine Corps Drill Instructors, also referred to as "DIs" were insane, sadistic, and terrifying.

Since I knew the basic marching drills from Army boot camp, I was immediately singled out and appointed as a squad leader. In short, this meant that not only did I have to square myself away, but I also had to make sure my squad was squared away as well. Within four or five days, I was fired along with all the other squad leaders for not anticipating the Drill Instructor's commands. We were the blind leading the blind, not that I would have dared to protest. Over the next week, the Drill Instructors turned over the squad leaders several more times until the platoon started performing at a higher level.

At the beginning of boot camp, the Drill Instructors appoint one recruit to the position of platoon guide. The guide becomes the recruit in charge of the squad leaders and the platoon when the Drill Instructors are occupied or unavailable. The guide carries the platoon guidon, a pole with the platoon flag. We started the first week with a guide who was an ROTC leader at his high school. He knew how to march, but other than that, he didn't command anyone's respect. The Drill Instructors spotted this immediately and fired him in front of the platoon.

Public humiliation is a big part of the Marine Corps boot camp experience.

"Give me that guidon, and get back in formation, Private Dumbass!" the Drill Instructor barked. To the rest of the platoon, he yelled, "Who is going to take his place? Which one of you candy-ass, wannabe Marines thinks he has what it takes to carry this guidon?"

It only took a nanosecond. A recruit jumped out of formation, snapped to attention, and yelled, "Sir! I do, sir!"

He was a stoic, tough guy from Chicago named Douglas, whom we already instinctively knew was the alpha of the platoon.

"Double time your ass up here and prove it!" one of the Drill Instructors commanded.

"Sir! Yes, sir!" Douglas shouted as he bounded up to the front of the platoon and onto a platform with all the DIs.

And it was on. The Drill Instructors took turns thrashing him with push-ups and mountain climbers in front of the platoon until he had a pool of sweat on the floor the size of a trash can lid. He then stood at attention for an hour while the DIs drilled him with question after question to see how much of the Marine Corps's core knowledge he'd memorized. Though he completely screwed up some of his responses, Douglas didn't flinch. Since we were only a week or so into boot camp, the Drill Instructors were more interested to see if he had the guts rather than the knowledge.

When they concluded, the DIs stepped into a small circle to compare notes. They looked at each other and nodded in approval; then, they handed Douglas the guidon.

"*Never* let this fall," the Senior Drill Instructor commanded. "Fall in and take charge of the platoon! You are the guide until you're fired!"

Then the Senior Drill Instructor turned to the rest of us. "Listen up, shitbags," he yelled. "This is your new guide, and he is authorized to kick the living shit out of each and every one of you for any reason he sees fit. If you are behind, he will put his boot up your ass. If you are not squared away, he will bitch-slap you until you're squared away! Are you receiving my transmission?"

"Sir! Yes, sir!" the platoon yelled back in unison at the top of our lungs.

From that moment forward, we collectively descended into a new circle of hell.

Douglas was a badass, about five foot nine, a good hundred and ninety pounds of solid muscle, and maybe 12 percent body fat. He was the recruit they wanted us to be like and look like. He could only roll his sleeves past his elbows because his biceps were too big. Douglas relished his role and was always in someone's face or punching another recruit.

For some reason, Douglas and I seemed to get along, but that's because I kept my distance and my mouth shut to avoid bringing attention to myself. I knew it was only a matter of time before I would have to deal with him.

Douglas was given license to dominate every recruit in the platoon, and he loved it. He was the Drill Instructors' private hitman, like Dog the Bounty Hunter back when he was in prison. If a recruit was out of line, the DIs would glance over at Douglas and nod. Douglas would stare through them so as not to telegraph anything, but we could always tell when those moments were going down.

After that, the recruit was marked for *extra attention*, a designation nobody in their right mind ever wanted.

Several weeks into boot camp, I developed severe stress fractures in my shins from running all day in boots. I was limping badly and was ordered to report to sick bay. The doc told me my situation would continue to worsen if I didn't minimize my activity. He then pulled out my chart and made a note with his pen.

"We're going to need to put you on medical hold for a few weeks," he said. "If all goes well, you'll pick up with another platoon next cycle to complete boot camp."

The thought of starting boot camp from the beginning again was unbearable. "No, sir. I can't do that, sir," I said. I lied, "It doesn't hurt that bad, sir. I can make it through. Are there any other options, sir?"

"I want you to report back in a week for reevaluation if you make it that far. That's the best I can offer you, recruit."

"Yes, sir," I responded gratefully.

A couple of corpsmen standing next to him tightly wrapped my legs from my knees to my ankles in shin splints, gave me some anti-inflammatory horse pills, and told me they'd done all they could do.

I hobbled out of the doc's office and felt the pressure of the splints up against my shins. At first, I took small steps without bending my ankle and then slowly increased my stride's distance in an effort to appear less pathetic. A few Drill Instructors who passed me on my way back to the barracks looked at me in a familiar, dismissive way as if to say, *He won't make it.*

For the next few days, I continued to hobble around while the DIs taunted me like a relentless pack of hungry hyenas.

I was consistently last to formation for runs. You don't want to be the last dumbass running out of the barracks—ever. It makes you look like the weakest link, the one that's about to get cut from the platoon.

When we formed up for PT—physical training—the next morning, we were all wearing shorts. The Drill Instructors looked at each other in disgust the instant they saw my shins wrapped. It happened that fast: they singled me out as weak.

As the days of extreme physical training intensified, the bandages holding the splints would loosen and slide down to my ankles. I frequently needed to stagger-step to pull them up, which made me stand out more and more. Now, not only did I look weak, I began to feel weak, and the Drill Instructors fed on this like vampires, sucking every ounce of motivation from me. *I'm not going to make it!* started sounding off in my head.

Within a week, I finally reached my limit. It happened while on a long run with the platoon. No matter what I did, I was in excruciating pain. I fell out of formation without permission and collapsed to the ground holding my shins. *I'm done!* exploded throughout my mind.

Immediately, two Drill Instructors fell behind the platoon and towered over me to size up my situation.

"Lookie here, we got our first casualty of the day!" one of them screamed with an emotion I could only classify as insane joy. "Boy, what in the hell are you doin'? You ready to quit?"

I couldn't think of anything else to say, so I lied. "Sir! Removing my shin splints, sir!" I yelled at the top of my lungs, trying to buy just a few seconds off my feet to let the spiking pain subside.

The other Drill Instructor lowered his volume into a sinister voice. "Hell, boy! This ain't shit. We're only four weeks in, and you got nine more weeks to go. You ain't gonna make it! No way! *And I'm gonna see to that*, you weak little bitch!"

That brought me back to a similar moment in Army boot camp, and I could almost hear the voice of the Senior Drill Sergeant yelling, "I'm gonna kick you out of my beloved Army!"

My father's disappointment and the shame of going home broken again jolted me to my senses. Just a shadow of a thought about my father sent a massive rush of adrenaline and hate blasting through me. Enraged, I began to pull and tear at the bandages and tore the shin splints entirely off of both my legs, struggling to my feet as I stuffed them into the waistband of my shorts. Removing the splints had taken the pressure off my injuries, and I was initially surprised to find there wasn't much pain when I stood. But within a few steps of walking and then moving into a shuffle, both shins exploded as if they'd caught fire. It felt as though my flesh was being torn down the entire length of both of my shin bones, like a Velcro strap pulling apart.

"Hurry up! Hurry up! Move it, move it, move it! You're movin' like pond water. Do you know how fast pond water moves, Private?"

"Sir! No, sir!" I responded with all the force I could muster.

"It don't, you *maggot*! Not only are you weak, you're also stupid, aren't you, Private? Say it, Private Fuck-Up: 'I'm weak and stupid!'" he commanded.

"Sir! I'm weak and stupid, sir!" I repeated.

"You ain't got what it takes, you worthless piece of shit. Get your ass back up to the formation," he screamed directly into my ear. Beads of spit hit the side of my face as he continued screaming and jumping alongside me.

To anyone outside the Marine Corps, he might have looked like a man who had lost his mind.

I hobbled behind the platoon for a good quarter mile until I caught up to my spot in the formation. I stuffed the pain into a place deep inside myself by visualizing my father's disgust. That, at least, empowered me to push through it as I blended back into the platoon and finished the run.

When we got back to the barracks, it took all I had left to avoid limping. As I approached the entrance, I pulled the shin splints from my waistband and looked at them for one last time. I hadn't washed them for days. They were grimy and ripe from my sweat. As I looked at them, I felt a sense of accomplishment. I hadn't been broken by the Drill Instructors, and I hadn't heeded my critical mind, screaming for me to give up and quit.

Courage is *at the core of my being!*

Not only did I finally believe it, I owned it.

The pain was at my threshold, but I could feel my mind toughening. I was becoming more determined than I had ever felt before, and the power and promise of it felt new and different. Something triggered inside of me, and it urged me to embrace the experience.

Take the pain! Take the pain! I let out a primal scream and dunked the shin splints into a trash can just outside the door to the barracks.

My renewed sense of determination propelled me forward. As I limped, I clenched my teeth. That seemed to help suck up the pain. My conviction went to war with my critical mind and my low sense of self-worth. Something was shifting inside of me.

I knew rage, but I had never before known how to channel it.

Suddenly, an image popped into my mind. I watched myself marching in the graduation ceremony that would take place nine weeks out. *Take the pain!* became my mantra from that moment forward.

I never reported back to sick call as I had been ordered to. There was no way; they would have to drag me away from the Marine Corps.

My pain reached its excruciating peak and remained that way for another three weeks. Eventually, my damaged shins began to numb and harden, and the pain started to subside. A six-inch-long indention ran down the outside of both shins where the flesh had torn away from the bone. But, like the welts I had as a boy from my father, my wounds healed. The process fascinated me. Eventually, my limping returned to a fuller stride, and I could keep up with the platoon.

I was no longer last out of the barracks. Now, I was close to the leader in the pack. There, I could blend in and choose where and when I wanted to stand out.

The Drill Instructors no longer addressed me as "Private Lamont," which stood for "Low Man on the Totem Pole." I was no longer the weakest recruit about to get cut from the platoon.

The stronger I showed up, the faster they looked for the next "Lamont" somewhere else, and that was fine by me. They had hardened me up and now hunted for weakness in the other recruits.

Now, my goal was to pass all the intensifying physical and mental tests, and I had a strategy that had worked for me growing up. Due to the dangers I experienced throughout my upbringing, I'd learned any display of vulnerability opened a person up to both emotional and physical pain. Therefore, I had become adept at concealing my shortcomings whenever I sensed trouble, and I learned how to avoid or handle most situations through this lens.

My awareness instantly tuned to my environment, and I began to sense the smallest of details in the rapidly changing conditions around me.

Through this heightened state of awareness, I developed ways to minimize my fear of failure and embarrassment to avoid appearing vulnerable. Whenever possible, I found a way to hang back and observe other people's actions and communication before speaking or attempting a task in front of anyone.

This strategy worked well, and I was surprised to find I could match or exceed most anyone else's best performance. I was no longer petrified of being singled out as inferior the way I was when I was a kid—terrorized by those who prey on weakness.

In the military, there were so many others ahead of me in practically every circumstance. I could observe and learn a great deal about their approach and body posture to see where they were weak and why they crumbled and failed. The lack of confidence on their faces and the awkwardness of their body movements telegraphed imminent failure. If I were ever labeled a klutz or singled out for being awkward and nervous, I would be discounted in the eyes of the other recruits. Worse yet, if the Drill Instructors observed weakness, I would be thrashed and belittled in front of everyone.

The last place I wanted to be was on the Drill Instructors' shit list, which meant extra PT and bullying from the platoon. To avoid this, I overcompensated for my insecurities by obsessing about how to mimic the body movements, attitudes, and communication of the best performers and toughest alphas I could observe.

When it was my turn to be tested on the ropes course, combatives, or water survival, I looked instructors in the eye, spoke clearly, and attacked the training exercises with conviction. I usually made the cut on my first attempt. I didn't understand then how my high-intensity overcompensation would pay off, but my confidence grew exponentially when my fitness exploded to higher and higher levels. The scared kid I once was began to fade off into the past.

My ability to concentrate was off the charts in physical and experiential training. However, my capacity to focus while reading and my ability to concentrate when studying was still an obstacle. I had great difficulty memorizing an ever-growing list of mandatory core knowledge that included a set of general orders.

At all hours of the day and night, Drill Instructors would snap us to attention, poking their fingers in our chests while screaming, "What is your fifth general order, Private? What is your eighth general order? What is the muzzle velocity of your weapon? What are the front and rear hand position measurements while marching?"

Chest poking was still a big trigger for me. I decided the Marine Corps must have been where my father adopted this behavior to assert his authority over me when I was growing up.

It's funny what we are capable of memorizing. One of our Drill Instructors had a particular obsession with word-for-word definitions around every aspect of our core knowledge, so we had to memorize them verbatim.

He would use this sadistic obsession to trip us up or stump us in our definitions, so he could thrash us with more PT. The same instructor would tower over us as we held in the front-leaning rest push-up position for eternity and yelled, "*I am a living God* creating professional warfighters out of you knuckle-dragging primates."

Suddenly, this crazy DI pulled me out of PT and pinned me against the wall, shouting in my face, "Private, what is the definition of *nomenclature*?"

Without hesitation, I yelled, "Sir! The definition of nomenclature, sir: a system of names used in the classification of an object or thing, sir!"

Unimpressed, he immediately followed with, "What is the nomenclature of your weapon, Private?"

Again, without hesitation, I shouted, "Sir! The nomenclature of my weapon, sir! The M16A1 5.56-millimeter rifle is a six and a half pound, air-cooled, gas-operated, direct impingement, rotating bolt, magazine-fed, fully automatic, shoulder-fired weapon with a maximum effective range of five hundred and fifty meters, sir!"

I was astonished I had pulled the information out of my head and delivered it with such rapid-fire accuracy.

As if we were in a scene right out of *Forrest Gump*, the DI yelled, "Goddamn, Private! You nailed it! Burn one! No, burn two!" He pivoted and marched away to find somebody else to harass.

It was the first time any of us heard a positive word come from that sadistic bastard's mouth. "Burn one" meant take a smoke break, and "burn two" meant take your sweet ass time about it. I savored those few minutes, silently gloating as the rest of the platoon was made to do a massive amount of push-ups. I leaned against the wall while all the recruits gave me the stink eye, and I slowly dragged on a couple of Marlboros.

I guess I'm not so stupid, after all, I thought with a sense of pride.

The Whiskey Locker

As we reached week seven of boot camp, our company was transported to the rifle range at Camp Pendleton. By now, I had a good sense of how Marine Corps and Army boot camps compared. In Army boot camp, after six weeks, I would have just graduated a week prior with a good level of fitness and some basic rifle and infantry training. In Marine Corps boot camp, I was just starting to continuously max and exceed my previous fitness levels and still had six weeks to go. In addition to pistol and rifle training, we would also be preparing for mountain training.

Camp Pendleton is a smaller, more isolated Marine base away from the central recruit training installation in San Diego, and there were far fewer officers snooping around and checking up on things. With the barracks being a little more secluded, it enabled the beatings from our platoon guide and squad leaders to continue, and they started getting out of control. This was the perfect place for the Drill Instructors to harden us up while having some sadistic fun.

Every night, anyone who got out of line throughout the day was dragged into the whiskey locker by the four squad leaders. There, our platoon guide, Douglas, waited to give the unfortunate recruit a beating. The whiskey locker was a small, five-by-five foot cleaning supply closet with a large deep sink. The room was dark and musty, with a single light bulb above the sink. It was intentionally left empty—a secret room, out of sight, where they would try to break us.

Anyone going to the bathroom—also called "the head"—would hear a small stampede of footsteps shuffling by. That was the sound of squad leaders dragging one of us past the toilet stalls and into the whiskey locker. Usually, this shuffling was accompanied by some whimpering, and you could hear the thump of body shots while people whispered, "Shut up!"

When the door to the whiskey locker closed, the sounds of simultaneous thumps, slaps, and muffled cries echoed through the shower room and the head but not loud enough to be heard in the squad bay or in the Drill Instructors' quarters down the hall. I heard grown men crying and whimpering, pleading for the abuse to stop.

But that was the whole point of this shit-fest: they wanted to break us down to find our rage. As far as they were concerned, anyone who couldn't handle it couldn't be a Marine.

Every time I saw someone the next morning after their beating, they were twisted inside. For better or for worse, the DIs were tapping into our rage, and you could feel the platoon's performance tightening as a higher and higher percentage of us went to the whiskey locker.

I remember one night going to the bathroom in one of the stalls, listening to yet another whiskey locker beating. They had just taken a guy inside. He was an easygoing guy everyone liked, but they thought he was too soft and that he smiled too much. I heard what sounded like a gut punch, and he let out a groan. *Thump, thump, thump*—I could hear him whimper with each blow. My eyes grew bigger as I gritted my teeth. *No way, I'm not cryin'.* I knew my time was coming.

The whiskey locker beatings by the guide and squad leaders gave the Drill Instructors deniability. It was nerve-racking for each of us as we waited for it to be our turn. Some of us got it more than once or twice if we failed to get our shit together.

My time came about a week after arriving at Pendleton. No one liked this one guy in the platoon from New Jersey; he talked too much and was constantly falling out of runs from exhaustion. I was squaring away my foot locker, and for some reason, he started giving me a hard time and kept getting too close. After warning him to back off, I smacked him across the face open-handed and stared at him in silence. He froze and stared back for a moment before walking away. I didn't think anything more of it until that evening when I got a slug in the shoulder from Bagget, one of the squad leaders.

"Go to the whiskey locker," he ordered. "The guide wants to see you. Now!"

This is it, I thought. Adrenaline bolted through me in a body memory of my entire upbringing at the hateful hands of my abusive father. Instantly, I went numb and empty, showing no fear or emotion whatsoever. I was ready.

My lack of fear made Bagget visibly nervous, and he stepped aside, so I could walk in front of him. Of the four squad leaders and the platoon guide, Bagget was the weakest link. He looked nervous and scared most of the time and tried to put up a tough guy front, but no one bought it. He marched behind me past the Dis' quarters, where the other three squad leaders were waiting. When they grabbed me, instead of resisting, I pushed myself toward them as we fast-walked down the hallway to the open door of the whiskey locker. There, Douglas was waiting with his arms crossed.

After shoving me in, the squad leaders squeezed past me to the other side of the deep sink. Douglas pushed me into the corner and moved to block the closing door behind him. With six guys crammed into this small closet, there was no way for me to escape. The edge of the deep sink pressed against the back of my legs.

Once again, like so many other times in my life, my words to Glad—*Why is this happening to me?*—flashed in my mind.

My knees shook, but I quickly steadied them and felt rage starting to boil inside me. *Here we go*, I thought and turned to stone as I gazed through everyone without expression. Everything slowed down. I could hear the echo of their voices and feel the shoves back and forth, but I just absorbed everything and gave them nothing.

Douglas got in my face, enraged over my lack of fear, and barked, "I thought you was cool, man! You nothin' but a punk-ass bitch. You think you're tough, punchin' another recruit in your squad?" The guide moved up nose to nose to try to intimidate me, but I'd seen this movie my whole life.

I looked right through his eyes with a blank stare and didn't blink. As I expected, that pissed him off. He tried to knee me in the groin, but I blocked him with my leg. He then tried to throw several punches at my face, but I dodged and sidestepped them. After this string of failed attempts in front of the squad leaders, he grew embarrassed. Now he was enraged.

Seething, Douglas grabbed me hard by the groin. When I bent toward him in pain, he grabbed me by the throat and picked me up completely off the ground—about chest high—and slammed me ass first into the deep sink. My legs and arms dangled over the edge, and I was up to my armpits. I looked up to see his fist crash me square in the cheek with a straight right. The back of my head slammed into the wall, and I saw stars. The bottom edge of my glasses embedded themselves into my cheekbone, and blood gushed down my face.

Then, the squad leaders joined in.

I took about ten or fifteen good hard punches to my face and the sides of my head. I didn't give them the satisfaction of seeing any tears. I didn't give them so much as a whimper.

I knew I could take anything they could deliver; they couldn't break me.

Years later, when the movie *Full Metal Jacket* came out, the blanket party scene sent me into a full-blown flashback. In that movie, a goofy recruit named Private Pyle was making the platoon work extra hard, seemingly oblivious to the impact his shortcomings had on everyone else. The platoon wanted some payback. In the middle of the night, a few recruits pinned his arms to the bed with a blanket and held a sock across his mouth to keep him quiet. The entire platoon ran in circles around his rack, beating him with bars of soap wrapped in socks or towels, like blackjacks. There was nothing Pyle could do but take it.

Every scene of Private Pyle from there forward showed him with his shit together and squared away, but the twisted, maniacal look on his face said everything.

The whiskey locker was instilling something within me far worse than rage: retribution. I had no fear. All I wanted was payback.

When the guide and squad leaders finally stopped their assault, I leaned my head back to the wall, eyes glazed and numb. I didn't break, a fact that pissed them off and puzzled them even more. That was fine by me. I almost felt a weird sense of respect emanating from them as they filed out the door and left me to tend to myself.

When I realized no bones were broken, my craving for retribution burned hot enough to melt steel. Just like Private Pyle, the worm had turned. I began to beat on the wall with my fists, harder and harder, raging and yelling; I know for sure the entire squad bay and Drill Instructors heard me.

Just an hour before, I was highly motivated and eight weeks into becoming a Marine. I knew I would make it. I visualized my graduation day, complete with my parents in the stands watching and my dad finally respecting me.

But now, I didn't care about graduation or anything else. I was numb and just wanted to destroy the men who'd assaulted me. I'd been dominated all my life, and I was all twisted up inside again, but one thing I knew for sure was that I was no longer willing to be a victim.

I slammed the whiskey locker door open and walked from the head into the squad bay, where one of the Drill Instructors was waiting for me.

"What happened to you, Private Shitbag?" he yelled.

I stood at attention and glared, wanting to annihilate him.

"I *said*, what in the hell happened to you?" he repeated, now just an inch from my nose.

"Sir! Nothing, sir!" I yelled back in his face.

"Don't you know it was lights out twenty minutes ago, Private Numbnuts? Get out of my face, clean yourself up, and get in your rack! Move!"

"Sir! Yes, sir!" I replied.

I staggered to the sink and looked in the mirror—blood was everywhere. I had a gash about an inch and a half long under my left eye where my glasses got buried into my cheekbone. Huge bumps were forming all around my head. A long gash across my nose was pouring blood over my mouth and onto my shirt. After washing my face, I grabbed a towel and held it in place as I walked to my rack. Every eyeball in the squad bay locked on me when I entered. As I walked, I intentionally locked in on each squad leader and then the guide as I went by them. Everyone was snickering and whispering insults.

That night—and every night until the end of boot camp—I laid in my rack with my gut in a knot, ruminating and obsessing over how I would sneak to the guide's rack to surprise him in his sleep. I wanted to put his lights out.

That night never came.

A feeling of betrayal from my fellow Marines and from the Drill Instructors I had idolized before the whiskey locker came over me, and I just wanted out of there. I wanted out of boot camp and out of being dominated.

It would take thirty years to untangle and transcend this experience.

As I look back, one thing I know I took away from those thirteen weeks—especially the whiskey locker—was the ability to channel my force of being. I found that my inner rage was a superpower that resided deep within me. It was a source of energy I could tap into at will.

When we finally graduated, as I had envisioned, my parents were there. My father was beaming with pride. When we shook hands, he looked straight into my eyes and nodded as if to say, *I'm proud of you.*

He didn't say it, but he didn't have to. I got it.

Without saying goodbye to anyone, my gut soured, and I pointed to the parking lot. "Let's go," I told my parents.

I had earned the title of being a Marine and had found my tribe. Still, I knew deep down that my lifetime of trauma and volatility would be a challenge to contain.

We spent the first night of my newfound freedom after boot camp at a beachfront hotel in San Diego. The next morning, I was catching up with my mother, and we called Glad for her to join us. Glad was delighted to talk with my mother and me, and I could hear the smile in her voice as she shared how proud she was over the progress I had made in my life.

At the same time, I could sense there was something making my mother nervous, and Glad wasn't giving anything away. My father never looked away from the TV. Something was up.

After our call, I looked at my mother. She sat on the edge of the hotel bed with a worried look on her face. Tears turned her eyes glassy, and she quietly opened a folder. Within it rested a piece of paper, and she carefully passed it to me.

"John, I think you know you have a child," she started, voice unsteady and fighting back emotion. "It's a boy, and his name is Danny. He's just a few months old."

Of course, I thought. It had been about a year since my former girlfriend told me she was pregnant. I shrunk inward, sad and ashamed.

"Yes, I know," I replied.

My mother took a deep breath and could barely choke out the words, "This is the legal document for Danny to be adopted by his great-grandparents."

"Danny's mother is only sixteen," she continued, "and is in some sort of trouble and mixed up with some really bad people. I've been told she is unable to care for Danny, so her grandparents have taken custody of him."

As she played with the hem of her blue dress, she said, "They are very insistent about the terms they have set for adopting Danny. They know you just entered the military and will be gone for a long time and have made it clear to your father and me that they don't want anything to do with you or any of us, and we are to have no contact with Danny or with them once the adoption papers are signed.

"They already have Danny's mother's signature allowing them to adopt him, and they need your signature as well."

She broke into tears. Seeing her pain was heartbreaking.

"I'm so sorry, John," she wept. "With my Parkinson's getting more severe, I couldn't care for Danny, and your father and I feel this is best. You need to do what is best for this child, John. Giving him the best possible chance of receiving the healthiest upbringing is the priority here."

I thought to myself, *The healthiest upbringing for Danny would be to have zero contact with my father.*

"Do you see this is what's best for him?" my mother implored.

I had just turned eighteen and would soon be heading to my first duty station somewhere in the world. I didn't know when I would return.

"Yes," I said quietly, and I signed the documents.

I spent the rest of the afternoon isolating myself in my hotel room. While it was painful to see my mother heartbroken to not have her grandson in her life, I was relieved that my father would be nowhere near Danny. This way, the monster who raised me could not abuse him.

At least he'll have a shot at a safe upbringing, I hoped.

CHAPTER 9

The Dude from Philly

After boot camp, my first duty station was radio school Twentynine Palms, a.k.a. "The Stumps." The base was in the middle of nowhere and, just like Phoenix, hot as hell in the summer.

When I arrived, the first thing I noticed was there were no Drill Instructors getting in my face or yelling at me—a welcome relief. I was no longer a recruit, and it felt good to show up as a Marine with all the others.

I was a green and freshly minted Marine, but I had made it.

Within a few weeks, I settled into the routine of barracks life on base. The squad bay I was assigned housed about sixty Marines. There were thirty on each side of a long squad bay with a large head and showers in the middle.

There were cliques of Marines clustered throughout the barracks: cowboys in one corner, Spanish speakers in another, African Americans in one area, and rockers and stoners in another. But we were all Marines, and regardless of religion or ethnicity, we talked smack about each other equally. No exceptions.

One Marine was from Philadelphia, so of course, his nickname was Philly. Several times a week, Philly would get seriously shit-faced and turn into an ass. His inner Italian tough guy would come out, and he got on everyone's nerves.

Alcohol was like liquid courage for him. Some guys bought it and backed off; most of us just ignored him. One evening before lights out, I was ironing my uniform for the next day and heard Philly and some other guys outside the window near me. At first, I didn't pay much attention.

BAM-BAM-BAM-BAM! Four firecrackers went off simultaneously as they flew by my head, sparkling and hissing with smoke. I was temporarily deaf in one ear, but I could hear them howling with laughter outside the window. I don't recall what I said when I yelled at them, but apparently, it was offensive enough for all five of them to encircle me within a few seconds.

Philly walked up close and went into his wise guy, Joe Pesci impersonation. His breath reeked of alcohol and cigarettes. "Who do you think you're talkin' to?"

Philly was wearing a hat with the front flipped up. It was one of those goofy-looking Rocky Balboa hats. He wore a white T-shirt, cuffed blue jeans, and shiny black boots. And, of course, his look included a black leather jacket complete with a belt hanging down on both sides.

He looked like he had just come from a *Grease* fan club rally. I was trying to size up how tough he would be to fight but kept picturing Fonzie from *Happy Days*.

Philly had a muscular, lean frame similar to mine, but he towered over me by a few inches. Naturally, he did the one thing tall alpha guys do: he got right up close, so I had to look up at him.

The entire squad bay got wind of a blood match, and within seconds, a crowd came from everywhere to form a big half-circle around us. All the cliques bolted to the circle from their respective corners, chanting at the top of their lungs, "Fight! Fight! Fight!"

I was blocked in with wall lockers behind me, a crowd of spectators in front of me, and the five firecracker-slinging wise guys right up close. Everyone was waiting for the gladiators to begin. It looked like something straight out of a prison movie.

My heartbeat pounded in my throat so hard my ears started to ring. As a panic attack began to build, I noticed there was something way more intense about Philly. His eyes were quivering, his pupils were massive, and he was grinding his teeth. When he cocked his head and looked at me with a maniacal expression and a big shit-eating grin, I knew this was going to end badly; they were all amped up on PCP.

Feeding off the crowd, Philly began to inch himself closer as he taunted me. Over and over, he kept pointing his finger close to my face, slinging insults.

I put my hands up about chest high, palms out toward him. "Hey, man. It's cool. I don't want any trouble."

"You should have thought of that before you disrespected us! You're not getting out of this. I'm gonna fuck you up!" Philly yelled, inching closer.

Nervous, I kept my hands up and leaned back, scanning the situation.

Suddenly, the chanting stopped, and everything went silent. The entire room whipped their heads toward the exit to the squad bay. There, the Duty Sergeant stood with his helmet, arm sleeve, and a flashlight, staring at us in silence.

I breathed a sigh of relief, thinking he heard the mob and was here to break things up. I relaxed and stepped back a bit.

Instead, he leaned against the wall in amusement and said, "I don't see anything."

I felt dizzy and disoriented as I looked back at Philly. *Why in the hell is this happening to me?* The old, anxious mantra flashed across my mind once again.

Philly stepped up right in my face, close enough that I could see every pore on his nose.

Feeling sanctioned by the watch guard—our senior by one or two stripes—the mob erupted into even louder chanting.

"Fight! Fight! Fight!"

Philly sensed my fear, and he wasn't wrong. I was terrified and could feel my knees shaking slightly. There was no way I was getting out of this, and I needed a plan.

I put my hands up to feign weakness and looked at his chin instead of looking him in the eyes. This made him even more confident. High on PCP and drunk with the power of the moment, he looked down at me with that big, crooked smile again; he thought he couldn't lose.

The dumbass looked over and winked at his buddies, then stepped out into a wider stance, putting his hands behind his back. Philly stuck his chin out at me and said, "Take your best shot 'cause I'm gonna pulverize ya." His shit-eating grin grew even wider.

And then, a miracle happened.

My hands were already up in a passive gesture, so I eased in closer, repeating, "Hey, man. It's cool. I don't want any—" *BAM!*

I elbowed him with everything I had, right in the upper part of his throat underneath his jaw. The impact took him up, and his feet left the ground as he flew back about six feet from me. He landed on the concrete with a thunderous *clap*, and there was a solid *thump* when the back of his head hit the floor. He lay there twitching, chok-ing, and hacking, with one hand holding his throat. The other hand cradled the back of his head. I thought he was done, but instead, he leaned up on one elbow and started wheezing.

Aside from Philly's choking, you could hear a pin drop. Everyone was in total shock. The Duty Sergeant popped off the wall and ran toward us with a panicked look on his face. It reminded me of an astonished, wild-eyed fan at a baseball game, as if he were coming off his seat at the crack of a bat hitting a home run. One second the Sergeant was enjoying the entertainment; the next, he must have been imagining all his precious stripes being ripped off his sleeve at his court-martial.

I kept my fists up and watched Philly like a hawk as he scrambled to his feet. He tried to speak, but he didn't have a voice. Instead, he managed to issue a whistling, wheezy scream as he plowed toward me, his head down, throwing haymakers. I gave him credit for getting back up, but I was done taking his shit.

He charged toward me, going for my waist in a wild effort to take me down. I fell backward to the floor with him over me, and I grabbed him in a chokehold. Wrapping my legs around his waist, I straightened my back and squeezed the choke tighter. His arms flailed helplessly as the lack of oxygen began to threaten his consciousness.

The Sergeant grabbed my arms, ordering me to let him go.

"Why the hell didn't you stop this in the first place?" I demanded.

"Gimme a hand!" the Sergeant commanded, and a few of the senior guys jumped in to unravel us.

I got to my feet, but Philly was down on one knee, still wheezing. Everyone was in shock. Suddenly, the crowd erupted, jumping around and high-fiving each other, screaming and yelling in excitement. A couple of buddies shouted in my ear and slapped me on the back. "Hell yeah! Way to shut him up."

After that, everyone gave me some extra space to operate, and I acted like it was no big deal. But it was. It was the first time I had ever had to coldcock someone.

That day, I learned to dig deep and stay calm.

The next morning when I woke and began to get ready for formation, Philly was fortunately nowhere to be seen. As I moved about, I noticed that a lot of guys throughout the squad bay were eyeballing me. A guy in the next bunk turned from his wall locker and fist-bumped me. "Respect!" he stated as he winked and nodded. We bumped our knuckles together. I nodded as I winked back.

Throughout the day, the experience from the night before reverberated through me, and all I kept picturing was my father standing in front of me instead of Philly. But in reality, Philly was yet another messenger offering me no other choice but the pain of growth. Breaking the paralysis of fear was like waving a victory flag in front of me. Now I was ready to look at what else my fear was holding to keep me small, which was my father. It was finally time to face him for the reckoning he had long deserved.

Taking My Power Back

As my father continued to age and I grew into adulthood and joined the military, an uneasy truce emerged between us. He no longer attempted to intimidate me physically, and I projected no fear toward him, but we both knew the time was coming for us to deal with our past.

For the most part, my entire childhood had been spent waiting and fretting in suspense to see what version of him was coming home from work each day. Whether it was morning or afternoon, I was preoccupied with five o'clock. Every afternoon was a riddle to figure out how I would need to deal with his constant volatility and abuse.

As the power dynamic shifted, I intentionally said less and became more serious when I addressed him. I didn't have it in me to become his abuser, but there was a sense of justice, a reckoning I was about to bring, looming over our tension.

It was as if, at birth, my father had taken my license to live and locked it away. Now it was time for me to take it back.

My confrontation with Philly was still fresh in my mind. I decided that the next week, while home on leave after graduating radio school, I would confront my father.

One morning when I was home, I poured a cup of coffee and casually asked my father, "I need to drive across town to pick something up; want to come with me? I need to talk to you." He looked up, puzzled, and reluctantly agreed.

As we pulled away, I found it interesting to have my father in the passenger seat. I had never been allowed to drive him anywhere—yet another example of the control he held over me. My resolve strengthened as we drove, and I began looking for a place to pull over to give us some privacy away from prying eyes.

When we entered the freeway and began to head to the outskirts of North Phoenix, I saw his fists clench, and his forearms flex. He was readying for combat, and I was already there. Approaching an off-ramp, I spotted an old abandoned gas station and decided this would be the place. As we pulled in, he asked in a direct but nervous tone, "What are we doing here?"

Remaining silent, I pulled behind the building, came to a stop, and slowly shifted into park. I didn't have a plan but noticed my absence of fear. My heart was pounding, but this time, it was from adrenaline pumping due to nervous anticipation. I turned and leaned my elbow over the seat, almost facing him.

Seeing my father anxious, fidgeting, and trying to compose himself made him appear childlike to me. I half smiled, and we remained silent in an awkward pause.

I suddenly realized my sense of self, filling and overpowering the space between us as he shrank smaller, fretting.

It was then I knew I had just taken my power back. I knew this was true as I felt my heart rate slow and took a slow, deep breath. *I no longer need to hurt him*, came to the forefront of my reptilian brain—the same part of my brain that had been readying me for battle.

I could feel Glad's approval as I calmed myself and smiled, puzzled by the twist of fate that had just occurred. I had shifted from rage to empathy, and my entire game plan for dealing with my father had just evaporated. All that remained was a void in my psyche, and I sat silent, trying to find what words needed to emerge.

"I need to talk to you about some things I'm struggling with," I said, not knowing what would come next.

"What is it?" he replied, reflecting my puzzled look.

A strange realization came next when I noticed the absence of fear in my father's presence. I didn't care what he thought, and I no longer feared what he could do to hurt me.

"I have a huge problem with authority, and I'm getting in too much trouble all of the time. Wearing glasses has always caused me to feel handicapped and inferior."

I'm unsure why I poured this out to him or what I expected. My father had never shown empathy when I tried to share my problems with him. His lack of care growing up trained me not to ask him for help or advice.

Where is this burst of vulnerability coming from? I'm supposed to be beating the shit out of him right now, I thought.

I paused as I wiped my eyes, expecting only a stone-faced look of emptiness in return. Instead, to my astonishment, his eyes were teared as well.

"I can't believe this," he replied. "These are the same things I have struggled with all my life too."

It was as if my dilemma had turned on a faucet of tears as he spoke.

For the next hour, I sat with a sense of compassionate suspense as he poured out his experiences growing up with his stern father and the tough streets of Fresno. His glasses made him the target of bullies, but unlike me, he grew more violent in dealing with his situation. Boxing was his path to dominating others—something I would later see echoed in my son, Danny. But what remained was my father's feelings of inferiority about wearing glasses and his lack of education. Because his family faced financial hardship when my father was growing up, he had to quit school during his eighth-grade year to pick fruit in the farm fields. He did it to help support his mother and eight siblings.

I was beginning to realize what had created the monster that raised me.

There was still his abuse toward our entire family and me, but I decided to set that aside for the moment. What I took away was immeasurable. I had taken my license to live back and felt I had settled a score that freed up immense levels of rage I had been directing toward him.

When he quieted, we sat in a new space of understanding each other. He didn't have any sage advice as a father, but what had just been conveyed were our relatable struggles and shared suffering.

Strangely, my father and I stood equal for the first time in our existence.

CHAPTER 10

Jump Wings

After radio school, I arrived at Camp Lejeune, North Carolina—my permanent duty station—on a rainy fall afternoon. During in-processing, the clerk opened up my file and said, "Radio operator, huh? Want to go ANGLICO?"

"ANGLICO?" I asked.

Pausing between each letter, he said, "A-N-G-L-I-C-O. It's an acronym for Air, Naval, Gunfire, Liaison Company." When I didn't say anything, he raised his eyebrows and continued, "I get a steady string of FNGs"—*Fucking New Guys*—"fresh out of radio school, and those who make it into ANGLICO love it. It's a badass unit that deploys a lot, and they're looking for radio operators. First Sergeant asks me to screen all the radio operators when they arrive to keep a steady flow of candidates coming to the unit.

"Here's the skinny," he went on to say. "Basically, ANGLICO embeds small, four-man teams into NATO assault forces from different countries. They also embed a lot with the Army 82nd Airborne out of Fort Bragg, a few hours away, and the 101st Airborne out of Fort Campbell, Kentucky. They act as a liaison team to coordinate fire missions between NATO forces and other branches while maintaining communication back to the Fleet Marine Force."

I leaned in to hear more, intrigued.

The clerk continued. "What's also cool is they get to parachute ahead with the NATO assault forces in advance of the Fleet Marine

Force and blow the shit out of everything. They can level an entire battlefield from a radio in their rucksack."

"You get to go to jump school?" I asked excitedly.

"Yeah, but it takes a while. The Marine Corps doesn't get a lot of jump billets like the Army," he explained. "ANGLICO is the only unit in the Marine Corps beside RECON that gets jump qualified unless you want to be a damn parachute rigger."

"That's badass," I stated.

He grinned at me and introduced himself. "I'm Grady."

"John," I replied as we shook hands.

"Man, I'm tellin' you," Grady continued. "If I weren't stuck here in admin and I was a radio operator, I'd be all over this. If you don't, you're gonna get stuck in some grunt unit with sixty other knuckle draggers in a squad bay. ANGLICO has a sweet barracks with one or two men per room."

That sounded great to me. "Jump wings, travel, luxury digs? Hell, yes! Sign me up," I said enthusiastically.

"There's just one catch," Grady said, tilting his head. "You have to pass an interview with their First Sergeant. And he is one scary sumbitch!"

I smiled. "Let's get this party started," I said, giving him a solid fist bump.

"Have a seat; I'm on it!" he responded.

A few minutes later, he yelled, "He's on the way. He'll be here in thirty minutes."

As ten minutes turned to twenty, my tension began to peak. My palms were sweating, and my heart was pounding.

"What the hell am I getting myself into?" I whispered.

Right at the thirty-minute mark, the First Sergeant bolted through the door and scanned the room, locking eyes on me as he walked to Grady's desk. The instant our eyes met, I understood precisely what Grady had meant. This man was a scary-looking freak of nature. He was about six-four, must have been at least two hundred and thirty pounds, and had maybe 10 percent body fat. He looked to be in his late thirties, and his face was chiseled with an iron jaw. His arms were too big for his uniform and stretched his sleeves tight and to their limits.

He snatched my file out of Grady's hand and gave me the stink eye as he walked straight toward me. I could feel him sizing me up like a hungry timber wolf.

I snapped to attention, and he walked right up just a few feet away and made me look up at him. As he looked down on me, I stared at his Adam's apple.

I was instantly triggered and felt irritated. I knew what he was doing; he just wanted to sense if I was intimidated. As was my experience with so many "tough guys," I'd seen this episode too many times. I went empty, gave him nothing, and stared right through him.

"I'm First Sergeant Bowman," he said in a deep, booming voice. "I understand from Lance Corporal Grady he's filled you in on some of the details of what we do, and you think you got what it takes to be in my unit."

"Yes, First Sergeant!" I responded. I kept my composure by focusing on the gold jump wings pinned to his uniform, glowing against the dark green of his fatigues. I was mesmerized.

When he noticed I was fixated on his jump wings, he looked down at them and said bluntly, "You want a pair of these, you got to earn 'em!"

"Yes, First Sergeant," I agreed.

Immediately, I determined I wanted those pinned on my chest, and I was going to make it into this exclusive club.

I think the first sergeant had done this drill so many times with prospects that he knew how to instantly hook FNGs into the fantasy of getting their wings. I bit, and the hook set deep. As they say in the South, "Big hook, big bait, big fish."

"Sit down," he ordered. I stepped back and took a seat as he continued to stand at parade rest, my file behind his back. Man, he was impressive. His uniform was impeccable, and he filled every square inch of it. Now he looked even more gigantic.

In rapid-fire succession, he began a series of quick, targeted questions.

"You married?"

"No, First Sergeant."

"Plannin' on gettin' married any time in the next few years?"

"No, First Sergeant."

"Got a girlfriend?"

"No, First Sergeant!"

"Plan on gettin' one?"

"No, First Sergeant!" That response was bullshit.

"Fitness—can you run four miles in boots and cammies in less than twenty-eight minutes?"

"Yes, First Sergeant."

"At least twenty dead-hang pull-ups?

"Yes, First Sergeant."

"At least sixty sit-ups in less than ninety seconds? Can you pound out sets of fifty push-ups?"

"Yes, First Sergeant!"

"Good," he replied. "'Cause until you go to jump school six months to a year from now, this is the daily drill every morning at zero four-thirty. And then you get to PT and run eight to twelve miles with the rest of the company at zero seven hundred."

He studied me for a few seconds. "You willin' to put in this level of commitment?"

Now I really wanted this. "Yes, First Sergeant."

"If you're bullshittin' me, son, and you can't cut it, I'll smoke your ass out and bounce you straight to grunts."

I looked him in the eye in silence. Then, he gave me a sinister grin.

"You scared of heights, aintcha?"

"No, First Sergeant!" I replied sternly, even though *hell, yes*, I was scared of heights.

"You got a problem parachuting out of planes and helicopters any time, day or night?"

"No, First Sergeant!"

"You got a problem being gone for months at a time?"

"No, First Sergeant!"

The back and forth went on for another twenty minutes. Suddenly, he stopped. The First Sergeant gave me one last once-over, walked back to the counter, and slammed my file down in front of Grady. "We'll take 'im," he said bluntly and bolted back out the door.

"Damn, son!" Grady said. "Congratulations. Don't hate me when they're thrashin' the shit outta you."

"I got this," I replied with slightly more confidence than I felt.

"They're sending someone to pick you up in a bit; hang tight."

About an hour later, a husky-looking Marine with gold jump wings stepped through the door, and Grady yelled, "Yo, brother! Your ride's here."

As I approached the Marine, he introduced himself as Lance Corporal Davis. "I'm assigned to take you through the orientation and onboarding process. First thing, we need to get you to all your check-in points and show you where the barracks and chow hall are located."

Davis was easygoing with a big smile and filled me in on the layout of the base as we drove. That night, he took me to The Nautical, a rowdy roadhouse bar just off base. When I saw the sign out front—*Four bucks for all the draft beer you can drink*—my mouth watered. *Sign me up!*

After a few giant mugs of ice-cold beer, Davis gave me the skinny on who to look out for, when and where to show up, and most importantly, what to expect in the coming weeks and months.

"You got to earn your place in line to go to jump school, and then you got to keep it. For any reason, you piss the leaders off or screw up, they'll hold your jump billet, and you'll go to the back of the line. Got it?"

"Got it," I repeated.

"The absolute most important thing to focus on is your fitness level," Davis continued. "In this unit, you're a military athlete, and if you don't have a perfect PT fitness score while you're in Junior Jump, you better be damn close if you want to hold your place in line."

Junior Jump is the fitness program for "Legs"—that's what you're called until you get your wings pinned.

"Every morning at zero four-thirty, no matter what the weather, you got to be standing next to the pull-up bars when they blow the whistle. Got it?"

"Got it," I replied.

"Don't expect anyone to treat you with respect until you are at least a lead winger."

"Lead winger?" I asked.

"All the military branches use the Army jump school at Fort Benning for parachute school. If you make it to jump school, you are awarded a pair of jump wings upon your fifth jump. They're silver with the wings folded upward—we call 'em 'lead wings.' Your goal is to get your gold wings as soon as possible when you get back. We do parachute jumps every Friday." I fixated on every word.

"When you complete five more jumps back here with ANGLICO, you'll get your gold jump wings. Any time you see a Marine with silver jump wings, it either means they are fresh out of jump school, or they just got lucky and found a way to get a jump billet. We don't think much of lead wingers in the Marine Corps, so get your gold wings as soon as possible."

The image of me getting my gold wings pinned sent a shockwave of adrenaline into my psyche.

Davis grinned. "And that's when you get to go through our rite of passage. Every gold winger in the unit gets to give you your blood wings. It's an old tradition."

I gulped my beer. "Blood wings?"

"Anyone in the unit with gold jump wings gets to punch you as hard as they want on the new gold wings pinned on your chest. And, since I'm onboarding you, I'm gonna be the first one in line to give you your blood wings."

He smiled, and we toasted our mugs with a loud *clunk*.

"Some of the hardcore guys in the unit take this over the top. They'll stand you up against the wall, step back a few feet, and slam you in the wings with a hammer fist to make the pins dig in and cut. But most of the guys will just give you a good thump and congratulate you. When the day comes, you better have a bottle of Jack and a leather strap to put between your teeth. It's gonna be a bitch!"

I spouted back, "If everyone with gold wings went through this rite of passage, then bring it on!"

"That's that," Davis declared. "That's your onboarding. I'm done. Now it's all up to you."

Within a few weeks, I settled in and got to know the other Legs in Junior Jump. We became tighter than ten toes in a sock.

Pretty much anyone with gold wings treated us like lepers. One Lance Corporal named Leighty got in my face for being a smartass. He was a husky, corn-and-grain-fed Marine from Ohio whom everyone respected. He walked up on me and poked me in the chest, saying, "Shut your mouth, or I'll throw you off this second deck, you little piss ant."

We later became good friends, but I didn't earn his respect until he pinned my gold wings.

A Big Fat Hen

Almost nightly, all the Legs in the unit were summoned by any number of gold wingers to The Nautical for hazing. There was an unspoken rule that certain tables were off-limits in the bar for Legs; they were reserved for gold wingers. I was explicitly told not to be the dumbass Leg who sat in one of those chairs.

The gold wingers made us participate in drinking games until we threw up, and they laughed their asses off. They knew damn well we needed to be at Junior Jump at zero four-thirty the next morning, and that was exactly the point.

One of the drinking games I will never forget was called "A Big Fat Hen." It took hundreds of beers to finally get it right.

We stood in front of a table lined with full beer mugs. The gold wingers would chant the game's words and phrases in unison. We were to memorize and recite what they said verbatim. As the point of the game was to repeat the words exactly, if we screwed up and missed a single word, we had to chug a mug of beer and start over.

"A big fat hen, a couple of ducks, um…"

"Drink!" they would yell.

I'd gulp a mug of beer and start again.

"A big fat hen, a couple of ducks, three brown, uh…"

"Drink!"

Gulp, gulp, gulp. By the second week of hazing, I finally nailed it.

They knew we wanted in to their exclusive club, and they worked extra hard to coordinate their efforts to make us suffer before earning it. They would often debate who and how they would tag team hazing us, always within earshot or simply right in front of us. We'd get back to the barracks by midnight or one in the morning and then freeze our asses off at zero four-thirty in the wet and slushy North Carolina coastal winter. It was an endurance game we played for months.

It wasn't long before I fell in with the rowdy nonconformists instead of the squared-away Marines who were in lockstep with the order of things. I see now that my need to fit in has gotten me into more trouble than anything else in my life. I can attribute some of the most avoidable and challenging events in my life to that drive.

If you combined my rage with my need to fit in, threw in an abundance of alcohol, a bunch of hard-drinking Marines who loved to fight, and shook well, voila! You'd get me: trouble and a never-ending string of serious disciplinary actions.

Being former Marines, Steve McQueen and Lee Marvin fit my image, and I related to their personas. Chesty Puller, the most famous Marine in history, was also one of my role models. Over the course of his career, he went from Private to General and kicked ass and took names the whole way. My favorite quote from Chesty was during a visit he made to a Marine base: "Take me to the brig; I want to meet the *real* Marines."

Jump School

Because my smart mouth had landed me a cozy spot at the top of most leaders' shit lists, I lost my place in line for jump school several times. Still, after about nine months of Junior Jump, my fitness level was insane. I finally got my billet to go to jump school. I guess they thought I would never give up, so they threw me a bone and told me not to screw it up. But, of course, I did.

I arrived at the Army's jump school at Fort Benning, where I met a small number of Marines who were sent from other units with direct orders: we were not allowed to fail or drop out of jump school. This was the main reason for Junior Jump. Our unit demanded we show up at Fort Benning and smoke the hell out of those Army bastards. We didn't hate them, but we wouldn't be shown up by them, period.

It was June in Georgia, and I was entirely unprepared for the extreme humidity. It was much worse than North Carolina. The air was thick and sticky, infested with bugs and huge mosquitos that could puncture right through our uniforms. When you smashed them on your arm, it would leave a blood stain the size of a dime.

On the first day of formation, we lined up and met our team of instructors. They were called "Black Hats." I was one of four Marines among around four hundred and eighty Army soldiers, as well as a few guys from the Air Force. We Marines were in camouflage uniforms, and all others were in plain green, so we stuck out. They called us "Trees."

There were also five Army trainees wearing big, white motorcycle helmets. At first, this seemed strange, but then the senior Black Hat made their reasoning abundantly clear. He stood the company to attention and gave us our onboarding speech. Then, in a thick southern accent, he yelled, "Gimme all ma Big Heads. Get up here!" The white-helmet trainees immediately broke ranks and double-timed to form a new line in front of him and snapped to attention.

"Sir! Big Heads reporting as ordered, sir!" they sounded off in unison.

As it turned out, their heads were too big to fit into the steel pot helmets the military otherwise issued, so they were forced to wear motorcycle helmets.

The senior Black Hat continued.

"You got big heads; that must mean you got mo' brains! Ain't that right, Big Heads?"

"Sir! Yes, sir!" they yelled.

"Well, do some push-ups, Big Heads!"

After laughing hysterically and thrashing them for a few minutes for no other reason than their collective skull sizes, he dismissed them and started in on the rest of us.

"Gimme all my Trees! Up here!" he yelled.

That was us.

We broke ranks, double-timed, and locked it up in front of him.

"Sir! Trees reporting as ordered, sir!" we shouted in unison.

"You are our guests here, Marines. I hope you will not be offended if we find it amusing to single you out and thrash the living shit out of you while you are here."

"Sir! No, sir!" we yelled.

"Gimmie a dive-bomber and count off fifty!"

"Ooorahh!" we yelled while springing into the air in a perfect set of dive-bombers.

A dive-bomber is executed by leaping into the air while kicking your feet up into the air over your head, causing your face and upper body to race toward the ground. The objective is to catch yourself with your hands on the deck with your boots hitting the ground last.

As our boots hit the ground, we counted off fifty push-ups aloud and in unison, then locked it up back to attention.

"Get out of my face, Trees," he commanded.

"Sir! Yes, sir!" Poof, we were gone.

The heat and humidity were miserable. To keep our body temperatures cool, we were either run through outdoor showers in full uniform or sprayed with fire hoses every twenty minutes. As we lay in the dirt doing never-ending leg-lifts and getting soaked, the Black Hats walked among our ranks with the spray hoses yelling, "Who wants to quit?" Within a few minutes, the weak stood, eyes to the ground, and wandered aimlessly to the edge of the formation.

Still dripping wet, the remainder of us were directed to run straight from getting soaked to the sawdust gig pits. That's where we would practice parachute landing falls. By the end of every day, we had sawdust caked everywhere inside and outside of our uniforms. Between the heat, the humidity, the soakings, and the sawdust, we lost 20 percent of the trainees the first week. It was crazy. They would just quit and stand up like zombies before walking away from the platoon, broken and defeated.

The three other Marines and I used this as fuel to drive us onward, never showing even a moment of weakness.

At the end of the first week, some new Black Hat instructors joined in for the next training phase. My RECON buddy, who hailed from Hawaii, Mark, jabbed me with his elbow to get my attention.

"Look at that one Black Hat, the new guy. He is your doppelganger, dude. Do you have a long-lost twin?" he joked.

Eventually, some of the other Black Hats noticed our resemblance and called me up to stand next to him. Neither of us liked the attention, and neither of us liked each other either; this was obvious the instant we locked eyeballs. I was a Marine; he was an Army man. In our world, that was reason enough. I was also a trainee, and he was a jump school, Black Hat instructor. I was certain things were about to get harder for me. And I was right.

Ten days later, sure as shit, my doppelganger turned out to be the lead instructor in charge of grading us on our door exits from the thirty-four-foot mock towers. We were to stand in the simulated airplane door with a jumpmaster telling us when to jump. When he yelled *go*, we were to push our static-line toward him, arm outstretched, so he could snatch it from us while we stepped to exit the plane through the door. Standard jump procedure dictated that we launch out of the plane's door, assuming a tucked position with our hands around our reserve chute, elbows in, and legs locked together straight out in front, forming an L shape.

We were judged by how tucked and rigid we were as we exited the door. It was obvious after most people's initial attempts that the majority of people had a serious fear of heights. I was nervous but not terrified.

The military had researched the height of the mock tower to determine the exact point where most people have maximum fear and anxiety. The thirty-four-foot towers were the result.

There were a surprising number of trainees who just freaked out every time they came out the door. A ridiculous number of trainees either quit or were kicked out almost immediately. Each time it was my turn, I could see my doppelganger, sitting with his clipboard in judgment, looking up at me with a smartass smirk. No matter how perfectly I performed, no matter how tightly I tucked, all I heard him yell was, "Fail!"

"You fail one more time," he warned, "and I'm gonna send you packing, Marine."

And no kidding, the next time I popped out the door, he immediately yelled, "Fail! Pack your shit, and go home, Marine."

I took my gear off and walked up beside him to watch several trainees pop out the door one at a time and saw them make several mistakes.

"Pass," he shouted at them, over and over.

I looked back and said, "You mean you passed that piece of shit? You're telling me *that* shitbag got a pass? One of his arms was down to his side, not tucked. My exits were tight!"

He glared at me. "You failed, and you're done! Shut up and get out of my face! Report to the commanding officer to out-process."

Several other Black Hats crowded around, grinning. There was nothing left to do but walk away and pack my shit.

I could not accept going back to my unit without passing, dishonoring both them and myself. The thought was as enraging as it was depressing. Because I wouldn't be jump qualified, I wouldn't be able to go on any deployments or missions. That meant I was sure to get bounced out of the unit and sent back to some grunt platoon.

I dreaded the walk to the commander's office. When I reported in, I sat in the waiting room for over an hour, contemplating my fate, when I finally got the call to report to the commander's desk.

There, two officers were waiting for me, looking through the rosters of people who washed out of the course. After I reported in, they told me to stand at ease.

"At least you can tell your unit you didn't quit but got washed out," the junior officer said with a smirk.

I looked directly at the commanding officer and said, "Permission to speak, sir?"

"Speak," he replied.

"Sir, in my unit, we are not allowed to quit or fail jump school. I can't return to my unit without passing this course."

"What do you mean, you can't?"

"Sir, there has never been a Marine from my unit that didn't come back with their jump wings, sir."

The commander sat for a second and responded, "If I choose to recycle you, son, you will have to repeat the entire course. You sure you want to do that?"

My heart rate quickened. So, there was still a chance. Without hesitation, I replied, "Yes, sir!"

The commander nodded toward the door. "Wait outside."

"Yes, sir," I barked and about-faced. I waited for an excruciating fifteen minutes and was finally called back in.

"Okay, Marine. You will be recycled and are set to pick up the next training company in two weeks. Here are your orders. Report to base maintenance in the next hour. They will get you started with the cleaning detail."

For the next two weeks, I became an expert with weed whackers, hedgers, and lawn mowers. There were oceans of grass to mow and endless miles of sidewalks to edge.

The steady flow of rubbernecking Army soldiers and officers driving by was hilarious. They were astonished to see a Marine in camouflage utilities edging their Army base's sidewalks.

The best part of being recycled was all the free beer. I had a lot of off-time and spent most of it at the enlisted club. Man, if I had a quarter for each Army guy who walked up and said, "I was going to join the Marine Corps. Can I buy you a beer?" I'd be rich.

When it was time for the next training cycle, I knew exactly how to pass through the course. Even better, my doppelganger was not one of my instructors, and so I made it through with no real difficulty.

Jump week was awesome. Going out of the bird for the first time at 2,500 feet by static line was exhilarating. We flooded through the door, pushing the guy out in front of us—asshole to belly button, they called it. I stepped into the doorway and sprang out to pop into a tucked position. Within a couple of seconds, I was sucked in the opposite direction with tremendous force, and the groin straps of my harness dug hard into my skin. My chute popped open with a *boom*, and before I knew it, I found myself floating on a cushion of air. Everything was super quiet.

The guy I'd pushed out in front of me was now at least a hundred feet away. It surprised me to discover we could still hear each other speak as if we were standing side by side.

For our fifth and final jump, we landed on the graduation field to kick-start the ceremony. It all happened pretty fast. We hit the ground, and within minutes, we were in formation and waiting to receive our lead wings.

As my wings were pinned, I thought about all the Marines in my unit who had hazed me. Besides making it through Marine Corps boot camp, getting my jump wings pinned on my uniform was the second most significant personal accomplishment of my life.

Glad flashed into my mind. She was right: I had found my courage. Having my wings pinned straightened my spine even further. Everywhere I went, people took notice. In the Marines, anyone with sparkling silver or gold wings stands out big time in an ocean of green.

When I arrived back at my unit, I was received with mixed reviews. Some of the guys congratulated me for sticking it out; others were irritated with me that I'd been recycled as they felt that meant I'd embarrassed them.

I didn't care. I was on my way to getting my gold wings. I was just five jumps away.

Every Friday was jump day, and my first jump was out of a single prop Huey helicopter, the kind of 'copters you see in Vietnam-era movies. We sat with four men on each side, our feet hanging over the sides onto the skids as we went up to about 2,500 feet. Nervous and exhilarated, I could feel my adrenaline spiking.

The jumpmaster slapped my shoulder. "Go!" he yelled.

Up and out I went, and then *boom*, chute deployed, and our small team of eight was in the air. As we plummeted toward the earth, I felt part of something bigger than myself. It wasn't just about getting my gold wings anymore; being part of the inner unit now mattered to me the most.

One of the next jumps was a night jump, again, out of a Huey, and again, there were four men on each side. As we climbed in elevation, the horizon was a beautiful, deep purple that stretched into blackness above us. The constellations that sparkled there were clear and crisp.

"Ten seconds! Ten seconds!" the jumpmaster yelled. Then, I received the slap on the shoulder I'd been trained to wait for. Spring loaded from the elbow, each of us popped up and out to avoid hitting the skids.

I felt much better when my chute opened into the night air. I could see the full moon illuminating the sky, punctuating my panoramic view of the deep purple, star-studded horizon. The silent bliss of floating in the night sky was beautiful and meditative. The purple was so deep you could reach out and touch it, and the stars popped and sparkled through the darkness like pinholes pushed through a dark blanket.

When the horizon went dark, I knew it was time to prepare to land. That darkness meant I had just entered the tree line and was about a hundred feet from the ground. Quickly gauging the direction I was heading, I relaxed and instinctively executed a right parachute landing fall (PLF) and rolled out on my back, looking up at the sky. The thousands of practice PLFs paid off from jump school. I landed in the dark clearing without a scratch. When the dust settled, I laid still to take in the moment.

Within seconds, the thrill bubbled up and out of me. "I get to do this! This is awesome!" I yelled.

One more jump and I would get my gold wings.

Blood Wings

The night before my tenth jump, the word was out that I was getting my gold wings pinned the next day. Everybody seemed to know and was eager to give me my blood wings.

I didn't sleep the night before my tenth jump, and when I finally got into the helicopter, my body was flushed with adrenaline and gratitude. It was exhilarating and disorienting at the same time. The instant I exited the helicopter on my tenth jump, I knew I had made it into the elite club I'd committed to qualify for and join almost a year prior. All that was left was to get my wings pinned.

Later that evening, the reality set in that my next few days would be about initiation into the club. I was about to allow well over fifty of my fellow Marines in the unit to remove the pin backings off of my jump wings to pound them into my chest. The blood-wings ritual is a rite of passage that could not be avoided.

Luckily, I understood the stages of trauma and healing I was about to go through. The first few days of dealing with the physical injury would be the worst part to endure. The coming days after that, the puncture wounds and surrounding muscle of my chest would begin to harden into a welt that would ripen with colors for a week to ten days. It was strangely nostalgic of my childhood. At least I could say my father had prepared me for this, and looking forward to the hardening stage helped me deal with what was about to take place.

The next morning in formation, I was called to the front of the company. Commanding Officer Colonel Sweetser pinned my gold wings to my uniform, and I felt a swell of pride as he secured it into place.

"Congratulations," the Colonel announced loudly as he gave a light thump on my wings with a hammer fist.

I looked down at my chest and couldn't believe my eyes. There they were, a pair of gleaming, golden wings affixed to my uniform, just as I had envisioned them.

They could never be taken; they were mine, and I had earned them.

As I stood at attention, looking out at the company, the men roared and erupted into applause. They grinned at one another with great anticipation over who would get to pin me next.

Some of the easier-going guys waited after formation to give me a mild thump and to issue their congratulations. For most others, it was initiation time. Throughout the day and everywhere I went, even at the chow hall, these sadistic bastards were waiting to hammer me with no mercy.

By the time late afternoon rolled around, my chest was bleeding through a bandage and the T-shirt under my uniform top from the punctures, and the colors of a massive blue, yellow, and brown bruise began to bloom across my chest. Just after dark, someone pounded on my door. *Bam! Bam! Bam!* "Report to the break room now, on the double!" they called out.

"Shit!" I yelled as I threw on my uniform. I knew I was in for another round of painful "congratulations."

Double-timing over to the break room, I found a good number of guys in the unit waiting for me. They were fired up and ready for my hazing.

The ritual began with one of my leaders recounting all the bullshit I made him put up with and emphasizing how much he'd been waiting for this moment. He then reached into my uniform top and removed the backings from my wings. With a hand on each of my shoulders, he backed me to the wall, reared back, and using the palm of his hand, slugged hard with a straight right, glaring at me nose to nose.

"OOOORRAHH!" I screamed in his face to absorb the pain. Everyone went wild, howling as they pushed and shoved each other to get to the front of the line to be next.

Someone handed me a bottle of Wild Turkey, and I chugged a few long gulps to prepare for the next primate to take his shot. This went on for about ten or twelve hits and over half the bottle of bourbon. By the time it was done, my voice was hoarse from yelling.

I was ordered to remove my uniform top and T-shirt, so the men could examine the damage. The soaked material stuck to my skin as I pulled it away. My chest was cut and riddled with pin-hole punctures, and everyone slapped each other on their backs in approval. Most of them crowded closely, trying to jab me in the chest with their knuckles as I swatted them away. Though I was in tremendous agony, I played it off by laughing.

The next morning, I could barely move. My chest was swollen and blazing with pain. As I looked in the mirror, the entire left side of my chest was pulsing under a massive, ugly bruise, dotted and streaked with scabs.

"Shit!" I cursed.

Regardless of my condition, it was time to fall into formation, and I would have to get from my room to the front of the barracks without getting punched in the wings.

Everyone had probably heard about the night before, and I was sure the few remaining gold wingers were eagerly awaiting my arrival. I decided to wait until the last thirty seconds before the company was called to attention before exiting my room. My plan worked, and I arrived just in time. All through formation and the announcements, though, I heard whispers and snickers from others in the ranks. Those who hadn't already pummeled me weren't shy about letting me know it was their turn next.

Because I was hiding out—not even going to chow—it took about three days for everyone to score a shot. I was relieved to discover most mid-level and senior leadership didn't participate in the barbaric ritual.

As predicted, in the following ten days, I fixated on the hardening of the welt that formed across my chest and constantly pressed on it through my uniform, remembering the wounds of my childhood.

Turns out, not long after getting my wings pinned, I heard a Gunnery Sergeant's lung had collapsed while getting his blood wings, and from there forward, the initiation was officially banned. But I've heard that, unofficially, it continues to this day.

Like Michelangelo chipping away to free David, a good amount of self-doubt fell away after the blood-wing crucible had concluded.

I had defied the odds and earned the jump wings I came for.

My self-worth evolved from needing my father's respect to finding self-respect.

CHAPTER 11

NATO Exercises

Turkey

When our unit got orders to deploy and embed with the Turkish Naval Infantry for a joint NATO exercise, it felt like I had won the lottery.

Just a year or so prior, back in my neighborhood, I was going nowhere fast. Now, I was deploying to Turkey with my unit. I attached my wings to my freshly starched uniform and put it on. For the first time in my life, I liked what I saw in the mirror. The overwhelming sense of pride was exhilarating and felt like my reward for all the suffering it took to get here.

Our briefing about the upcoming mission with the unit leaders had a nostalgic sense of all the military movies I had seen growing up. The seriousness of the leaders orchestrating their parts to convey how the operation would come together was impressive. We would embed with a battalion of the Turkish Naval Infantry and travel with them to our destination on a WWII-era ship the US Navy had given Turkey after the war.

When we reached our destination, we were to disembark from the ship by climbing down large nets into the amphibious boats pulled alongside the ship—just like in the movies. We would then assault the beach with the Turks and move across a mountain range to our final objective, about twenty miles inland.

A few days before the exercise, we arrived at a port in Turkey to board our ship. I could see the Captain and the entire crew packed on the outer deck waiting for us as we pulled up in our transport. As we exited our vehicle, the Captain and crew immediately snapped to attention and saluted. They collectively held their salute with pride until we ceremoniously returned the gesture.

Our small team had three Marines and a Navy Lieutenant: Lieutenant Richards, Corporal Border, Lance Corporal White, and myself. We immediately shuffled into a small formation and took our positions directly behind the Lieutenant. We snapped to attention, returning the salute. The contrast between how the Turks salute differed dramatically from ours. Theirs was clean and well executed, but when Marines salute, it is intense, lightning-fast, and razor-sharp, with a clean and straight edge down the forearm from the tips of the fingers to the elbow.

The Captain and the Lieutenant marched toward each other, stopped, saluted again, and exchanged friendly greetings. The Lieutenant then executed a crisp about-face and ordered us to grab our gear and board the ship.

When we arrived at our living quarters, there were bunks six high up to the ceiling. The Turkish soldiers crowded around us, smiling and curious, pointing at our uniforms and whispering to each other. As the horn sounded to signal that we were pulling away from the dock, the ship began to sway with the ocean waves. As we took on some speed and forward momentum, the left-to-right swaying stopped, and the front of the ship began to porpoise up and down into the breakers.

The word "Turk" had me imagining large, serious, and fierce-looking warriors, but I was surprised that almost all of them were shorter and smaller than I had anticipated. I stood just over six feet, and most of the Turks were less than five foot eight. Instead of appearing as intense and aggressive as I had anticipated, they were gracious and friendly, smiling and shaking our hands while nodding their heads in approval of our presence. We were immediately put at ease and invited to share a meal with them.

In front of us was an open floor with four large, round serving trays about four feet in diameter. Each was heaping with mounds of what appeared to be fried yellow rice mixed with meat and vegetables. We were handed metal plates but no utensils and were puzzled until several of the Turk leaders sat down cross-legged, gesturing for us to join them. They could see our confusion and quickly filled their plates using pieces of flatbread, gesturing for us to join in.

We were starving and immediately dug in. The food was sticky and clumped together, making it easy to pull apart with small pieces of torn flatbread. The array of flavors and spices immediately expanded our senses, and our eyes widened as we smiled back in approval. Our hosts were pleased, and the officers motioned for the other Turk soldiers to sit and eat. Sharing a meal with our Turkish hosts was the best team-building experience we could have planned. Everyone was smiling, and the Turks began pointing at our uniforms while pointing to their gear, repeating, "You trade? You trade?"

Immediately, I nodded in agreement as I ripped off my utility belt with a canteen, gesturing to one of the Turks who had his belt and canteen at the ready. We shook hands with a smile as we exchanged possessions, nodding in unison.

"Good," he said.

"Yes, good," I replied.

For the next day and a half, we would be traveling in close and constant proximity with our hosts, and we were invited to dine with the officers that first evening for dinner. The display of respect was humbling, and the array of exotic foods was strikingly colorful and rich. Unexpectedly, shot glasses filled with a milky white liqueur were placed in front of us. Our hosts smiled and gestured for us to pick them up. The Lieutenant nudged us, whispering, "Raki. It is Turkey's national drink, also called 'Lions Milk.' Sharing Raki is a gesture of great respect. Don't refuse. Smile, and drink."

We toasted and never broke eye contact as we gulped our shots. Raki is a strong liqueur with an intense, black licorice flavor. It burned going down, and we smiled and winced. Our hosts chuckled in amusement and refilled our glasses the instant we placed them on the table. This was just the first of what would be a continuous series of toasts they would make throughout our meal and late into the evening. Throughout the night, we continued trading our gear, and the entire group had loosened up to the point of joyful laughter in our newfound camaraderie.

We didn't have to speak each other's language; the common sentiments of peace and goodwill were all said with our eyes, calm voices, smiles, and warm gestures. At nineteen, to be receiving such a worldly understanding of diplomacy was a maturing experience.

Late into the evening, we left the officer's galley and headed to our sleeping quarters. Unfortunately, the sleeping arrangements for us on this old ship would be the only negative part of our seagoing experience. We were assigned to sleep in the top bunks, about two feet from the ceiling. When I first laid down, within seconds, something small and crawly either fell or jumped from the ceiling onto my cheek and freaked me out. After brushing the bug off my face and over the side of the bunk, I pulled the sheet over my head. I could feel tiny little insects scattering about on the sheet the entire night and rose well before dawn to escape the torture.

When I arrived on the outside deck to take in the ocean air, I was greeted by a few guards who eagerly handed me an English-Turkish translation dictionary. They wanted to converse and offered me some incredibly strong black coffee.

Smiling and nodding, one of them read from a notepad he had been scribbling on while studying his translation book, "NATO... America, big fish. Turkey, little fish."

I smiled, confused.

"No choice," the Turk continued with a troubled look.

All I could do was look back at them sympathetically.

Another Turk piped in and exclaimed, "Roots!" The third said, "Yes, Dallas."

Now I was even more puzzled. I frantically looked through the pages of my translation book and found the word "roots."

"Sebze?" I asked.

"Yes, sebze," they responded in unison.

There was no reference in the book for Dallas, so I looked back and gave a gesture of confusion. "Dallas?" I asked.

Eventually, we acknowledged our mutual confusion and the futility of continuing, but all was well as we continued to sip our coffee and gaze out to sea.

Within an hour, the ship came alive with crew members and soldiers moving about and prepping the nets for the coming beach assault. Our four-person squad of Marines was led to the galley for breakfast, and as we sat down, one of the guards I spoke with earlier looked across the food trays and pointed at me, blurting, "Dallas," and then pointed to my two fellow Marines and said, "Roots." All of us looked at each other and were puzzled. We looked over at one of the officers who spoke fairly clear English and asked him to help us understand what they were so adamant about.

He sheepishly looked at his soldiers and back to us. "You see, we have only a few American TV shows in Turkey, *Dallas* and *Roots*."

American TV. *Dallas* and *Roots*. I looked at the other Marines first in confusion, and then, suddenly, we all got it.

Two of our team members were African American, and the Lieutenant and I were white. Immediately, my stomach soured, and I felt a sense of shame over our country's heritage that quickly ricocheted into empathy for what Border and White must have been experiencing. To my surprise, they burst into hysterical laughter, and the Lieutenant and I joined in.

Suddenly, one of the Turks then took it up a notch by pointing at Border, saying in a puzzled way, "Kunta Kinte?" and then to me, "JR?"

"No, no, no, no," we all replied, waving our hands in front of us.

Our hosts were still puzzled while the officer tried to understand our explanation: that it was an old TV show and not how America is today. Still, we acknowledged that it was a historical trauma of our country's past.

I was sad that our host's only definitive impressions of America were from old TV shows and that they were a "small fish" in America's big pond.

Our exchange was suddenly interrupted by alarms; it was time to prepare to disembark the ship for the beach assault.

Our gear had been staged on the outside deck. We grabbed it and headed to our designated positions. As I looked over the side of the ship, our amphibious transport boat was pulling alongside us. It was rocking in the turbulent waves while several Turk seamen attempted to tie it off. A large cargo net was strewn over the ship's side, hanging down into the waiting boat.

First went the Turks, up and over the side, climbing down like spiders, some were more reckless than others, and one got his foot hooked and fell downward until he was snared, hanging upside down. Their leaders were not pleased with their troops' lack of skill and efficiency.

When it was our turn, the entire boat was filled with the Turks waiting to see how their American counterparts would do. The Lieutenant grabbed us in a quick huddle. "Take your time. You got this. Now show them how it's done."

We went over the side of the ship in two pairs as the Turks watched in silence. Confidently, we spider-straddled the netting in unison down to the slim top deck of the boat and then jumped the five feet down to the deck. When we stood to face the Turks, they remained silent as their leader smiled and gave us a thumbs up.

The deafening and powerful engines of the amphibious craft pulling away from the ship vibrated the deck beneath our feet. Large waves began crashing against the outside walls, soaking us from above as we rocked front-to-back and side-to-side. Within seconds my breakfast signaled it needed to come back out, but after a few deep breaths, my stomach began to calm. However, the taste of salt water and the smell of vomit in the air from others close by was difficult to endure.

I kept my focus off in the distance toward the shore. A mile or so away, I could see other landing craft washing up on the beach with troops spreading in all directions toward the hillsides above the shore. The front of our vessel thrashed up and down, giving us sporadic glimpses of the approaching coastline. Eventually, there was a thunderous crash when the front gate of the craft opened and dropped, slamming into the sand.

Instantly, waves flooded into the boat as we all let out a roar and began pouring out through the surf onto the open beach. The Lieutenant motioned our team with a hand signal to move toward a designated point on the ridgeline with velocity. Our adrenaline was pumping ferociously, and we hardly noticed the soft wet sand slowing our pace.

We staged up under a small cliffside where the surf had created a dugout and radioed our command to check in.

Once we checked in, it was time to again move with velocity to our next objective, twenty miles inland. Marching with the Turks felt like we were respected warriors with a bigger purpose on their home turf. At all times, they were genuinely respectful and gracious to us.

After the completion of our successful exercise, we were transported back to the coast, where the Turks gave us a lavish dinner they had prepared to celebrate our unity as a combined force.

We entered a large white Arabic tent that strained in all directions against the relentless coastal wind. Surprisingly, the inside of the tent was calm and quiet in comparison. Before us was a colorful array of food covering the entire span of a gigantic twenty-foot banquet table lined with oversized high-backed chairs. Every few feet, servers dressed in white robes gestured for us to be seated. Our goblets were immediately filled with red wine from giant glass jugs wrapped in thin woven baskets. There were mounds of roasted chicken, large pans of aromatic rice dishes, sauces of all colors, and a separate table piled high with breads and fruits. It was more food than we could possibly consume.

Our hosts were, once again, toasting us relentlessly with our favorite newfound elixir, Raki. The feast lasted well past midnight. While we were sad to say goodbye to our hosts, I was already beginning to anticipate where our unit's next adventure would take us.

I could feel Glad's presence and her pride in my adventures and in who I was becoming. Something was happening bigger than me, and I was no longer swimming against the currents. I was learning to swim with them.

Spain

It had been months since our deployment to Turkey, and all we were doing was physical conditioning training and cleaning our vehicles and gear, over and over, waiting.

During this time, the rumor mill amplified about where we would be heading next and what the mission would be. It was always interesting to compare supposedly "leaked" information from our command in advance of announcements with the facts. One leak that turned out to be true was that we would be involved in a mass tactical air assault on an upcoming deployment to Spain.

While waiting to enter the briefing room, I overheard one of our platoon Sergeants talking with a group of his men behind me. He stated bluntly, "For those of you who've only heard about mass-tactical air assaults in jump school, listen up and pay attention. In a few minutes, you will hear about a jump we will be making at 750 feet, the lowest possible altitude to deploy a parachute. There will be 700 jumpers in the air all around you within about one minute."

He went on to explain, "You must be focused and alert to execute your exit from the bird perfectly because there is no time to pull your reserve chute if you screw up going out the door. There is very little hang-time, so as soon as your chute pops, you will pop your quick-releases and your rucksack drop, so it hangs below on your eight-foot line. Your ruck will hit the ground first to absorb some of the impact of your landing."

He then paused to ensure all of their eyes were on him.

"A mass tactical air assault," he shared, "is a high-casualty solution when a piece of enemy real estate needs to be taken. The objective is to put a significant force on the ground as quickly as possible. As I said, the jump typically happens at the lowest altitude possible, 750 feet. In an actual combat situation, it is anticipated that a third of the force will be shot and killed in the air before they land. Another third will be killed in combat on the ground taking the objective, leaving the final third to complete the mission."

As I listened, I thought, *I hope we never have to do one of these for real.*

About this time, the doors opened to the briefing room, and we were waved in. When we were all settled, the room was called to attention to begin. "Take your seats," ordered the First Sergeant.

The company commander stood, and the room fell silent as he walked to the large map board, pointing at a set of circles inside the borders of Spain.

In his booming voice, he announced, "All preparations have been made. Two months from today, ANGLICO will participate in mass-tactical air assault with the 101st and Spanish Airborne as an exhibition for the King of Spain near Torrejon Air Base."

Mesmerized, I replayed his words in my mind, *Exhibition for the King of Spain?* I imagined Glad sitting alongside the Spanish royalty, beaming with pride.

The Colonel continued, "We will embed teams of five ANGLICO Marines into units of the Army 101st Airborne Battalion. Together, we will demonstrate a combined NATO show of force, jumping with the Spanish airborne for the exhibition.

"Once on the ground, all units will force march to a mountain-top objective approximately twenty miles away. Our ANGLICO teams will remain in continuous radio communication with the fleet Marine force to coordinate fire missions throughout the day. The entire mission will begin before dawn and conclude just after dusk."

I scanned the room to read the vibe, and the energy was electric with anticipation.

As planned, two months later, we arrived at Torrejon Air Base the night before the jump. The following morning before dawn, we arrived at the flight hangar to 'chute up with our gear.

We each had a ruck weighing sixty to eighty pounds that was to be hooked to the D-Rings below our reserve chutes which would make it hang down in front of us below our knees. The only way to walk was wide-legged hobbles on both sides of our rucks, carrying it just above the ground. It took a lot of back strength and was an effective way to get airborne troops out the door of the airplane with the least amount of injuries.

When we hobbled up in the bird, all eyeballs were on us. We were five Marines in camouflage uniforms in contrast to the ninety-five Army paratroopers wearing flat green. The ways in which we stood out were awesome: our uniforms, our insane fitness levels, the intensity of our focused mindset, and how we operated as a small team.

When we were all strapped in, the ramp closed and seven C-130 cargo planes lifted off the runway with a hundred jumpers in each. It only took about twenty minutes to reach the jump zone, which did not leave much time to ruminate on what could go wrong at the lowest possible jump altitude. The red light came on, indicating we were just minutes from exiting the bird. All eyeballs were locked on the jumpmaster as he raised both arms and yelled, "Stand up!" followed by, "Hook up!"

The sounds of the propellers just outside the door were deafening, but the jumpmaster's hand movements directed our actions. We all connected our static line clips and stood facing the door. The red light was still on, and the jumpmaster yelled while pointing at the two immediate jumpers to his left and right, "First jumpers, stand in the door!"

My ears were ringing with anticipation, and my temples were tingling from the adrenaline rush.

When the light switched from red to green, the jumpmaster slapped each jumper standing in the doors on the shoulder and yelled, "Go!" They quickly exited and disappeared, followed by the next jumper. One by one, we pushed each other toward the door.

The jumpmaster and I locked eyes for a nanosecond as I approached him. Then, I stepped toward the door, extending my hand with my static line for him to hook with his arm.

The jumpmaster used a circular motion with his arms to gather the large volume of static lines coming toward him. He kept the looping movements high enough to allow each jumper to shove the static line toward him, chest high. The jumper would immediately grab the sides of the open door, pop out, and tuck his body tightly while the chute automatically deployed outside the plane.

We had practiced our exits a thousand times in training, but this time was different. When I shoved my static line chest high toward the jumpmaster, instead of snatching my static line, he slapped my forearm, and I went out the door with my arm extended and outstretched, causing the static line to loop around my wrist and forearm. About ten feet out the door, the line snapped tight and pulled my shoulder with a severe jolt, and I dangled along the side of the bird. The next jumper whipped by, barely missing me.

When you are a "towed jumper," as it's called, the jumpmaster will look out the door at you. If you are conscious, you are to look at them and slap your helmet twice, signaling to cut the static line so you can deploy your reserve chute. If you are unconscious, they pull you back into the plane by your static line.

For a split second, I looked up at the door and rotated my wrist around the line, and suddenly, I popped loose, and the plane pulled away as I fell back and then sucked upward as my chute deployed. I let out a roar from the pain and cursed that jumpmaster all the way to the ground.

At 750 feet, there is very little hang-time in the air. My shoulder was on fire, and I struggled to use my left arm, but at least everything was still attached. I popped my quick-releases, and my ruck dropped down below me about ten feet, hanging by the strap. The ground was coming at me within seconds. My ruck hit first and absorbed a big part of my momentum. The wind stretched the line as I hit the ground.

I lay flat on my back in agony for a moment, trying to assess the damage to my shoulder. Ed, one of my teammates, was on me within seconds, asking if I was injured.

"My shoulder," I replied. "The jumpmaster hit my arm as I went out the door, and my wrist got wrapped around my static line. I got towed!"

We got my gear off and examined my arm and shoulder's range of motion. "It's not dislocated," Ed stated. "Man, you are lucky."

As I rolled over and stood, the team circled up. Suddenly, Ed grabbed my helmet strap with a couple of tugs to get my attention and repeated sternly, "It's not dislocated! You gotta suck it up. Let's get moving!"

My shoulder felt seriously screwed, but my adrenaline was pumping, so I focused on my mantra, *Take the pain*. Ed helped me throw on my ruck, and as the weight settled, it pulled my shoulders back. Surprisingly, it felt more bearable with the extra pressure.

Within seconds, we were moving as a unit at a fast pace to join the assault force. The sun was scorching, and we were sweating heavily. Within about an hour, we came across a sprawling valley of vineyards stretching for miles. My shoulder had swelled, restricting my movement as we forcibly marched for hours through long rows of vines toward our objective. Fortunately, all around us were massive clusters of large green grapes, a little smaller than ping-pong balls. I'd not seen grapes this large, and we were grateful for the hydration and sugar. One after another, we snipped off the large clusters and stuffed them into the fronts of our baggy uniform tops to provision us for the journey ahead.

I stuffed my wrist into my harness strap as a makeshift sling in an effort to isolate my shoulder. After ten hours of force marching, we still had one final ascent to reach our final objective.

Looking up, it was a steep, jagged climbing trail cut in the dirt and stone up the side of a cliff. Our team leader shouted, "Let's set the pace and show these bastards!" In a true Spartan mindset, we all grunted in unison. I pulled my wrist out of my harness to check my range of motion and straightened my arm down to my side. A stabbing pain shot through me. Fortunately, I could move my arm in front of me almost chest high, but I couldn't reach above my shoulder. With only a few minutes to get it together, I devised a climbing strategy to minimize my left arm's movement. I would compensate with my right arm—it would do most of the reaching and grabbing. My left arm would be used to grab the rocks directly in front of me. Ed was close by and climbed just below me to shoulder some of my weight when I needed to rest. About halfway up, we caught a break and perched on a boulder for a good rest while the others yelled down at us to hurry it up.

We made it to the top of the mountain just after dusk, and after checking in with our other teams, I grabbed a handful of Motrin from one of our corpsmen and rolled up in my poncho, using my ruck to rest against, and I passed out.

Truth be told, the closest we came to the King of Spain was about a mile away in our parachutes. But imagining what it must have been like for the Spanish royalty to see this stunning exhibition of military force captivated my thoughts as I faded off to sleep.

Puerto Rico

It was a welcome relief when our unit received orders to go to Puerto Rico. We were to embed small teams with the Puerto Rican National Guard. We would conduct a joint NATO exercise, and our small teams would liaison between the guard unit and the Fleet Marine Force, providing continuous radio contact and calling in fire missions.

I had an image of what the Caribbean islands would be like from pictures I'd seen in magazines, and I imagined us sitting on a white, sandy beach against a deep sapphire blue ocean, sipping Coronas. The entire unit was in extreme anticipation during the weeks before our departure.

Preparations and staging of equipment and supplies began weeks in advance, and on the day of departure, everything loaded into the massive C141 cargo plane in a blur of organized chaos.

I loved the moment of liftoff the most. It signified we were finally en route to our next adventure. The instant the wheels left the ground, the entire unit erupted in a frenzy of excitement.

After takeoff, I quickly unstrapped myself from the uncomfortable cargo netting seats and climbed up onto a large canvas-draped pallet of supplies to stretch out. In the military, I had learned to catch a few winks wherever I could. Although it was uncomfortable, the humming vibrations from the jet engines lulled me to sleep within minutes. I don't know how long I slept, but I suddenly got a slap on the arm.

"We are approaching the island. Get down and secured for landing," one of our Sergeants commanded.

Looking out the window at the beautiful coastline of Puerto Rico, I wondered what was in store for us in the coming hours and days. The ocean was a beautiful, deep blue that faded into the shallow waters and beaches of white sand. I smiled and thought, *Wow, this is just like in the pictures.*

When we landed and walked down the ramp onto the runway, I immediately felt the hot sun on my face. The heavy humidity opened up my pores, but it was much more bearable than the wet stickiness of the Carolinas and Georgia.

We stood in formation for about thirty minutes while the aircrew unloaded our equipment and gear. Our platoon leader had a sudden stroke of genius and barked out the one thing that would inspire us into immediate action: "As soon as we get checked in and our gear is secured, there will be plenty of cold beer." We all looked at each other and immediately jumped into action. As the sun began to set, we completed our tasks and formed up to receive our final instructions for the day. In plain sight, just a hundred yards away, was an outside picnic area. There, as promised, at least twenty large garbage cans filled with beer packed in ice awaited us.

I was so hypnotized by the thought of cold beer that I couldn't recall anything we were being told while in formation. I was instantly jolted into a full sprint at the long-anticipated word "dismissed."

Like a hoard of Vikings descending upon a village to conquer, the entire unit collided with the trash cans, knocking most of them over and scattering beer bottles onto the grass, where we fought our way into the dog pile, each grabbing three to four beers. I found a shady area under a tree and laid down in the grass to cool down. I placed two ice-cold bottles under my uniform directly on my stomach and chest, holding the third against my forehead while chugging the fourth. By the time I downed my last beer, I felt my body cooling in the shade and a steady ocean breeze.

It was hard to believe my previous life back in the neighborhood compared to sitting here in paradise. These were the moments where I took stock of the hardships I had endured to survive my upbringing and what it took to become a Marine.

The following day, just before dawn, we awoke to the swarming activity of troops and machines preparing to depart to the airbase. A large group of CH 46 helicopters awaited us. We would load our Jeeps and equipment into the helicopters that would then transport us to a remote area of the island.

I was among four Jeep drivers. Each vehicle had a trailer in tow, loaded with provisions and gear, strapped, and tied down. The flight crew carefully guided us to back our rigs up the ramp and into the cargo area of the helicopter, where we strapped and secured them. When it was time to depart, the unit squeezed into the cargo netting seats surrounding the Jeeps that lined the walls of the bird. As the large cargo ramp raised and closed, we lifted off with six other 'copters, quickly ascending into a formation for the ride ahead. Looking through the porthole windows to the landscape beneath us, I could see the vast jungle and rolling hills stretching to the horizon.

Eventually, I dozed off to the soothing vibration of the synchronized engines and props but suddenly awoke to a slap on my helmet. The platoon Sergeant towered over me, motioning with both hands, fingers outstretched in front of my face, shouting, "Ten minutes!"

Glancing out the window as we descended, the hills were growing closer, and the bright green canopy contrasted against the darkness of the thick jungle beneath. Preparing to land, we fell even more rapidly, like a roller coaster plunging, and my stomach was instantly queasy. We lowered to a small opening in the tree line where a landing area had been cleared for us. The wheels set down with a jolt, sending a shockwave of adrenaline through my body, snapping me to a hyper state of alertness.

It was go time.

We quickly began unbuckling and releasing the chains and straps securing our vehicles as the large cargo door lowered, exposing the jungle from ground view.

Tactical insertions are rapid and well-orchestrated. This is to get troops and equipment on the ground and to ensure the bird is back in the air as quickly as possible. As soon as the door fully lowered, we rapidly drove our vehicles down the ramp into the thick foliage and disappeared into near darkness. Immediately, the bird's engines and rotors roared. It lifted off the ground as the ramp raised. Within seconds, it was ominously hanging directly above us. It gained altitude and pulled away.

Everything went silent as the bird flew out of sight over the steep hills surrounding us. We huddled up with our maps and compass on the hood of one of our Jeeps to find our location and plot the direction we would take to our objective: to meet up with the Puerto Rican National Guard a few miles away.

At first, we crept along, zig-zagging through the openings between the bushes and small trees, but after being bogged down and taking too much time, our team leader ordered us to move directly through the tree line by creating our own trail. Until then, I had only driven Jeeps on smooth roads with no off-roading experience. Nervously, I braked, clutched, and stomped the gas to get up and over the first large hedge of bushes with the trailer jumping and banging around behind. Once we got the feel of the ruggedness of cutting the trail, I gained more confidence and skill. Soon, we moved along with more speed to make up time. My lifelong love for off-roading was born in this formative experience.

We arrived at the base of a steep hillside marking the entrance to a dark horseshoe gorge. There, our team leader signaled for us to shut down our engines and circle up. A few Marines stayed behind to guard the vehicles, but the rest of us made our way down a narrow path to a large camouflage tent in the darkness. As we approached, we detected movement all around us. Suddenly, the shadowy silhouettes of dozens of soldiers holding weapons became visible under the foliage moving up the hill. A single figure emerged from the tent's entrance and approached us as our team leader greeted him. They spoke for a few moments while glancing at a map, and the soldier pointed up the hill to where we would be staging our equipment.

Looking up at the steep terrain around us, we could sense hundreds of the Puerto Rican soldiers we would be training with. They were all around us and almost completely concealed.

Over our five-day operation, we didn't spend as much time with our guardsmen hosts as I had hoped. Still, I found them friendly and curious. We spent most of our time practicing fire missions, calling in air support and naval gunfire.

One of the highlights of our time on the island was on our final day after completing our joint training exercise. Our unit began a ten-mile run in formation around the base under the scorching sun. It ended like an epic movie scene. Unexpectedly, as we approached the beach, the company commander ordered the entire unit of hundreds of Marines to run in formation directly into the ocean. The first platoon entered the surf with velocity and swam out as the rows behind them rapidly packed into the waves—one of my fondest memories.

I could not have filmed a better scene to end our adventure.

Words cannot capture the sense of pride or how lucky I felt to deploy around the world with such an elite team of military athletes in the prime of our lives.

"Once a Marine, always a Marine" and "Marine for life" are not just slogans; they are a mindset and ethos instilled through our most formidable moments and experiences that define who we are and what it means to be a Marine. Every military branch has a similar sense of pride, but the Marine Corps intentionally takes this lifetime identification to the extreme. Even though I was a hell-raising and, at times, unmanageable Marine, I am proud to be a Marine for life.

CHAPTER 12

"Gon' Kick You Out Ma Marine Co"

In the early months of being in the unit, a leader I liked, Staff Sergeant McGaha, decided to have a one-on-one sit down with me. He noticed I was struggling with some of the junior leaders disrespecting me during Junior Jump's hazing period.

"We can handle your storm," he said, "but you need to channel your rage. The most important thing to us is that you can be relied upon in combat." The fact that he took the time to give me some private and respectful advice elevated him in my mind and earned him my utmost respect. *He could lead me anywhere*, I thought.

After receiving and digesting his sage advice, I developed a mental checklist that I felt offset this shortcoming of being out of control at times. Very high fitness scores: check. Can carry a heavy pack for as long as it takes: check. Can be relied upon to hit what I shoot at: check. Will run toward machine gun fire on command: check. Can channel my rage into the tip of a spear when necessary: check. In my mind, that was what being a Marine was all about. The only thing I lacked was more beer.

Looking back, I can see that my rage against my father inspired my every reaction to authority, and it all caught up to me one early and cold January morning after formation. I was ordered to report to the First Sergeant's office at zero nine hundred.

I arrived early and paced around the hall, nervously waiting to learn what I was in trouble for this time.

When the door opened, and the First Sergeant stepped out, he gave me a hard look and a head shrug, indicating for me to get in his office. As I entered, a Navy officer in a white uniform was seated next to the First Sergeant's desk.

Now I had a verifiable reason to be nervous. I tried to recount my last interactions and incidents. What had I done? Or, what had one of my buddies roped me into?

The First Sergeant got right to the point. "This is Captain Rohn. At my request, he is here to conduct a psychological evaluation of you."

My heart began to pound. *I'm getting booted*, raced through my mind.

The Captain piped in. "It won't take long. I just want to ask you a few questions." He stood and gestured toward the door.

Though I tried to maintain my composure, my anxiety and heart rate spiked. *I'm getting booted, I'm getting booted*, repeated like a mantra. We walked down the hallway, got some coffee, and entered a small conference room.

When we sat down, he relaxed and said calmly, "Here's how this works, son. I'm going to ask you some questions about your time in the Marine Corps so far and anything else that might be relevant. You're free to answer as little or as much as you like. Fair enough?"

"Yes, sir," I responded.

"Let's start with why you decided to join the Marine Corps."

"My father, sir. He was career military. He was in the Marines in Korea and then in the Air Force in Vietnam as a reconnaissance photographer. I went into the Army when I was seventeen but got separated on medical discharge just before graduating boot camp. When I healed up, I was able to reenlist and decided to join the Marines."

"What does he think of you now?" the Captain asked.

"Becoming a Marine is the only thing I've ever done that he's been proud of, sir."

The Captain leaned in. "He's a Combat Vet. What was he like as a father growing up?"

I squirmed in my seat and blurted, "Violent and abusive to everyone and drank a lot. Sir."

We talked about my father for a while, and I was completely honest and transparent about my upbringing. I gave some pretty detailed accounts of violent incidents that stood out to me the most.

"Tell me where you grew up and what that was like," the Captain said.

"Southwest Phoenix, sir. It's a bad neighborhood. High crime, gangs, drugs—most of the guys I ran with are either in prison or on their way there. Some are dead. I was the only one without a felony. The military was my ticket outta there, sir."

The Captain nodded at me. I probably wasn't the first person he'd spoken to who had come from a violent situation. "Let's talk about some of the trouble you've been having with superiors and your fellow Marines," he said. "The First Sergeant said you had a steady string of confrontations and some alcohol-related incidents at the barracks. If you were to string all these incidents together to look for a theme, what would they all have in common? Is there something that sets you off? Something you can put your finger on?"

"Being disrespected or bullied, sir," I immediately blurted. "I just don't know how to deal with it. Most of my problems in the unit stem from when I first joined as a Leg during Junior Jump. There was a lot of hazing, and I had to take it. But now, even though I've got my wings, some of them still keep it up."

The Captain was listening intently. After I finished speaking, he asked me to give him a moment to take some more notes.

When he was done, he looked up, seemingly satisfied with how things had gone. "That's all I need. I don't think we'll need to meet again; thank you. You can return to your unit now. Good luck to you, son."

As I stood, I nervously asked, "Am I being kicked out, sir?"

"That's not my call," he told me, "But your First Sergeant is heading in that direction."

And that was that. I left the meeting feeling conflicted. It had felt nice to get some things off my chest, but I couldn't shake the feeling that I had just given the First Sergeant more ammo to build his case against me.

I knew my days were numbered, and I had to think fast. Back at the barracks, I asked around for advice. After a few days, I narrowed it down to only one option I could use, as all others were hopeless. There was a long-standing tradition in the Marine Corps I could turn to: requesting mast—a formal protocol for handling disagreements between Marines and superiors.

I found some details on requesting mast in a regulations manual I borrowed from one of the squad leaders. If a Marine disagrees with a superior's disciplinary decision, the junior Marine may officially request mast to have their case addressed by their superior officer's next-level superior. Requesting mast would allow me to go over the First Sergeant's head and give me an opportunity to appeal to the company commander directly. It was my only shot.

Colonel Sweetser was our company commander, the same one who had given me my gold wings. He stood at least six-five, had a gentle smile, and maintained a calm and steady leadership style. I respected the hell out of him. He communicated in a way that made the men feel heard and understood but was also known for being firm when necessary. I had a few conversations with the Colonel one on one as his driver in the field a few times. He would always ask questions about where I was from, and we talked about my father being a Marine. He took an interest in me and how I was doing.

My only chance was to plead my case in front of him.

About a week went by before I got a heads-up from my squad leader. "First Sergeant wants you in his office, double-time!"

When I arrived, the First Sergeant motioned me into his office and sat behind his desk with that same smirk, eyeballing me in silence as I reported in.

He gave a good long pause before a full smile came across his face.

"Gon' kick you out ma Marine Co'," he said firmly while patting his hand on my file. "Yo' days of grabassin' and screwin' off in my unit is ova!"

I had prepared for this moment and took a deep breath, thinking, *Am I actually going to do this?*

"First Sergeant," I stated directly, "I would like to request mast."

First, he blinked, then his eyes got bigger. Even so, he continued to grin and now seemed amused. He reached into a filing drawer, pulled out a document, and offered it to me from across the desk. "Don't matta what you do. CO's already on board with it," he said dismissively.

The mistake I made in that moment was how I plucked the paper from his fingertips.

"Thank you," I said with a hint of sarcasm and a slight grin.

His eyes got huge, and his giant arms inflated inside his uniform as they flexed. I could feel his rage radiating off his body as he stood up behind his desk, clenching his fists.

"Stand at attention, and freeze!" he ordered.

My eyes locked on his intense stare. He was serious.

"Get your eyeballs off me! I said freeze! Eyes front!" he barked.

He growled, "You just assaulted me," and he slowly began to walk around his desk toward me. Out of the corner of my eye, I could see him approach the side of my face. He brandished his knife hand—all four fingers pointed with the thumb tucked in—about an inch from my nose. "You just *assaulted* me!" he repeated in a sinister tone.

I was nervous but didn't think he would hit me, so I relaxed and went empty, staring straight ahead. When he sensed I was unfazed, he tensed up even further.

Suddenly, like his fist was spring-loaded from his shoulder—*BAM*—he smashed me in the jaw with the force of a mule kick. I staggered backward in shock, and the look on his face told me he was going to kill me.

I freaked out. There was no way I could take him in a fistfight. I crouched and darted under his guard to grab him around the waist, putting his weight back on his heels. Clearly, he didn't expect me to go on the offensive, and I was shocked I was able to get under his guard so quickly. Lifting his heels just off the ground, I fireman-carried him across his office, issuing a battle cry at the top of my lungs—"Aaaaahhhhhhh!"—as I created as much speed as I could to plow both of us into his wall of plaques and memorabilia. The force of the impact exploded his prized wall hangings everywhere, and I was sure the commotion alongside my yelling would be felt and heard through most of the building.

I held onto him for dear life. He was starting to peel me off and roaring about breaking me in two when the door slammed open, and suddenly, hands were grabbing us everywhere.

Instantly, Colonel Sweetser and a group of officers and senior enlisted leaders crammed their way between us.

As we were pulled apart, the First Sergeant yelled, "He assaulted me!"

Restrained by both arms and without thinking, I screamed back at the top of my lungs, "I assaulted you? *Are you crazy?!*"

"Lock it up, Marine," Colonel Sweetser commanded.

Immediately, I came to my senses and snapped to attention, eyes front. *Shit*, I thought. *Now I'm going to get written up for assaulting the First Sergeant and for disrespecting him in front of the Colonel. I'm screwed!*

Colonel Sweetser stared a hole right through the First Sergeant and gave me a direct order. "Get out of here, Marine, and wait outside my office! Now!"

"Yes, sir!" I responded. I picked up my cover off the ground and bolted through the door. Even standing outside the CO's office down the hall, I could hear their booming voices arguing back and forth for almost fifteen minutes.

The door to the First Sergeant's office suddenly slammed open, and all the officers followed the Colonel down the hallway in single file. They walked by me into the CO's office without saying a word. The door slammed, and though I heard the murmur of a conversation on the other side of the wall, I couldn't make out what they were saying.

As I awaited my fate, time slowed down. Each second felt as though it lasted an eternity. The First Sergeant's door suddenly swung open, and he quickly marched down the hallway in my direction, burning a hole through me with his stare. He was carrying what looked like my file. He growled as he walked around me to knock on the CO's door to announce his presence. *Bam, bam, bam!*

"Come in," the CO commanded, and the First Sergeant entered.

The murmuring continued for a good while, then the door opened, and an officer peered out and paused.

"Enter," the Colonel commanded.

Aw, shit, I'm fucked, flashed in my mind.

I marched crisply to his desk and locked it up to attention, eyes front.

The First Sergeant was to my right, and the group of officers stood shoulder to shoulder behind me.

The Colonel was sitting at his desk. He already had my file open before him. He studied it and looked up, giving me the stern look of a disappointed father. I hated myself for this. I loathed my father, but Colonel Sweetser reminded me more of my grandfather, whom I loved dearly.

This time, though, his usual pleasant demeanor wasn't present. He was rigid and angry.

"Do you know why you are here?" he asked.

"Yes, sir, I do. The First Sergeant wants to process me out," I replied.

"That is correct, and I am inclined to agree with him. Setting the assault the First Sergeant is accusing you of aside, your behavior and volatility won't be tolerated any longer. Do you have anything to say on your behalf?"

Respectfully, I asked, "May I speak freely, sir?"

"You may," he replied.

My tone was direct but sincere. "Sir, my father was career military. A Marine Combat Veteran of Korea and a reconnaissance photographer in Vietnam. I was told not to come home with anything less than an honorable discharge. I'm responsible for my actions, and I'll take whatever discipline is called for, but you can't kick me out, sir!"

The Colonel leaned back in his chair, staring back at me for a long time. I gathered my response was not what he expected.

The First Sergeant's veins were popping out of his neck, and I could almost hear his teeth grinding. He could sense the CO was deep in thought, and the idea that my dismissal was no longer a sure thing was clearly upsetting him.

"Sir—" the First Sergeant interjected, but the CO put his hand up, gently yet firmly cutting him off.

Puzzled, the Colonel's eyes darted to the others in the room and then back over to the First Sergeant.

After what felt like an eternity, he said to me, "Wait outside."

"Yes, sir," I replied. Heart pounding in my throat, I about-faced and bolted from the room.

Once again, I could hear the sounds of a full-throated debate taking place inside the CO's office. The First Sergeant's voice boomed the loudest. I think that was a mistake because the Colonel's voice halted the conversation abruptly. "We're done!" were the only two words I could clearly make out.

The door opened, and the First Sergeant exited the room. He almost grazed me with his shoulder as he stomped back down the hallway.

"Enter," the Colonel commanded.

It's strange what can flash through the mind in a nanosecond. I rationalized what a colossal mistake it was for me to join the Corps in the first place. I just didn't understand how incapable I was of dealing with authority figures. Joining the Marines was my golden ticket to defy the odds and truly make something of myself, but I feared I'd just blown it.

"Once a Marine, always a Marine," rolled off my lips in a whisper as I took my first step forward. I loved being part of this tribe, but I thought my situation was hopeless and would no longer be able to stay in the Marines.

As I entered the room and stood at attention in front of his desk, the group of officers quickly filed out behind me and shut the door on their way out.

Colonel Sweetser thumbed through my file again before looking up. "I'm supposed to process Marines out if they get three Article Fifteens—and not many do, I can tell you that. You have four. The only way I can maintain respect and discipline with the unit is if you are gone."

My heart sank. My mind went blank, and I could feel my body going numb to brace for a devastating ruling. My father's stern and disappointed face flashed in my mind, followed by Glad's. She looked sad for me.

"This is now out of my control, and I can't look out for you any longer," he said frankly.

"Yes, sir," I replied with the miserable certainty of a man who knew his life was over.

"The only thing I can do is get you out of this unit. I'm giving you orders to Okinawa."

I was visibly stunned, and my mouth dropped open, unable to speak. *Okinawa? What the hell?*

Colonel Sweetser continued, "You have just a year left of your enlistment. If you keep out of trouble, you can make it to the end of your term. Do you think you can do that?"

I wasn't being kicked out. Again, Glad appeared in my mind's eye. This time, she was smiling. Shocked, I replied with enthusiasm, "*Absolutely, sir!*"

Colonel Sweetser raised an eyebrow and gave me one last look-over. "You leave in two weeks. Dismissed."

Almost quaking in shock, I ran at a full sprint back to the barracks, locked myself in my room, fell on my bed, hyperventilated, and cried uncontrollably.

God is love. The phrase returned to me after all these years, and still, I didn't understand it. I had been sabotaging myself my entire life without ever understanding why. At the time, all I could think of was that Colonel Sweetser had given me one last chance to pull myself together, and he had probably saved my life. In that moment, I promised myself I would not disappoint him. He was the first great man in my life who stood by me when no one else would.

Again, I thought of Glad. "Sometimes the courage to continue is all you have, and you are never too young to dream big dreams and to have the courage to follow them—no matter what your life feels like right now. You have lots of courage inside of you, and I know this is true already, John."

Courage had inspired me to speak up. Courage had saved me. I now had a fresh start to focus on. I took a deep breath and finally smiled.

Holy shit, I was going to Okinawa.

Before I left, I took a few leaders aside and thanked them for watching out for me. I gave my sincere and special thanks to Staff Sergeant McGaha for his sage advice when I had arrived at the unit two years prior. He showed up at the right time to look after my well-being.

Throughout my time with ANGLICO, I pissed off most, if not all, of my leaders, as my unaddressed trauma made me nearly impossible to manage. They were all great leaders who deserved better from me. I'd lay my life down for any one of them in a heartbeat.

CHAPTER 13

An Interruption to My Life's Trajectory

It had been a year since Colonel Sweetser granted me the opportunity to complete my enlistment. I don't know how my life would have turned out had he decided otherwise. It was abundantly clear to me that Glad's guiding influence had brought Colonel Sweetser to my aid.

Fortunately, I managed to stay out of trouble during my year in Okinawa. Now, it was time to prepare for separating from the military.

The idea of what lay ahead in my transition to the civilian world took me through emotional swings ranging from great anticipation to its opposite: extreme apprehension. *What will I do? Who am I?*

I had forged an identity in the military and loved the adventure and camaraderie that came with it. Being part of something bigger than myself had inspired me, and the leaders I respected knew how to tap into my determination, loyalty, and motivation.

When led by people I respected, I was all in. But when certain leaders tried to wield their rank and authority over me with flagrant disregard and disrespect, I met them with defiance and disinterest, leaving them irritated, to say the least. But when I transitioned back to civilian life, who would lead me?

I loved being a Marine but was clearly not meant to be a career Marine. Occasionally, when the thought entered my mind of being a lifer like my father, I cringed. Deep down, I knew if I stayed, there would be an inevitable confrontation between a Marine senior and me that would destroy all the progress I had made. I had no choice but to face the uncertainty of civilian life that awaited me.

I didn't realize I was facing a dilemma that has plagued transitioning Veterans since well before Homer wrote the epic tales of *The Iliad* and *The Odyssey* twenty-six hundred years ago. Young men and women leave home to be galvanized into warriors. Families await their eventual return, but the identity, ethos, and values forged when serving most often become a warrior's greatest block during their transition back to civilian life.

What makes someone successful in a military environment through pain, training, and experience often creates barriers to acclimating to civilian life. It can be incredibly challenging for Veterans to show any form of vulnerability during their transition back to family, education, employment, and community. Ego strength in one environment is necessary to instinctively run *toward* danger. At the same time, ego blindly projected in new and unfamiliar civilian environments can stereotype Veterans as stubborn, confrontational, and one-dimensional.

For most Veterans, navigating the trials of transition ranks among the greatest challenges of their lifetimes. Looking back, I was no different. Adjusting to civilian life would, for me, mark several incredibly difficult years of getting in my own way.

I needed to leave the military, but I knew nothing else. Everything I knew for sure about myself had been wrapped around my identity of being a Marine, and I was proud of this. But who was I as a civilian? I had no idea.

Every day in the military, I had a mission to accomplish and a constant sense of direction. What would be my new mission? What would give me direction?

In the Marine Corps, I had a purpose, and that gave meaning to my life. The Marines instilled a loyalty ethos that deeply resonated with my values: Unit—Corps—God—Country. A Marine's first loyalty is to the Marines fighting by his or her side. Their second loyalty is to the Marine Corps, third is their loyalty to their god, and fourth is their loyalty to the United States.

What would provide me with meaning and purpose more significant than this? At the time, I couldn't comprehend that it would be solely up to me to forge my own personal ethos as a civilian. I wish the military had invested in preparing me for the journey home with the same commitment they invested in making me ready for battle.

What scared me the most was the rage and ferocity I had forged and channeled into an explosive force. Where would I direct this ferocity, and how would I contain it as a civilian? In the Marine Corps, rage is a necessary force one channels and directs toward an objective. Even so, I had struggled to successfully and appropriately channel it. What was my new objective? Most likely, whatever it would be, it wouldn't require channeling my rage.

With only two weeks left until my flight from Okinawa to be discharged, these dilemmas relentlessly churned in my mind. To kill time while I waited, I logged a lot of hours at the USO on base drinking beer, celebrating, and saying goodbye to friends.

Then, in the time span of about five to ten minutes, my life changed forever.

A few of us who were out-processing pulled a few tables together near the bar to talk about what we were going to do back home. The beer was flowing, and so was the bullshit. The topics ranged from entrepreneurship and starting an import-export business to being relegated to finding a job in law enforcement or firefighting. Somebody mentioned becoming a correctional officer due to our lack of transferable job skills. We had no real plan but lots of exciting ideas about the new chapters we were preparing to open in our lives. We had no clue whatsoever of the identity crisis and the trials of transition we were about to encounter. Rough waters were ahead for most all of us.

In retrospect, we all seemed to share the same naive point of view. We trained to be unstoppable and to accomplish our objectives. Therefore, we concluded our fortitude and training would, of course, translate easily into success in civilian life. At that moment, anyone could see we were part of an elite and special tribe with a heritage that spanned over two hundred years. However, the average civilian didn't understand the things we held dearly, and frankly, they didn't care. This was a blind spot for all of us, and nobody prepared us for it.

We were under a spell of misplaced conviction, believing we would be successful at whatever we set our minds to doing. But really, who were we outside of this deeply ingrained identity? This was about to be tested.

While we were slapping each other on the backs and laughing our asses off, unbeknownst to us, a warrant officer leaning against the bar just behind us had been eavesdropping on our conversation. Warrant officers have a distinctive and well-respected status in the military. The gold bar on their collar with red squares signifies they were once enlisted, just like us, but then left the ranks to attend college to later re-enter the service as an officer.

When I approached the bar to get another pitcher of beer, the warrant officer and I exchanged glances, and he nodded.

Seeing my jump wings, he asked, "RECON or ANGLICO?"

"ANGLICO, sir," I replied as the bartender slid me a new pitcher.

"Getting out soon, I gather?" he said in a friendly tone.

"Yes, sir! Just a couple of weeks now."

He sipped his beer and asked, "Mind if I share some advice with you?"

"Not at all, sir," I replied. *When a warrant officer offers advice, take it*, I thought.

He looked directly into my eyes and said, matter-of-factly, "Within a couple of weeks after getting home, you're going to have a big realization, and here it is: the world is exactly the same, *but you've changed*." He paused to see if his words had sunk in. "You've changed because of your experiences, but the world is exactly the same as before you left home—that's what I'm getting at."

"You're right, sir!" I replied in ignorance. "I have changed a lot, but when I went home on leave a few times, all my friends were still doing exactly what they were doing before I left, which was pretty much nothing but drinking and smoking weed, going nowhere."

He leaned in. "Here's my advice: if I were you, instead of sitting here drinking and laughing with my buddies, I'd go to the closest bookstore and find the self-help section. I'd look for anything that jumps off the shelf at me and start reading about who I'm becoming."

I wasn't expecting that. Reading wasn't exactly a prized quality in the Marine Corps. His message reverberated through me as I waited for a punchline. *Where is this heading?* I wondered.

He stared at me more intensely, like he wasn't talking to me but, rather, my future self, the one he was trying to help. "Focus on who you are becoming. Don't just see yourself as a Marine or a Veteran. You need to wake up!"

Buzzed as I was, his message was sobering. Pointing at my wings, he said, "Sooner or later, you're going to realize the world doesn't really need another hard-ass Marine who can parachute out of helicopters at night and carry big, heavy packs. You need to reinvent who you are as a civilian, as a person, in addition to being a former Marine."

"Self-help section of the bookstore? What's that, sir?" I felt embarrassed to ask. The last time I could recall being in a bookstore was with my mother. When I was a young boy, she would take me with her to shop for comic books or Prince Valiant literature. Since then, I had not set foot in one.

"It's a section of every bookstore that has to do with personal development," he explained. "I'm not going to tell you what to look for or tell you anything more than this. You will not be in the military any longer. You will need to find out what gives you meaning and purpose. The *self-help* section, not the psychology section. Start there."

We talked for a bit longer, but I was deep in thought, processing and trying to make sense of what I had just heard.

The warrant officer laid some money on the bar and reached out to shake my hand. "Good luck to you. I hope this was helpful. Before I decided to become a warrant officer, a mentor of mine gave me this same advice. It changed my whole perspective; I'm just paying it forward."

I could only feel a sense of gratitude and awe that he had chosen me to share this with.

He looked into my eyes again. "I want to write something down to give you, and I suggest you commit it to memory. I did when it was shared with me, and my life got much easier."

He produced a small notepad and a pen from his side pocket, and he began to write. When he was finished, he tore the paper free and handed it to me. On it, he'd written:

"In times of change, learners inherit the earth, while the learned find themselves beautifully equipped to deal with a world that no longer exists."
—ERIC HOFFER

"Be a learner," he told me once I looked back up. "Be curious instead of stubborn, closed-minded, and *learned*. I wish the military did a better job preparing Veterans who are transitioning out."

He then shook my hand again, and I nodded to confirm I understood.

"Thank you for the advice, sir. I will commit this to memory," I stated sincerely, holding his note.

He turned and sauntered through the exit while I stood at the bar in a daze. It was the sort of resolute wisdom Glad would have shared with me or anyone else in need. I smiled and acknowledged her guiding these precious moments.

Walking back to my seat with my beer, I experienced a sense of anticipation. A total stranger had offered up this advice, asking nothing in return. *Why me?* I thought, as I sat with my buddies, disengaged and deep in thought.

His words had hooked me, and I decided I needed to investigate the mystery of what he had shared. I tapped my buddy, Chuck, on the shoulder and said, "Hey, it's important. We need to roll. Suck down your beer."

Within minutes, we were heading toward the exit. "I'll explain this in a minute," I said as we exited the building.

Chuck and I had met back in the States a year prior on our flight to Okinawa. I remember the first time I'd spotted him. Standing there in the ocean of camouflage uniforms, his gold wings got my attention instantly. I introduced myself with the usual, "Who were you with to get your wings?" He was a parachute rigger, and we became tight from that moment forward, sharing stories about jump school and parachuting out of planes, jets, and helicopters.

Chuck and I came from contrasting backgrounds. He was born into a third-generation family business where his father was the CEO. After his discharge, he was expected to go to college before coming to work with the family business. As for me, I was going home to an anxious father who claimed it was "Reaganomics," meaning there were no jobs. I could tell my father wished I had stayed in the service and made it my career.

"We need to get to the bookstore before it closes," I said to Chuck as we flagged a taxi. Not surprisingly, there were no bookstores on the Marine base, so we headed for Kadena Air Force Base, about six miles away.

We arrived and headed straight to the cashier to ask for directions to the self-help section. As we followed her through a maze of rows, I was reminded of the public library I frequented (hiding out) near the park and shopping center when I was being chased by bullies. The only reason I went to the library was because it was safe, not because I was looking for books.

The cashier was friendly and gestured to the section titled "Self-Help" as she walked by it and continued on her way.

And there we were, standing in front of a long section of books about five rows high and about twenty feet long. I still had no idea what self-help really meant, and I decided to jump right in, scanning from the top left shelf and working my way to the right. Row by row, I read every single book's spine and selected the titles that caught my eye.

There were many. In fact, I was amazed by all of the attention-grabbing titles. I started setting books aside in stacks of potential picks to buy and take home. I had taken the warrant officer's advice to heart: "Find what jumps off the shelf at you."

I cracked a few of my selections open, and the smell of musty paper delighted my senses. I felt immediately transported back in time to the excitement of exploring the old books Glad sent me each Christmas.

As I went through my stacks, my excitement grew, but I could only afford three books. The process was painstaking, but I managed to narrow down the selection to the three titles that spoke to me the most.

The first book I chose to buy was *The Magic of Thinking Big* by David Schwartz. The second was *Think and Grow Rich* by Napoleon Hill. Again, what a great title. It was just what I needed to see. The third title was so strange I had to pick it up and read some of the introduction. It was *Psycho-Cybernetics* by Maxwell Maltz. Maltz was a plastic surgeon who made people beautiful, but inside, they still felt ugly and damaged. I guess I related to this because I looked completely squared away and impeccable in my uniform, yet underneath the surface, I had so much anxiety, rage, and frustration it was severely impairing my life.

This book needed to find me.

Chuck also picked up some books and seemed thankful for their insights. During our taxi ride back to our barracks, I thumbed through the indexes and read my note with the warrant officer's quote over and over. *I am a learner*, echoed in my mind, and a bolt of excitement filled me with hope.

That evening, after lights out, I went to the squad bay's laundry room. There, the lights were on all night, so I could sit and read. I remember opening the treasures I had found with a great sense of anticipation. After devouring a few chapters of my first book, I realized this was really my first experience of wanting to read. Up until then, I had been forced to read in school and forced to read in order to pass the exams for my military vocational schools. Reading without a purpose put me to sleep almost immediately. This felt completely different. *This* was by choice, and it was liberating to imagine where this would take me. My concentration waned at times, but I was always brought back to the pages as a burning sense of curiosity ignited within me.

Little did I know at that time, self-help and personal development would completely transform my life and provide the healing and growth I desperately needed.

A five-minute conversation with a complete stranger—actually, in retrospect, an angel—interrupted the entire trajectory of my life. My openness to him and to what he was saying provided even more evidence of Glad's wisdom and impact. Her insight to watch for messengers who were here to help me would be forever present in my life.

As I continued to read, my mind was on fire with new ideas and knowledge. Until this point in my life, I had read only a few books cover to cover. I think it had to do with my self-image. I didn't see myself as intelligent because my father continuously told me I was stupid. He had torn me apart and dragged me down from infancy. I could make excuses and say he didn't know any better, but he did. Being raised himself by an abusive Combat Veteran father didn't absolve him from being guilty of being an abusive father himself.

My father, the very person who was supposed to nurture, teach, and protect me, had instead instilled within me a negative, critical self-image and a low sense of self-worth.

Many years after leaving the military, I decided to talk with a number of my relatives about my father to better understand the monster I feared and hated. I got a good glimpse of his upbringing from a couple of my aunts. As I'd already learned from my conversation with my father in the car years prior, he had a violent and abusive childhood and had to drop out of school in the eighth grade to pick fruit in California's Fresno Valley. He later joined the Marines as a demolition technician. I was told he suffered through some extremely traumatic experiences in Korea—experiences he could never speak about. After returning home from Korea, he transferred to the Air Force as a reconnaissance photographer and served a tour in Vietnam.

Throughout my childhood, when anything came on TV about Korea or Vietnam, he would change the channel immediately. If my mother had the remote and he could not immediately change it, he would march out of the room.

After my mother passed many years later, my father remarried and made my stepmother promise him she would never share anything about his time in the military until after he had died. At least he found someone to share his pain with, but I resented that he didn't tell me these things, father to son.

After my father passed, my stepmother shared he had seen too many of his friends die in Korea. She told me he was shot down with his pilot over Vietnam while on a RECON photography mission. To evade capture, they hid in the jungle and swamps until they were rescued. I often wondered why he was so uncomfortable around water and never got in the pool with us.

I wasn't called to combat during my enlistment, so I think he wanted to spare me from his traumatic experiences. Of course, that didn't stop him from bestowing traumatic experiences upon me of his own invention throughout my childhood.

Fortunately, the warrant officer from the bar had awoken a sleeping giant within me. He chose to share his insights with me out of all the other Marines at the USO, and I wish I could thank him one more time. Once again, I cannot imagine how my life would have turned out if I hadn't met this incredible man.

And most of all, I am thankful to Glad for sending me messengers in perfect synchronicity when I needed them.

CHAPTER 14

Homecoming

When I arrived home as a civilian, virtually everything was just as the warrant officer had predicted. The only exceptions were that most of my friends had grown pudgy and now had facial hair.

Unlike my return from the Army, this time, my father welcomed me into our family home to help me get settled. Our tumultuous relationship had evolved to a level of tolerable neutrality, and the days of being physically abused by him would never happen again. He was becoming far less aggressive toward me and stopped any attempt to take me on physically. I think he knew I was as volatile as he was, and not only did I tower over him by four inches, but I was also in supreme physical condition and knew how to defend myself. His day would come, but I was focused on trying to find some direction toward the next chapter of my life as a civilian.

Spring was turning into summer, and the Phoenix heat was beginning to build. My brother Russ worked construction as a framer and was able to get me work as a laborer, schlepping panels of sheetrock off trucks, into buildings, and up flights of stairs all day. The work kept me fit, and I quickly outpaced the other workers.

Within a couple of weeks, I met up with most of Russ's friends, a pretty big network of local drug dealers. I already knew one particular dealer friend, Fred, from a few years before joining the Marines. I'd bought my first car from him when I turned sixteen—for fifty bucks. It was a Plymouth Satellite with a 318 Mopar. Fred had used it to transport huge trash bags of weed. As a teenager, I would often help him load his trunk, and he'd toss me at least a four-finger bag as payment. He kept the car running well but never washed it intentionally. The outside was grimy and oxidized, so he could blend into low-income neighborhoods when he made deliveries to smaller dealers.

The instant he saw Russ and me, he burst out laughing, howling about how I had destroyed his car years ago. So, of course, he needed me to tell him the details. It had taken place just a few weeks after I drove the car away from his house.

He passed me a lit joint and said, "Come on, man, you're not in the military anymore; you got to tell me this story. All I got was sketchy details from your brother. I want a firsthand account!"

I couldn't remember the last time I smoked pot, and Fred was known for having the best weed of anyone around. All it took was one toke to remind me why. Within a few minutes, the three of us had the giggles, and I launched into the story of buying Fred's car.

I had just turned sixteen. After getting my first driver's license, Russ got permission from my father to help me buy Fred's Plymouth. Over the next few weeks, Russ helped me turn it into a hot rod by raising the back end a few inches and adding wider tires with larger, Cragar rims. It took a few days of elbow grease to buff out the oxidation in the paint, but eventually, the cosmetic transformation was complete. We determined it needed new brakes and some other minor repairs, but other than that, it was ready. It wasn't super quick off the line, but it looked awesome.

In the late '70s to early '80s, cruising Phoenix's Central Avenue was the biggest thing to do on Friday and Saturday nights. Thousands of teenagers and young adults converged on the strip to cruise and congregate as rival high school cliques regularly raced and taunted each other. The TV series *Happy Days* and movies like *American Graffiti* and *Aloha, Bobby and Rose* had been out for a few years, so the cruising scene and what was defined as cool at the time was well ingrained in my group of friends and our neighborhood. We were all starting to get cars, and I couldn't wait to be part of the cruising adventures each weekend. Russ was already a regular on Central with a souped-up Vega station wagon that had been modified with a 400 small block racing engine. It was among the fastest and hottest cars on the strip.

Unfortunately, my cruising only lasted a few weekends before I totaled the car. It was a Friday night, and I was out driving with five of my buddies jammed into the car. We had a couple cases of beer, and after an hour of chugging, everyone had to take a leak. I pulled into a residential neighborhood alongside a property with a large hedge near an alley and idled while everyone piled out.

Suddenly, I had a harebrained idea and sped off, leaving everyone pissing next to each other on the curb of the street. I planned to race down the street four or five houses and then speed back to a screeching stop like in *Starsky and Hutch*, but it didn't work out as planned.

As I slowed to a stop about five houses away, I put the car in reverse. The tires chirped as I began to back up. The cars parked on both sides of the street began to whip by as I accelerated, and then my car began to swerve. I looked over the seat behind me through the rear window but didn't realize how the slightest movement of my hand on the wheel could make me swerve, so I pressed the brake to slow down, but the pedal went almost to the floor.

Russ had warned me not to drive the car until I had made enough money to buy new brake shoes, but eager to fit in, I'd driven it anyway. Now I realized the gravity behind my brother's warning. The brakes were pretty much gone, and I panicked.

Everything went into a time warp and slowed as the car continued to swerve back and forth at a rapid, uncontrollable rate. Freaking out, I grabbed the steering wheel with both hands and pulled it as hard as I could toward my chest while stomping my foot on the nearly worthless brake pedal. My shoes hit the floor, over and over while I tried to stop. I think I recall looking down and seeing the speedometer, and it read about thirty miles an hour.

Helpless, I stared straight ahead and shut my eyes, waiting to sideswipe or slam into one of the parked cars. Suddenly, I felt the car bounce as it jumped a curb, smashing through a fence in the front yard of a home. Out of control, the car sped diagonally across the entire length of the front yard. It slammed into a corner of the next house's retaining wall ass first and with a violent impact, halting my momentum instantly.

I came to my senses within a few seconds and found that my seat had broken and bent back into an almost reclining position. My shoulders were pressed against the back seat, and my head was cocked forward with my chin in my chest. I wiggled my fingers, toes, and limbs. When I felt no pain, I slid forward and pulled myself up by grabbing the wheel. Disoriented, I looked around to assess the situation. Everything was super quiet except for the smooth purr of the engine—*vroom, vroom, vroom.* The green lights of the dash illuminated the interior with a surreal, alien glow. The beer cans my friends had left on the front dash were now splattered across the back dash and window.

Belatedly, I noticed the lights inside this and the surrounding houses had started flickering on, and then the gravity of my situation sunk in. Of course, my father's rage was the first thing that came to mind as I looked down in a daze at the column shifter. It was still in reverse.

Holy shit!

Without another thought, I jammed the shifter into drive, stomped my foot to the floor, and prayed the car would move. Miraculously, it climbed off the bricks and dug into the yard. It took all my strength to pull on the wheel to hold myself up as the seat back bounced around behind me. I could see the tire tracks my car had made across the yard, and I followed them back out to the street, skidding sideways through the broken fence.

I sped toward my friends a couple of hundred feet away, and I could see them bent over, laughing hysterically.

"Get in!" I yelled frantically as I slowed alongside them. I didn't stop for fear of getting caught. Unfortunately, the impact of the collision had jammed the doors shut, so I idled down the street while everyone crammed through the windows. Even while they were hanging out of the car, they were still laughing. It must have been a sight to see: five sets of legs dangling out of my windows as we sped off and out of sight. We were able to escape, but within a few miles, the car began to overheat because the impact had caused the motor to blow a freeze plug in the engine block.

The car was totaled and needed to be towed home. It looked ridiculous. The entire back end was completely caved in and smashed upward with a tall, vertical crease in the center from the corner of the building. The next morning, my father's ominous presence towering over my bed woke me without him uttering a word.

"What happened?" he demanded.

I made up a story, but he didn't buy it and stomped out in disgust.

A few days later, I borrowed my grandmother's car and parked it across the street from the house I thought I'd demolished. Fortunately, the major damage to my car was caused by the concrete retaining wall in front of an elevated flower garden. It was crumbled on the corner where I'd crashed, but there was no damage to the house. I was relieved it wasn't as bad as I imagined but couldn't get up the nerve to knock on the door. It was a sad moment. My car was gone, and I slowly pulled away, chalking it up to a bad experience.

When I was finished telling the story, both my brother and Fred sat pie-eyed. They were baked from the weed.

Fred and I caught up a little more, then he stood and said, "Come take a look at what I've got in my garage."

My brother had been telling me about a race car Fred had been building. Now it was time to see it. They both had a thing for Chevy Vegas, and this time they had built a hot rod far better than Russ had years before. This car was a Frankenstein. A '74 Chevy Vega with a 454 small-block engine. The unibody had been cut out and replaced with steel tubing to deal with the motor's flexing. The body had been modified with fiberglass fenders, a custom scoop on the hood, and a slick-looking wind fairing on the back. It was right out of *Hot Rod Magazine*.

I noticed Fred and Russ were looking at each other as I sat in the car. "What?" I asked.

"Fred needs to score some keys, and we're way short," Russ said, referring to the kilos of weed they needed to acquire. "He needs to sell the Vega. If you buy it, I'll do all the work to finish it."

Fred pulled out a huge binder and plopped it down in front of me. "Over thirty-two thousand dollars in receipts," he said. "Even if you decide not to keep it, you could part it out and make a killing."

"Sorry, no way do I have enough money to buy this," I admitted. They were disappointed but undeterred, and they wanted to know exactly how much money I had. After we went back in the house and smoked weed for the rest of the afternoon, I eventually revealed I only had twelve hundred dollars. Three hundred of it was already earmarked to pay to my father, as I owed him for a few months of food and rent.

Russ took me aside to tell me they'd gotten behind paying a biker gang Fred was connected with, and they were about to get their asses kicked if they didn't come up with the money today. They were out of time, and I was their only option.

"We need nine hundred dollars," he told me. "Nine hundred and the car is yours."

I felt I needed to look out for Russ and didn't have a choice, so I went to the bank, withdrew nine hundred in cash, and bought the Vega. After sitting in the car for a while, I couldn't believe my luck. Though I wasn't a teenager anymore, I kept imagining cruising this beast down Central on Friday and Saturday nights.

Parting My Hair with a Bullet

I drove my new hot rod only a few times because it kept overheating. I ended up parking at Russ's house, so he could work on it, but after four months of asking him to fix it as he had promised, it became clear nothing was getting done. Frustrated and fed up, I decided to go to his house one afternoon to retrieve it and tow it to a garage.

I arrived with a mutual friend of ours named Dave, who had a truck and a tow strap. He waited on the street as I walked to the front door. I popped my head in through the screen door, and I made eye contact with Russ. He was sitting on the couch.

"Hey, Russ, got a minute?" I asked, gesturing for him to come out front. From the hard look he gave me, I could tell he was already triggered, thinking I was about to bug him to fix my car again. As he launched through the door, it was clear he thought I was calling him out for a fight and became aggressive and enraged.

Within a second, he was towering over me, looking down into my eyes.

"This is about your car again, isn't it?" he said through gritted teeth. His voice was dark and sinister.

He'd looked down on me for my entire life, always in an effort to intimidate me. But we weren't kids anymore, and this time he could see I was unfazed. A lot had changed for me during my time away, and I sensed a nervous hesitation beginning to crack his tough-guy façade.

"It's been four months," I replied evenly. "I bought and spent all of my money to help out you and Fred, and you said you would do the work. Are you going to do the work or not?"

In spite of any trepidation, Russ grew more hostile and came closer to my face. "I'm sick of you bugging me about your stupid car. I'm going to grab a torque wrench and crank on the heads till they crack."

Then, he made a big mistake. He leaned down, sneering, and glared into my eyes. Once our noses almost touched, he smiled and asked, "What are you going to do about it?"

He thought this shit would still fly, and I'd back down. I almost pitied him for his ignorance. He was an idiot to get this close to my face, especially with his hands down. I feigned intimidation and put my hands up to convey I was backing down. As I expected, he became all the more intense to prove he was the alpha.

It took about a nanosecond before I clocked him hard with an elbow to the chin and shocked the hell out of him. As he turned his shoulder away from me, I popped him with three hard left hooks to the jaw, and he fell over the hood of my car trying to cover up. Grabbing his waist, I threw him on the ground, which wasn't easy. He was huge and went down hard on his back with a thunderous *clap*, hitting the concrete with me in full mount. I pummeled him at will with no response, and for the first time, Russ knew he was helpless and defenseless against me. When I saw the recognition in his swelling eyes, I popped him one last time to punctuate the lesson.

"I hurt my back; get off of me," he complained, defeated and embarrassed.

This was a tone I had never heard from him. I suddenly realized what had just taken place. A sickening feeling welled in my stomach, and I felt sorry for what I had done. In just a few seconds, I had just changed our relationship forever. I was no longer his little brother to pick on and take advantage of, but I had a feeling this also meant whatever closeness we once shared was now destroyed.

From this place of compassion, I decided to let him up—big mistake. I should have held him down with my fist cocked until I secured some agreements from him regarding how he would behave from here forward.

He stood and turned away from me without saying a word, disappearing back through the doorway into the house. I stood in silence, shocked by the both of us, and still trying to fully comprehend what had just happened.

Evidently, Russ had come to a very different conclusion than I had hoped. Within a few seconds, the screen door exploded into the wall. He charged through the door with a nickel-plated, .357 Magnum pointed at me. His mouth and beard were dripping with blood, and he stepped right up and pressed the muzzle of the firearm to the middle of my forehead.

"You son of a bitch!" he roared. "You just jacked up *three thousand dollars* of dental work I had done last week."

The metal of the gun was cold against my skin, and I was beginning to black out from rage. "You shouldn't have pulled that shit with me again, dumbass," I yelled back, pressing the barrel back toward him with my forehead.

He cocked the trigger, and I stared into his eyes, trying to comprehend how we got here. I gave him all of my money to keep him out of trouble, and now, not only did he not keep his word, he was holding a gun to my head, expecting me to cower to him.

I was really pissed.

"Do it!" I yelled with all I could muster.

Boom!

I felt the velocity of the bullet part my hair almost down the middle. I blinked and flinched but didn't otherwise move as I refocused our eye contact. My ears were ringing.

Boom! Boom! Boom! Boom!

In rapid succession, my brother emptied all the chambers but one, each shot fired just barely above my head.

At the sound of gunshots, Russ's wife burst out the door toward us and freaked out when she saw the blood dripping from her husband's beard.

My ears were ringing from the shots but even more so from the massive rush of adrenaline. I chuckled and ran my hand through my hair. "You done? I'm taking the car with me. Right now," as I bent down to throw a tow strap around the frame.

Dave, our friend I brought with me, stood in the street slack-jawed, trying to comprehend what had just happened.

"Stay in the street until I get the car hooked up," I yelled to Dave. Now, my ears were ringing even louder as I walked toward Russ to back the truck into the driveway. My brother's wife began examining the damage on his teeth, and with each passing second, she grew more agitated and furious.

As I hooked the strap around the bumper hitch, I heard a familiar "click click," the sound of a trigger being cocked. Russ had reloaded and was again pointing his weapon at me.

His wife lost it. She dropped her hands from Russ's face and grabbed a wooden two-by-four.

"You *bastard!* My father just paid three thousand dollars for his dental work!"

I looked at her and shrugged as she proceeded to pummel the windshield of the Vega, bashing the glass with all her strength.

I let out a belly laugh. "He started it!" I yelled over the sound of the wood connecting with my car.

Russ walked up closer and pointed his weapon toward my chest. The insanity of my situation seized me as I hunched over, propping my hands on my knees, now in a full, eyes-watering, hysterical belly laugh.

I noticed movement some distance behind him. Most of his neighbors down the street were in their front yards, lining the street in all directions to watch the spectacle.

Refocusing on Russ, I reigned in my laughter and told him, calmly, "Put that down, and I'll give you a beating you'll *never* forget." He let out a roar and blew a couple of rounds into the ground at my feet. "Get off of my property! If you ever come back, I'll kill you!" he threatened.

"Okay, tiger," I said, issuing a dismissive laugh.

About this same time, his wife had finished beating on my windshield. Exhausted, she stood near my brother, shaking, looking at me with a death stare.

Crouching down into the driver seat, I gave Dave the signal to pull ahead with the Vega in tow. I kept an eye on Russ through my rearview mirror as we pulled away. He looked beat up and defeated with his head down and his gun hanging from his hand by his side.

As we rounded the corner, I found my emotions were mixed. I felt torn from the experience, but I had also known it was only a matter of time before we would collide. I was my own man, and the men in my family seemed to struggle with that.

We spoke only once after this incident. Just one year later, my brother was killed in a motorcycle accident. For years, I had difficulty processing the fact that I finally gave him what was coming—and he surely deserved it—but he was *my brother*, he was gone, and I had always loved so much about him.

I feel lucky we *did* have one last conversation. One day, Russ unexpectedly popped by my apartment with some beer. After some awkward small talk, he looked at me and put out his hand. We shook and remained quiet, but both understood what we were acknowledging: we were brothers, and we were good. There was no bad blood between us any longer, and afterward, we had our first and only conversation as grown men.

Russ shared that he loved me while explaining why he had also hated me so much for so long. I couldn't believe I hadn't put two and two together before. He had a dream of joining the Navy since early childhood, and everyone in our family knew this was his destiny. Around age fourteen, he was hit by a car during his paper route. The vehicle struck him at a high rate of speed, sending him over the hood and knees-first into the gravel. He landed hard and needed to have the gravel removed from his kneecaps. His patella tendons were severely damaged, and he'd needed thirteen operations over several years to help him walk again without crutches.

As he shared this with me, I remembered the incident with heartbreaking clarity. Within moments of the accident, our phone rang. My father had picked up the phone and then suddenly dropped it and sprinted out the front door, almost taking it entirely off the hinges as he bolted down the street. By the time I got out the door behind him, he was already two house-lengths away.

I had never seen him run and couldn't keep up. By the time I rounded the corner three blocks away, my father was on the ground beside Russ, cradling my brother with a look of fear and pain I had never seen or even thought possible for him.

Unfortunately, this was probably the closest moment my brother ever shared with our father.

As Russ shared this vulnerable part of himself, I could see how watching me join the Marines had twisted something in Russ that he couldn't stomach. Russ believed my father was so proud of me, and in Russ's mind, I was modeling myself in his image. He hated me for that, so his rage toward me always bubbled just under the surface.

After our soul-searching conversation, we were good, but I couldn't look at the hot rod Vega anymore. Just the sight of it made me ill, so I parted it out and made my nine hundred dollars back, plus a thousand-dollar profit.

Russ's Passing

Late one evening, my father called to tell me Russ had been in an accident. He told me to get to the hospital immediately.

I wasn't surprised at first. Russ had endured a string of accidents over the years. He was always working on cars, trucks, and motorcycles and frequently required stitches and emergency room visits for his injuries. As I drove to the hospital, I obsessed over what the hell he had done this time. We hadn't really spoken since our reconciliation in my apartment, and I looked forward to seeing him.

When I arrived, my father was waiting for me outside. He had a look on his face I had never seen before, something haunted, miserable, and stunned. He was nervously pacing with his hands in his front pockets as I approached him. We walked in together, and I finally asked, "What now? How is he?"

My father stopped, looked at me, and said, "Russ is dead. We are here to identify him."

His words hit me like a slug in the gut. "Russ is dead?" I repeated as I slid down the wall and into a ball, unable to breathe.

In moments, a guy wearing scrubs walked up to my father and said, "This way, sir." I realized Dad had been waiting for me to arrive before going in.

We meandered through a maze of hallways to the back of the hospital, where we were escorted into the morgue. And there he was, my brother, laid out on a long steel table with a crisp white sheet covering most of his body. The stench of the sterile environment and strange odors made me breathe through my sleeve. Russ was much taller than the table's length, and his feet hung off the end. One of them was pointing in an odd direction.

I wanted to shake him awake, but he was gone. *But where did Russ go?* I wondered, overwhelmed with grief.

We returned to the waiting room. My mother was inconsolable and collapsing each time she attempted to stand, shaking her head and pulling her hair. It was too much for her to handle, and my father escorted her out of the building to take her home.

The shock of losing Russ and the shock of *seeing* him like that left me numb and unemotional. By sunrise, I was a zombie and decided to go to the accident scene on Dynamite Road in North Phoenix. The police were there just after dawn, taking photos. It was then I heard the details of what had happened.

Russ and a group of his dealer buddies were riding their motorcycles in the desert. My brother had just bought a new motorcycle with a reversed throttle, which meant instead of pulling down on the hand throttle to accelerate, it pulled up in the opposite direction to give it gas. This was supposed to make it easier to drive in the dirt and better at handling bumps.

All of the guys in Russ's group were tight. They were also always snorting too much coke, drinking, and smoking too much of what they sold. I wasn't surprised when the autopsy report revealed Russ was full of cocaine, and his alcohol level was way over the limit.

From what the police could gather, Russ was riding parallel to the busy, two-lane highway in the dirt, waiting for an opening in the traffic to cross to the other side. His front wheel went into a rut, and the reverse throttle made the bike accelerate. The motorcycle bolted forward straight into the freeway and into the grill of an oncoming semi-truck traveling about seventy miles an hour. He wasn't killed instantly and had a faint pulse when the paramedics arrived.

I stood on the spot where the EMTs had tried to save him, still in disbelief. There were syringes left by the paramedics, and a large amount of debris was still scattered around from the collision.

I retreated into my familiar numbness and buried my emotions with Russ.

CHAPTER 15

The Warrior's Wisdom

I was in my mid-twenties, I had left the military, and I was becoming more and more immersed in personal development. I came across an adventure retreat called "The Warrior's Wisdom," developed by a British-Sicilian author, Stuart Wilde. The premise of the retreat was to learn the mindset of the ancient Mongol warrior. Strangely, though, as I read through the descriptions offered about Mongols, it referenced participation in a Native American sweat lodge ritual.

I was mesmerized by the images in the brochures and quickly determined I had to do this! It would involve navigating seven days of challenges and obstacle courses, mostly outdoors in the cold and snow of Taos, New Mexico.

After registering, I began consuming all the information I could find on the Mongols. They were the fiercest warriors of their time and dominated most of the known world during the late twelfth and thirteenth centuries. Stuart's event was about the Mongols' superior mental strength and focus, and I was stoked.

The anticipation was killing me in the weeks leading up to the event. I didn't sleep a wink the night before my flight and was wired up on caffeine the whole way to Albuquerque. I rented a car, and as I ascended the mountains during the drive, the landscape began to morph from a cold and drab desert into steepening, snowy hills and towering pine trees. With each passing mile, my anxiety grew.

As I pulled into the sprawling mountainside lodge, I felt the same butterflies as when I'd arrived for parachute jump school at Fort Benning. This was going to be challenging, and I was up for it.

After checking in, I went to the bar to grab a beer, hoping to meet some other participants. As I walked into the bar, I noticed that the richly lacquered wooden lodge had the aroma of tobacco and musty leather. There were large couches, animal pelts, and trophies on every wall. Small circles of people in winter clothing were warming themselves in front of the fireplaces surrounding the great room, sipping cocktails and smoking cigars. The bar began filling with people just off the ski slopes and arriving for the event.

I scanned the room and could feel eyes exchanging glances, sizing me up. They were a rugged-looking bunch of mostly alpha males with a small number of women who looked fit and adventuresome. I sat at the bar next to a few guys standing shoulder to shoulder, talking with their beers at their chests. I signaled the bartender, who immediately delivered a draft beer in a frozen mug.

As I turned and sipped my beer, one of the guys next to me asked, "You here for the event?"

"Sure am. Just flew in from Phoenix," I replied. "No idea what to expect, but here's to doing it anyway!"

We toasted our beers and nodded in unison before chugging them down the hatch. Immediately, I felt accepted and joined the circle, ordering the next round of beers.

Our talking and laughing cloaked our nervousness, creating an element of anticipation and excitement.

Everyone had butterflies.

Awareness and Presence

The first morning began at 4:30 a.m. We were instructed to walk in silence to the entrance of a large set of doors in the main lodge, where we were to wait. When I realized what was happening next, I recoiled and felt instantly triggered into anxiety. Each of us was blindfolded by staff members dressed in black with hooded robes covering their faces. Though I was nervous, I allowed myself to be blindfolded. I was escorted into a room and seated on large pillows on the floor. Soft music began to fill the space, and soon I could hear an angelic woman's voice from the Celtic group Clannad, singing "Theme from Harry's Game." Her voice had an almost instantaneous calming effect, and my heart rate calmed down.

The room thickened with smoke, and the aroma was instantly recognizable: sage and incense. I descended into a deep state of curiosity and awe. Somehow, I knew I was meant to be here, experiencing this moment.

The sounds of chanting and the gentle shaking of rattles began to fill the room, coming from all directions. The event had finally commenced. My butterflies returned in waves, churning from anticipation to apprehension and uncertainty.

The rattles drew closer and soon surrounded me. A hand gently took mine in theirs, and I felt another touch me softly behind my elbow, gesturing for me to stand. They guided me to outstretch my arms, and I could feel the wisp of feather movements near my face and on my clothes. A man chanted while wisping thick, pungent waves of smoke all around me from the burning sage. I was being smudged in the Native American tradition to clear any negative energies and thoughts I may have brought with me.

Someone placed their hand, warm and gentle, on my chest and pressed over my heart. The chanting grew faint, and I was guided back down to my pillow. As I sat, I noticed someone's hand on my shoulder, gesturing for me to sit and be still. The music was soothing, and I soon became lost in thoughts of anticipation of what was to come.

As the smudging ceremony concluded, the rattles became more rapid. Something gently brushed my eyelashes, and I realized how aware I was of all my other senses. I began to hear faint hissing sounds quietly whispering all around me. As my awareness opened further, I determined there were three individuals slowly moving around me. One was gently blowing incense toward me; one held feathers, almost imperceptibly fluttering them near my face; a third, who stayed silent, was projecting an energy that mystified me.

This was a test. My senses were being probed, piquing my awareness even further.

The music began to fade and was followed by a long silence until a deep, soothing British voice said, "Describe what you have just experienced."

After a long silence, a participant spoke from across the room. "The smell of burning sage."

Another person said, "Someone very close."

The next shared, "Rattles shaking close by."

The British voice grew nearer until I felt a hand on my shoulder, and someone whispered in my ear, "Speak."

"Three people were moving closely around me," I said. "One was blowing incense, another was wisping me with feathers, and a third was moving in silence."

One by one, we all shared our experiences. When the last person concluded, we were instructed to remove our blindfolds.

Stuart sat on the stage, sitting on a tall chair, gazing at us. From the pictures of Stuart I had seen, he looked true to form. Stuart wore a black, wide-brimmed Spanish hat straight out of Zorro, with long, dark hair tied at the nape of his neck. He wore a black, long jacket, black shirt, black slacks, and all-black boots.

Before him stood three cloaked figures facing us. They were wearing Arabic-style black robes with black waist sashes and covered faces that revealed only their piercing eyes. One held a smoldering lantern of incense dangling from a rope. Another had large eagle feathers in each hand, and the third held a giant, white snake across his shoulders. The serpent was wrapped around both arms, resting its head in the palm of the person's hand, outstretched toward us. I knew I had sensed something strange with this third person and had felt a connection to something observing me moments before.

I looked around and saw hundreds of glowing candles warmly lighting the room. The participants lined the room's edge in a horseshoe, seated on pillows and facing the center where Stuart presided.

The air was still thick from the incense and sage, and the fog from the smoke formed faint halos around the candles' flames.

Stuart gazed around the room with his steely eyes and then calmly spoke. "You are here to experience life, not escape it." He paused. The room was mesmerized by his message. "You!" He pointed at an audience member. "Why are you here?"

The startled participant put her hand to her chest and looked around in confusion.

"Yes, you. Please stand."

She reluctantly stood, looking nervous. Her flowing red hair and colorful robe captured the room's attention. She mumbled something in a low voice we could faintly hear.

"It's okay," Stuart assured her. "Be nervous, but speak up, and speak your truth. Why are you here? What do you hope to get from being here?"

A staff member handed her a microphone. "I want to stop living small, and I want more out of my life," she stated, though it sounded like she had to cough up a hairball to get through it.

"Say that again, but step into your conviction."

"To stop living small and to get more out of my life!" she said firmly.

"Yes! That's clear, spoken with sincere conviction! How did that feel to step into your power and speak your truth?" Stuart asked boldly.

"Great," she replied with a smile.

I was living small! I screamed inside my head. *That's why I'm here! I've been playing small my whole life and am too comfortable hiding out. Step into my courage!* echoed from Glad from somewhere deep within me.

A surge of energy bolted through me. *This is why I'm here*, began repeating in my head.

I can't remember a word of Stuart's introduction after those first few moments. I realized that I had experienced a lifetime of hiding out and protecting myself from being seen. I felt the knot of resentment in my gut I'd been holding inside my entire life.

As the knot melted into magma and continued to build, I realized that I'd seen this movie before and knew the ending. Get fed up, commit to change, then eventually settle back into hiding out and being comfortable.

I was living my life with the same hairball that woman had coughed up—only this moment was different for me. I was at this event, hearing her message at this exact moment, and it was precisely what I needed.

Suddenly a voice sprang forward from within me.

Go first!

I could feel my eyes grow bigger at the thought.

Go first! Echoed in my mind.

I took a deep breath, filling my lungs. *Go first! Whenever possible during this event, go first!* No excuses; this was the answer I had been waiting for from the universe.

No more playing small! I thought. *No matter what, go first.* The simple act of acknowledging this declaration gave me a charge of confidence.

I was stepping into the unknown without understanding what I was about to do or what would be thrown at us in the coming days. All we were told was to dress warmly and expect physical challenges.

The lady Stuart called upon had tapped into my psyche, and it woke me up. During the break, I thanked her for sharing and told her I felt the same.

She responded, "I didn't expect to be called upon, but that was amazing." We smiled, and I nodded in agreement.

After the break, we gathered as a large group and walked to an area not far from the lodge. Four men were standing in front of what appeared to be an aerial ropes course positioned high off the ground. I smiled, thankful I could see how my life had prepared me to participate in this. It was our first exercise, and I had a lot of experience navigating obstacle courses.

"This exercise is called 'The Perch,'" Stuart began. "A forty-foot telephone pole with a small disc bolted on the top to stand on. While harnessed up with a safety line, the goal of this exercise is to climb the pole and work your way onto the top to a standing position on the disc, arms outstretched. The second step is to spring outward from the top of the pole to grab a trapeze swinging toward you."

I could feel the tension rising in the group as my butterflies returned. I thought of jump school and tried to steady myself. From the ground, all the riggings looked pretty complicated.

Stuart's flair for showmanship and his dramatic setup was all by design.

He continued, "Remember what was shared earlier. You are here to experience life, not to escape from it. Who will go first?"

"I'll go!" I yelled, springing through the group to the front.

And in that instant, as everyone's eyes studied me standing before them, I was the leader. My boldness provided the first piece of evidence that stepping up and going first was exactly what I needed to do.

Two instructors immediately approached me, carrying ropes and a rappelling harness. They were relaxed and confident as they sized me up and helped me into the equipment.

The lead instructor stepped forward to address us. He looked like a serious climber—sunburned face and hands, chapped lips, and he was wearing climbing boots.

"First,"—he grabbed my harness and turned me around—"this rope, clipped to the back of his harness, is called a belay line." He pointed up the rope to another rope, horizontally tied to two trees where the belay line hung over and down to the belay instructor standing below. "The belay instructor continuously manages the belay line from the instant you begin climbing. The rope will not be held tight but just loose enough to allow you freedom of movement, enabling you to perform all of the steps of the exercise safely."

I believed him, but my heart was pounding.

Stuart continued. "To successfully complete this challenge, you will need to complete the following objectives:

- "Climb to the top of the telephone pole.

- "Pull yourself up, one foot at a time, onto the disc and stand on a disc on the top of the pole. The disc is not fixed but has a bolt in the middle allowing it to rotate freely, so you need to stabilize yourself as you mount the top of the pole. You may not use the belay line to balance yourself or pull yourself up onto the disc.

- "Once standing, you are to put your arms in an outstretched position, facing the trapeze swinging toward you.

- "The next objective is to observe the trapeze as it swings toward you. Gauge when it is approaching its closest point to you.

- "The next objective is to leap from the pole to snatch the trapeze.

- "Once this step is completed, the belay instructor will tighten the belay line and wait for you to release the trapeze, then they'll lower you to the ground."

I was relieved there was a belay line; we had used them in the Marines a few times in training. The lump in my throat began to shrink as I swallowed, but still, getting to a standing position on a small, eight- to ten-inch disc was going to be a challenge. The idea of jumping from the pole was making my heart rate spike. A panic attack suddenly gripped my chest, and then, just as suddenly, I realized what was happening. It wasn't the exercise that was panicking me; I had lots of experience with this sort of thing. It was that I had not laid back to watch how others failed and succeeded. My safety step of observing and mimicking was gone. I had no reference points, and the thought of failing and embarrassing myself in front of others was the true source of my panic.

I felt a sense of rage building and channeled it into action. People may have hurt me, shamed me, and made me afraid, but I suddenly realized it was my responsibility to live my life and persevere, regardless of my past.

Let's do it! No more playing small! my inner voice screamed.

"Climber, are you ready?" the instructor barked.

"Yes," I replied as I looked up at the top of the pole. *No more playing small!* I moved to the base of the pole.

Small wooden blocks were nailed to each side of the pole, designed to grab and stand on. I gripped a block with one hand and wrapped my other arm around the pole as I took one last breath on the ground.

"Go!" the instructor shouted.

And I was off. I had only been out of the service for a few years, so I was still in pretty decent shape, and my legs were powerful. I moved up the pole rapidly, and the adrenaline, along with blood pumping into the large muscles of my legs, gave me a sense of being fully alive. It was coupled with just the right amount of fear and brought me back to the adrenaline rush of parachuting out of a helicopter at night.

I reached the top of the pole and grabbed the disc that spun quickly. I paused for a moment to catch my breath and assess the situation. At first, it felt awkward as I tried to pull myself up and over the disc onto my belly with my legs dangling, but once I put my left foot on the last wooden block near the top, I regained my sense of balance.

As I bench-pressed my body upward to get my knee onto the top of the disc, the pole started rapidly wobbling and swaying from my weight and movement. I took a deep breath and let it out slowly to lower my heart rate. I took a second breath, in and out. The military had taught me to center and calm myself using slow and deep tactical breathing, and I'd practiced it plenty of times on ropes courses.

As the wobbles slowed and the pole became still, I quickly pulled my right knee onto the disc. The wobbles returned, sending my heart rate pounding again, but a sense of determination overtook my fear.

More deep breathing once again slowed the wobbles. I took my left foot off the block and pulled my left knee onto the disc.

I froze for at least a minute to catch my breath and try to figure out how to balance myself enough to raise my right foot onto the disc. In my head, the minute lasted a lot longer. My monkey mind became distracted, wondering what the group was thinking.

"You're doing fine," the lead instructor shouted. "Take your time."

I bench-pressed myself up and attempted to raise my foot as the wobbles returned. The sole of my boot caught the edge of the disc, and I fell back. I had one knee on the disc, and my other leg was dangling straight below, trying to find the block.

I made it onto both knees on my second attempt. Once on top, it was easier than I'd thought to put one foot on the disc while gripping the edges and then the other. Slowly, I raised into the standing position with my arms outstretched.

The view was spectacular. I took in the entire mountain range of Taos as my chest filled with fresh, clean, and crisp air. I looked straight ahead to assess the trapeze swinging toward me. It came five to six feet from me at its closest point, about chest high. I waited for about six swings to time my jump and sprang into the air with my hands outstretched. I caught the trapeze with both hands only to discover that a thick ice layer on the grip had formed from the rainy night before, making my fingers slip off instantly. The ground came at me with such velocity, and like the backward pull of a parachute opening, the belay line jerked me back and halted my fall. I let out a yell in excitement.

The instructor stepped up next to me. "The purpose of the exercise is to attempt or complete all of the steps required. The learning is in the process of dealing with and moving through your fears."

My confidence soared, and I felt reborn. "Bring it on!" I yelled as the instructor unstrapped me. I walked through the group, fist-bumping and high-fiving.

Over the next five days, my "go first" declaration instilled a life-changing sense of certainty that has never left me.

Another memorable "go first" happened the following day. We were going to rappel down a river canyon off a 300-foot cliff, and I took the lead. I had enough rappelling experience to test my equipment quickly. Once reassured and confident in its security, I walked to the cliff's edge. When I turned to the group, the instructors were the only ones who didn't appear nervous or afraid. I tightened the rope and leaned back over the cliff, hopping a few times for one final test, and *zing*, the rope slid through the carabiner. I felt invincible as I bounded down the ridge to the canyon floor. Within a few moments, I was back up to the cliff's edge with everyone cheering. Not knowing what to expect at any time but going first anyway was the most significant part of the experience.

I Am Alone

As the sun set on our first day of The Warrior's Wisdom, Stuart instructed us to relax for a few hours in preparation for an evening exercise that would last until dawn.

"Dress warmly," he said. "You will be out in the snow the entire time.

"The exercise tonight is called 'I Am Alone.' The purpose of this experience is to take you away from the distractions of your life and quiet your mind to allow the insights you seek to manifest."

As I scanned the room, there was a vibe of nervous curiosity about what our experience would bring.

Later that evening, under a bright full moon, we were broken into small groups and driven into the steep, isolated wilderness surrounding Taos, packed with fresh snow. When we reached the peak of a steep mountain road, the driver stopped the van and turned to give us our instructions.

"Each time I stop," he said, "one of you will depart the vehicle. You are to walk into the wilderness from the road only as far as a few hundred feet into the snow and remain there until we come back to pick you up in a few hours. You are not to move more than 100 feet in any direction until the van returns. Understood?"

"Yes," we acknowledged.

While he was speaking, determined to go first, I grabbed the door handle, anticipating when he would ask for the first volunteer. Before he could finish the question, I popped the sliding door open, stating, "I will!" and put one foot out of the van.

As I stood outside, a freezing wind cut across my face and neck as I watched the taillights disappear into the darkness. I didn't think much of the exercise. *I Am Alone? Be by yourself in the snow? What's the big deal?* I thought.

About a hundred feet from the road, I could see the crest of a small hill and decided this was where I would spend my time. Departing the road, I walked into a small, open meadow area and immediately sank into the snow, past my knees. Moving to the crest of the snowbank was challenging but only took a few minutes. Looking around, I was in complete isolation with not a city light in sight. With nowhere to sit, I dug a space into the fresh powder and fashioned a large recliner to sit in for my stay.

Sinking into my ice-packed La-Z-Boy, my gaze softened as I looked to the sky. The starry galaxy above took my breath away. The stars were so close that I could almost touch them. The Milky Way, with all its vivid, celestial colors, blanketed the sky in every direction. It was beautiful.

I felt small and insignificant in the universe but in awe that I was also a part of it. My thinking mind attempted to find meaning at the moment, but the spaciousness of the universe echoed nothing back.

There was only silence. Just an awesome and infinite silence.

I then realized that I was not exactly alone. There were wolves and bears in these mountains, and I suddenly felt hypervigilant and vulnerable. The thick, dark woods and snow drifts created a sound chamber that resulted in a reflective, acoustic effect with even the slightest sound in the environment. I listened in a heightened state of paranoia for at least an hour, trying to sense any movement in the deep snow around me—there was nothing but stillness. Eventually, I relaxed and leaned back, feeling safe, allowing myself to breathe into the moment.

As I stared into the abyss above me, I noticed that any noise I made reflected off the snow chamber around me and amplified. I hummed a few bars, starting and stopping sharply to feel the sound resonate within my chest and echo in my ears from the wilderness.

It felt as though the heavens could hear me.

I sat in total silence for hours, breathing and softening my energy. I felt small and temporary in the timelessness of the galaxy.

Why am I here? I asked myself in wonder, gazing deep into the abyss. *Why do I exist?*

Who am I?

It was then I realized the purpose of this midnight experience and why 'I Am Alone' was an appropriate title for the exercise.

The hours of silent meditation deepened my sense of curiosity and awe. We were given no instructions, but I somehow instinctively knew exactly what to do with my time alone.

Although I wasn't spiritually evolved enough to answer these existential questions at the time, I was awestruck at my ability to recognize they were being presented to me by the universe.

"Thank you, Stuart," I whispered.

Around three in the morning, the van returned, and I didn't want to leave. I had found my place to be with the heavens and loved it.

The night had served its purpose, and my quest to discover my answers had begun.

Within a few hours, it was dawn, and we gathered to speak of our experiences. My mind was calm, and the connectedness to my experience was still fresh and clean. I decided to be silent and to keep my realizations to myself.

Snow Mountain Sweat Lodge

The next memorable experience came the following evening. We drove into the mountains surrounding Taos. We stopped in the darkness at the top of a steep hill and received our instructions to exit the vehicle. Six of us stood in a circle, shivering in the cold, waiting for the driver to speak.

He handed each of us a large bath towel. "You are to remove all clothing and shoes and leave them here," he said, pointing to a small wooden stand with a slanted roof and a bench beneath it. "You are to walk down this road until you come across a thatched dome where you will see three men tending to a fire. One of the men will open the entrance. You are to enter the dome one at a time, offering respect before entering and turning only to the right to move around the circle to your place inside. That is all." He said this as he turned and stepped back into the van.

Confused, we stared at each other for a moment before throwing off our jackets and clothing. There were four men and three women, so we grouped and staged our clothing while waiting for everyone to finish.

Now the cold was bone-chilling. With only a towel around each of us, we began to hop and dance around as we froze.

"Ready?" I asked, willing my teeth not to chatter. Everyone nodded. "Let's go!" I declared. Everyone began to stagger together in a mob for warmth.

Barefoot on a rocky and snowy road was painful initially. Still, as we continued, we seemed to acclimate as our feet began to numb from the ice.

About a quarter-mile down the road, the glow of a campfire caught our eye, and we quickened the pace.

A few group members struggled to tolerate the cold. I was worried they would soon become hypothermic, so we immediately pushed them to the front of the line so they could enter first.

From what I could see, three large-statured Native American men were facing us in front of the fire. They were dark shadows with orange flames at their backs, but I could make out their long hair and some of their features. One of the men held a shovel, another a pitchfork, and the third chanted in a rhythmic, Native American way while pounding a large round drum to a steady beat.

One of the men put down his pitchfork and reached to the fire, producing a large, smoldering bundle of sage. Its pungent smoke curled through the air as he began to circle the first person in line, wisping the smoke around her outstretched arms and body. She went to stand near the dome's entrance when he finished smudging her.

"Shit!" one of our group said. "I gotta get in there; I'm freezing!"

"Shh!" I whispered in his ear. I didn't understand what this ritual meant but knew this was a sacred ceremony and not to disrespect our hosts. "Suck it up!" I added.

I was suddenly struck by the realization that I was standing on the side of a freezing mountain with three naked women and a couple of guys wrapped in towels, waiting to enter a sweat lodge. I chuckled; I could have never predicted this in my wildest imagination.

The smudging and chanting continued until we were all cleansed. Only then were we allowed to enter.

The man at the door threw a large flap of heavily stitched animal skin up and over the dome's entrance, gesturing for the first of the three shivering ladies to enter.

It was easy to see the group was suffering from the cold, so I hung back to allow everyone else to enter before I approached.

Finally, when it was my turn, I entered the sacred space and glimpsed the silhouette of a fourth man in the darkness. As I crossed the threshold, I put my forehead to the ground in a gesture of respect. When I raised back up, a young Native American man in his late teens faced me cross-legged, motioning for me to sit.

The group was circled around an empty fire pit, shivering from the cold. My feet were numb, and I rubbed them to get the circulation going.

Within a few minutes, the flap opened, and a large smoldering boulder was slid into the fire pit by a pitchfork. The boulder was red hot, glowing, and pulsating with intense heat that began to warm our skin.

The young man introduced himself as "Grandson," explaining that his grandfather was a great tribal Elder. I listened in reverence, grateful for his willingness to lead us through this experience.

"Through this ceremony," Grandson began, "the womb of creation opens to us, bringing clarity, insights, purpose, and joy into our lives. Through fire and sweat, we purify and dissolve our inner conflicts and harmonize with the forces of nature. The physical release of negative thoughts and feelings creates peace and contentment and leaves us in a place of deep gratitude." He paused to let his message settle.

"During this ceremony, you will have moments of suffering and laboring." As he spoke, he poured a ladle of water over the boulder filling the dome with a thick, steamy fog. He then pulled a small branch of leaves from his medicine bag and ceremoniously placed them against his forehead while chanting a prayer before placing them on the smoldering boulder. The leaves immediately disintegrated into smoke that merged with the steam filling the dome, creating an overpowering aroma of eucalyptus that burned our nostrils and lungs. I fell over onto one elbow, suffering and laboring to breathe.

I need to get out of here, raced through my head. My lungs were on fire.

"Breathe in," he encouraged. "Feel the burning in your lungs to know the purification and the purging have begun. The discomfort will pass as you calm your mind and allow the cleansing to purify your being."

My lungs felt scorched, and my body was overheating from the smoldering boulder just a few feet away. My first instinct was to crawl out of there, but I sat and tried to calm my mind.

Suddenly, the animal skin over the door flung open again, and another smoldering boulder was placed in the firepit. A rush of freezing wind filled the dome, giving our burning lungs a reprieve. After he dumped the smoldering stone, his pitchfork retreated out of sight, and the skin was thrown back over the door.

Again, Grandson poured a ladle of water over the red, glowing boulders, intensifying the steam, followed by more leaves disintegrating into the fog.

I gazed at the glow of the rocks and went into a trance, captivated by the energy they held. They were smoking with orange, yellow, and red colors and pulsating around where Grandson had placed the leaves. It was hypnotic, and time stood still.

Grandson began to chant and play a large round drum, deepening what was now a group trance we all shared. The pain in my lungs subsided, and my mind felt free. I became lost within myself, captivated by the moment, and detached from my physical pain. The ritual repeated for what seemed an eternity until a total of six boulders were shoved into the pit.

Each time the door was flung open, the fresh cold air granted us a much-anticipated relief. And, each time, Grandson would share, "This is the dream of your life, sweeping into your being for you to seek comfort and warmth. But do not fall back to sleep, back into the dream. The true journey of your life is one of preparedness and strength to meet the challenges we must face."

The young shaman then paused and motioned in the four cardinal directions.

"Aho."

The ceremony was complete, and we all bowed our heads in respect.

This time, when the door flung open, he gestured for us to depart. Once outside, our bodies repelled the cold initially, but within seconds, the sweat from our soaked bodies began to freeze from the brisk wind as we made our way back up the trail for the long walk to the van, which was already waiting for us when we arrived at the top of the mountain. We dressed frantically, eager to escape the elements that had frozen the world around us.

The van was warm and welcoming. Inside, hot coffee, snacks, and water awaited us, and we were completely drained and almost unable to speak.

Chasing the Pig

Stuart devised a unique exercise for the following day to put us into the mindset of how the Mongols functioned as cohesive and interdependent units.

He began with an overview of the Mongol horde of the 1200s and early 1300s and how they were organized. He explained that from the bottom up, the Army was broken into units, called Arbans. They consisted of ten Mongols with one in command. Ten Arbans were then organized into a larger unit called a Jagun which would move as a large square formation of horsemen on the battlefield.

Stuart emphasized that on the battlefield, highly efficient Arbans proved to be the real power of the Mongol cavalry. The Mongol Army could travel fifty to sixty miles per day, often at a full sprint, and he chuckled as he compared the Mongols to a British Army in the 1800s. Back then, the British could only travel approximately twenty miles a day if they were in full retreat.

During training, the Mongol riders rode with their ankles tied together to keep the horse formation tight and moving as a wall. This hindrance helped to train the Arban riders to be disciplined and efficient in battle. Moving independently, each Arban was able to move in strategic, geometric patterns across the battlefield on command. When commanded again to regroup, they could effectively reorganize back into the square Jagun.

Stuart again compared the British Army of the 1800s to the Mongols. Western troops fought in fixed positions, facing the opposing force, beating drums, and playing bugles with lots of fanfare. In contrast, the Mongols would ride toward an opposing Army at full gallop in their square formation, breaking into geometric patterns as needed, all in total silence.

Stuart posed, "Can you imagine if the British Army would have encountered an Army like the Mongols on the battlefield? How intimidating." And then he punctuated the point with a belly laugh. "They woulda been pissin' their pants, they would!"

We laughed with him until Stuart abruptly shouted, "Follow me," as he jumped off the stage and headed through the audience. He flung open the facility's double doors to lead us outside.

As we threw on our jackets, I thought, *Okay, here we go*, wondering what was in store for us.

Like the leader of a marching band, Stuart forced marched the audience of over a hundred participants across the main thoroughfare of Taos. We walked down the road until we reached a fenced baseball diamond, where he proclaimed we had arrived. He stood near home plate. It was covered in a thick layer of hay with a large wooden cage containing what appeared to be a chubby, pink, and white juvenile pig.

"We are going to simulate the Arban experience!" Stuart declared. "Line up, single file."

He then counted us off into groups of ten to organize us into Arbans. "This is your Arban," he declared. "You will function together in these units from this point forward until the end of the event."

He then picked five Arbans, mine included. He instructed us to enter the baseball field and to space our groups evenly from first base to third base, facing home plate. Short pieces of rope were delivered to each team, and Stuart instructed us to tie our ankles together.

This detail was unexpected and met with a good number of complaints and curses from the groups.

Stuart chuckled as he approached the cage. He opened the door and kicked the side of the wooden enclosure, scaring the pig. It hopped outside, snorting and sniffing around near his feet.

"The goal of this exercise is for your Arban to encircle this pig, pick it up, and carry it back to home plate. The Arban that does this first wins."

We all glanced at our legs and started laughing. Stuart interrupted us and yelled, "Go!"

Most everyone on the field initially froze in confusion, then suddenly attempted to break into a run toward the pig. Every few feet, a person or two in each Arban would fall, which resulted in a chain reaction that brought the entire Arban tumbling to the ground. Everyone was yelling commands to get everyone else in step, and it took at least a few minutes for the groups to learn how to walk as one.

After some trial and error, we realized it helped to keep our hands around each other's waists. We succeeded at assuming a decent walking pace and then upgraded to a shuffle. Our straggling bunches of legs finally began to move in unison. As our horde converged on the confused pig, it ran to the dugout gate and turned to stare at us, confused and terrorized. When the first Arban ahead of us encircled the pig, several people dove at it and created a dust cloud.

The rest of us started laughing so hard that we got out of step. At that very moment, the pig bolted through the dogpile, running straight toward us at full speed, squealing frantically. Now, laughing hysterically, we screamed, "Get it!"

The pig easily dodged us and took a hard turn, making a beeline to the right field.

It was a sight to see—all five Arbans converging on the right field at full speed, running with that poor pig squealing even more frantically.

I glimpsed over my shoulder to see Stuart hunched over on his side on the bleachers holding his belly. He was laughing just as hard as we were.

As the Arbans arrived in the corner of the field, we collided like a full-contact rugby team, shoving, elbowing, and knocking each other to the dirt while trying to keep an eye on the pig.

I grabbed the animal's leg for a split second, but its skin was oily, and the creature slipped right out of my grasp.

"Shit!" I yelled. "It's been greased!"

The pig was off again, heading toward the far corner of left field. We looked at each other, more determined now, and started moving. This time, we quickly discovered a confident cadence and found our rhythm. We hit a full stride and saw we were in the first position to reach the pig. This time we encircled it against the fence and got on our knees to minimize any escape openings. I was in the middle of the Arban and dove on the pig, pulling it into a bear hug. It stunk horribly and was squealing as it jerked and rubbed its greased head and neck against my face. It was truly disgusting. Hands were everywhere, grabbing its legs, tail, and ears, trying to hold it down. I picked the thirty-pound porker off the ground to rest it on my knees, still in a tight bear hug.

We rose off the ground as a group, and the pig kicked its legs, ripping the shirt of a guy near me and badly gouging his skin.

Nevertheless, we got a secure hold of the animal's every limb and walked across home plate. The crowd erupted in cheers, and we put the pig back in its cage. My oily clothes reeked of pig shit, and my hands, face, and neck were greasy and grimy from rolling in the dirt. Still, we were the victors. We chest-bumped and bear-hugged while the members of the other Arbans stood silently, demoralized, while quietly untying their ankles.

This exercise was ridiculous and fun but clearly illustrated how most people have no clue how to work together as a cohesive team toward an objective.

Fire Walk

On the afternoon of the final day, just after lunch, we assembled in the center of a large parking lot outside the lodge. Before us was a long, gigantic pile of wood stacked about six feet high by ten feet wide and stretched about forty feet in length.

As Stuart spoke, four staff members began to light large wicks and kindling along the base of the pile.

"Tonight, the last night of The Warrior's Wisdom, we will fire walk," he said, then he paused to observe the smoke and fire beginning to blaze. "How many of you have walked on fire before?"

No hands went up from any of the participants. I felt a lump of nervousness in my throat.

"Good, then you will all be fire walkers by the end of this evening," Stuart said. "It is the final test of The Warrior's Wisdom, and I can assure you, this is entirely possible for everyone. We will spend the rest of the afternoon preparing your minds. This evening, we will return when the fire has reduced to coals and prepare to walk."

We returned to the lodge. There, Stuart began to share the process he would take us through to prepare for the event.

"The temperature of the coals we will be walking on is approximately one thousand degrees. An aluminum engine block melts at approximately twelve hundred degrees." I could tell Stuart's description had impacted the group. Most people looked puzzled. How were we supposed to do this?

"I see some looks of concern," he acknowledged with a grin. "People have been fire walking as a spiritual practice dating as far back as the Iron Age, back in 1200 BC in India. So, how do they do it? On the surface, fire walking is mind-bending and unexplainable. Still, when you understand how to strengthen your mind, the body follows what you have set your mind to do. The fire walk is about changing your perceptions and limiting beliefs about yourself and what you believe is possible for you. The fire walk is a symbolic experience of triumph over your mind, proving that if you can walk across thousand-degree coals, you can do anything." Stuart asked, "What has been holding you back?"

I thought to myself, *If I could do this, I could do anything!*

After another suspenseful pause, Stuart asked, "Are you ready to take back your power?"

"Yes," the audience responded loudly in unison.

"Come on! You're going to need to muster more commitment than that. Say it with conviction, loudly. Are you ready to take back your power?"

"Yes!" we shouted in unison.

"Stand up, and take off your shoes and socks," Stuart instructed. "I want you to walk around barefoot on the carpet. Notice how it gives a little with each step. Feel the softness of the fibers beneath your feet. Now, as you walk, I want you to imagine you are walking on a beautiful green field of damp, cool moss. It has recently rained, and the wet, cold moss squishes between your toes as you walk. Feel the coolness of the wet moss and the softness under your feet. This image is the secret of fire walking; you are simply preparing your mind to transform the coal's heat into a long bed of cool moss. As you walk, I want you to begin to chant, 'Cool moss!' Now, keep repeating this as you walk."

Stuart asked us to line up into our Arbans and gestured for us to spread out on the room's open floor.

"In front of you is a distance of about thirty feet, which is the length of the fire walk. I want you to walk, one at a time, the length of this space while chanting 'cool moss'—loudly. All others in your Arban will be chanting as well. When you complete your fire walk, you are to turn and chant to the other members of your Arban to encourage them."

This all seems a bit silly, I thought.

"On your breaks this afternoon," Stuart continued, "I want you to go outside in your bare feet and walk on the cold concrete. Step into the snow to feel the cold. When you return to walk on the carpet, you will feel like you are walking on cool moss. It will be more real when you can feel the cold on the bottoms of your feet."

We lined up, walked, and chanted for the next several hours until dinner. The repetition helped relieve the stress of what I was about to do, but my concerns never entirely departed. After dinner, we reassembled in the lecture hall and kept the pressure on to practice our firewalking mantra. The lingering doubt we all felt was still present. Yet, even so, the camaraderie we had built gave the room the adrenaline boost of conviction we needed.

Around 8:00 p.m., Stuart arrived and took the stage, commanding, "We are going to do this! Say it loudly."

"We are going to do this!" the room confirmed.

"Let's go," he commanded and stormed across the room. "Follow me!"

We nervously followed him through the door and into the darkness, chanting loudly, "Cool moss! Cool moss! Cool moss!"

Once again, like the leader of a marching band, Stuart led us to the long fire pit, clapping his hands, yelling, "Cool moss! Cool moss!" at the top of his lungs.

I was the second person in our Arban, and a lady ahead of me was becoming more nervous as we approached the coals. She froze when we got to the starting point and stopped chanting altogether. When I offered to go first, she smiled and nodded yes in silence. Her eyes were wide and panicked.

I swallowed as much of my fear as I could handle. Looking around, wild-eyed at my Arban, I yelled, "Let's do this!"

My adrenaline was pumping. I felt a familiar jolt of energy surge from my temples and across my chest. To me, it signified how monumental this was.

The large fire pit was now a thick layer of red, glowing embers, and it was an ominous sight. Several staff members were shoveling and preparing for our walk. As we drew closer, the heat became more and more intense despite the plentiful, fresh snow blanketing the ground.

My heart pounded against my ribs like it was trying to escape my chest. We formed two lines, each with five Arbans. At this point, everyone was screaming, "Cool moss! Cool moss! Cool moss!"

Go first flashed across my mind over and over as I chanted.

Stuart bolted in front of us barefoot, shaking his fists and hopping up and down. He also chanted, "Cool moss! Cool moss! Cool moss!"

He then turned to the coals and power walked across them, shouting the mantra at the top of his lungs.

Astonished, I saw no sign of physical harm during his enthusiastic march.

He reached the end and wiped his feet on a carpet. "One at a time, come on!" he yelled, gesturing for us to follow him.

Without hesitation, I stepped up, roaring, "Cool moss!" with the crowd. The coals glowed and looked wavy beneath the heat that rose from their fiery depths. Adrenaline flooded my system, and with a jolt, I bolted into a power walk, growling the chant as loud as I could muster.

"Cool moss! Cool moss! Cool moss!"

The coals crunched like popcorn under my feet and between my toes. Still, incredibly, I experienced absolutely no perception of heat whatsoever. Elated, I made the final step off the coals. Immediately, a staff member holding a hose splashed cold water over my feet.

I turned to Stuart and swept him into a grateful bear hug that lifted him off the ground. We were both euphoric. I released him, and we turned to the oncoming fire walkers, screaming our chant into the night.

For all my joy, I also felt suspended in bewilderment. I struggled to come to grips with the seemingly superhuman feat I had just accomplished.

I ran alongside the coals and up to the halfway point, clapping and chanting to encourage the reluctant woman who was next in line. Her eyes became intensely focused forward. She bolted onto the coals, stomping across them fully until she reached the end, screaming and jumping with pride.

Seeing is believing. The entire group was in a frenzy, eager to have their turn. As I looked around, the parking lot was full of hundreds of people who had seen the spectacle.

After the last fire walker crossed, Stuart gathered the group back in the lodge's great room. He recited a poem by Guillaume Apollinaire that described a group of nervous children who were spying on an older man who lived on a cliff in the mountains. He coaxed them to the edge, and when they nervously looked over it, he pushed them off, and they flew.

Stuart raised his hands in a gesture of completion, and we erupted into cheers.

The celebration began immediately, and we drank and partied almost until dawn. We agreed that this was indeed one of the best nights ever!

I came away from The Warrior's Wisdom with a newfound sense of conviction; I knew I wanted to live my life differently. No way was I going to fall back asleep, as Grandson had warned at the sweat lodge. The sensations of aliveness and decisiveness welled up in me. It was time to bring my transformed, new self back into the world I had known.

Before and throughout the retreat, Stuart prompted us to consider the major and minor aspects of our lives we had avoided. I decided there was something in my life I was avoiding—I was not being true to myself.

I needed to find the son I had fathered eight years prior.

In Memoriam

I dedicate this chapter to Stuart Wilde (1946–2013) with deep appreciation and gratitude. Stuart, you were Marco Polo reborn.

My only regret is that I could not join you on the adventure we envisioned. We planned to retrace the invasion routes of the Mongol hordes on horseback across Asia and didn't get the chance.

Thank you for helping me wake up. Thank you for the motivation and encouragement to see that I needed to jump in and go first.

I have never fallen back asleep.

CHAPTER 16

Finding Danny

My plane ride home from The Warrior's Wisdom was completely preoccupied with my decision to find Danny. Upon arrival back to Phoenix, I immediately called Glad to tell her of my plans and seek her advice. We had never spoken about Danny, but I remembered her talking with my mother just before I was presented with Danny's adoption papers.

After exchanging greetings, she asked in her usual, engaging tone, "So, John, how are you?"

"I'm fine, Glad," I replied, "but I have a serious matter I need to ask your advice about."

"Of course, what is it?" she replied.

"I know you are aware that I have a son named Danny who was adopted by his great-grandparents before I joined the military," I said matter-of-factly.

"Yes, I am aware of this. Is everything alright?" she asked, inquisitively.

"Yes, Glad, everything is fine," I replied. "You see, I just returned from an event in New Mexico that really stirred up my resolve to clean up things in my life that are unresolved or that I've been avoiding. The first thing that came to mind is somehow finding a way to connect with Danny, but it was made clear as a condition of signing the adoption papers that neither I nor my parents were to have any contact with Danny or their family. I had no choice in the matter at that time, but I'm feeling I can no longer keep this agreement. Something inside of me is telling me to find him, regardless of the consequences. I just want him to know who I am and that I am here if he wants to have a relationship with me. I don't want him looking me up when he's grown to confront me about why I didn't care enough to be in his life."

Glad patiently waited for me to finish before saying, "I think you are right to feel these feelings, and you are now old enough to understand your parental need to connect with Danny." She continued. "I remember a number of conversations with your mother and father when the adoption papers were presented to them. Your mother was deeply hurt, and your father was very angry about the way they were dismissed by Danny's relatives. But your mother's health was declining, and it wasn't possible for them to co-parent with Danny's relatives; otherwise, they would have fought for joint custody."

"Glad," I said, "I need to face the guilt and shame I've been carrying about not being in Danny's life. I could hide behind the fact that I didn't have a vote from before he was born, but now that he's eight years old, I feel a sense of urgency to find him. Even if he hates me, I need him to know who I am and that I want to be in his life—if he'll let me."

"Then you are clear on your purpose and your intention," Glad replied, "and now you must do this. It will be difficult but important."

I left our conversation feeling validated and empowered to unburden myself from my shame.

Going about finding Danny was a process of connecting many puzzle pieces from my past. The only thing I could recall of where they lived was from about ten years prior when my brother and I had once dropped Danny's mother off at her grandparents' home in northwest Phoenix. I wasn't sure if they still lived there, but it was all I had to go by. Though I knew the vicinity, I couldn't recall the exact street. As I slowly drove past house after house, my inner sense told me I was in the right place but none of the houses looked familiar.

I pulled over and sat in my car for a good while, gazing down the neighborhood street, wondering if I would recognize Danny if he walked by.

My decision to find him, regardless of the outcome, was the right thing to do, and I sensed it would go one of two ways: I would be met with anger from the family, and it would end there, or there would be a willingness to engage and find ways to come together for Danny's benefit. Either way, I'd come this far. It was time to wade into the situation and find out.

After driving through the neighborhood for a while longer, I decided my only option was to start at one end of the six blocks and canvas the area door-to-door.

I had a hard time approaching the first house and paced in the street for a couple of minutes before mustering the nerve to walk up the driveway. Heart racing, I knocked on the door. Almost immediately, a rough-looking guy answered, asking, "Yeah? What can I do for ya?"

"My name is John," I said in a sincere tone. "I'm a relative of a boy named Danny, whose grandparents live on one of these streets. It's been years since I've been here, and I can't remember which house is theirs, but I know it's nearby. Would you happen to know who I'm talking about?"

"Nope, doesn't ring a bell," he responded.

"Thank you," I replied, and I stepped away.

As I retreated to the street, my heart rate slowed. *That wasn't so bad*, I thought as I stepped up my pace to the next door.

I made it about halfway through the houses lining the third block. When I approached the next home and rang the doorbell, a kind elderly woman answered with a smile. When I asked if she knew Danny, she tilted her head.

"How are you related?" she asked inquisitively.

"I'm Danny's father, ma'am," I said. My interest was piqued—no one else had answered me that way.

"Wait here just a minute," she said cautiously as she closed the door.

When she reopened the door, she pointed over my shoulder. "Go to that house across the street."

I smiled and thanked her.

As I walked toward the house, I felt nervous butterflies in my stomach. Unsure of what to expect, I approached the door with caution. Before I could knock, it opened, and a white-haired, older man stood in the doorway. He was smaller than I was, and he was wearing blue work clothes. *Probably a maintenance man*, I thought. His sunburnt cheeks were peppered with gray razor stubble. He gave me a half-smile and a skeptical look and said, "You must be Danny's dad."

Surprised, I said, "Yes, sir."

"I'm Rich."

"I'm John," I replied as we shook hands.

"Please come in," he said, stepping aside and gesturing for me to enter. I felt guarded and cautious as I stepped through the door.

He led me to the living room. It was decorated simply and with no frills. I detected the faint odor of dust. As we sat down, his tone became much more direct.

"Who put you up to this?" he asked, sounding skeptical. I was taken aback, but he was still smiling at me, which left me confused.

"What do you mean, *who put me up to this?*" I replied, trying to keep my confusion and irritation out of my voice. I didn't think this man had any idea what it had taken—emotionally or physically—for me to find my son.

"Strange things have been happening lately," Rich told me. He brought his arms together and folded them on his chest. "Strange things—with Danny's mother and her crazy Vietnam Veteran boyfriend—and the timing of your visit is very suspicious. Did they put you up to this? How did you find us?"

"I don't know anything about what's going on with Danny's mother or her boyfriend," I replied honestly. "I found you because I remembered dropping her off somewhere around here about ten years ago, but I couldn't remember the street. The only thing I could think to do was go door-to-door until I came across your neighbor, and she called you."

His suspicious stare didn't let up, but he raised an eyebrow and uncrossed his arms. To me, that was a good sign. He was lowering his guard.

"I'm here because I didn't want Danny to go another day wondering who I am and thinking I don't care about him," I continued. "That's it; there is no other story. I have no relationship whatsoever with his mother, and you can believe me or not."

Rich shook his head. "I'm not sure I believe you just showed up out of the blue," he said bluntly. I bit my tongue to keep myself civil. Part of me could appreciate how hard he was working to protect Danny from drama. "How do I know you won't just vanish like everyone else? You can't just walk in here and act like you're his parent. My wife and I have been parenting him since he was three months old. We are his great-grandparents, and we legally adopted him. His mother was in all kinds of trouble, so we took responsibility."

About this time, an elderly woman appeared from the other room. Rich introduced her as Madge, Danny's great-grandmother. She half-smiled and said hello but stood at a distance, giving me a cynical look before turning away, back to the kitchen.

I took a deep breath. I could feel my patience waning as the magma began to build. *This could get ugly real fast*, I thought.

Rich paused in frustration and then dug in a little deeper. "Can you imagine what it must be like for him to get dropped off and picked up by us at school? And to have all of his teacher conferences attended by his elderly great-grandparents, not his parents? Do you have any idea how difficult this has been for him? Where the hell have you been all this time?"

"Rich," I said, keeping my tone even, "you only know one side of this story. Let me tell you the other side. I offered to marry Danny's mother when she told me she was pregnant, but she told me she needed to run away from home. And she did, with a neighbor I knew who was a drug dealer—a guy who worked with some motorcycle gangs. There was nothing I could do, and I didn't have a choice. I decided to go into the military, and now that I'm out, here I am!"

Rich thought for a moment, then stated bluntly, "I'm telling you, if you want to come into Danny's life, you better not abandon him like everyone else has."

Just as he finished his sentence, the front door opened and Danny came through the entrance with a backpack flung over his shoulder. He was a little pudgy with bright, blond hair. My breathing completely stopped as I waited in suspense for what would come next.

He stared directly at me and came to a halt.

"Danny," Rich said, "this is your father."

In slow motion, my son and I took in the gravity of the moment. He looked at me nervously.

I stood and slowly approached him with my hand out. This was the moment I had ruminated on since he came into the world. "Hello, Danny."

"Hi," he replied, smiling as he shook my hand. His smile was all I needed. My heart swelled with love and joy. I had a sense of where we could go from here.

Rich asked us to sit, and I repeated what I had said earlier. "Danny, I didn't want you growing up any longer thinking I don't care about you, and I just wanted you to know that. I know you must have lots of questions, and we don't have to talk about everything right now. But if you decide you want to see me, I want to see you, and I'll answer any questions you ask, and I promise to tell you the truth."

Danny seemed understandably anxious and didn't know what to say. Rich suggested he take his things to his room and see his grandmother in the kitchen.

It was becoming clear to Rich how serious I was about being in Danny's life. The awkwardness of the situation subsided, and we were able to talk about visitation and how I needed to comply with the rules and routines they had established.

I spent the next few months proving my intentions and reliability by showing up and respectfully following their rules. Over time, I was able to venture out on some day trips with Danny. He was curious and engaged in our conversations, and it began to feel like he was really starting to open up.

In the back of my mind, I had been saving a crucial conversation to have with him when the timing seemed right. That moment came one summer day while we were driving to go rafting down the Salt River outside of Phoenix.

"I need to talk to you about something very important, Danny," I said.

"Sure," he replied. "What is it?"

I pulled off the road and put the car in park. "I want to make an agreement with you that can absolutely never, ever be broken. All of my life growing up, my father was violent and physically abusive to me. To this day, I still have problems because of it."

Danny looked at me with big eyes, listening closely.

I told him, "I will *never* let this happen between us. When I was just about your age, I made a promise to our aunt Glad that, when I became a father, I would never hit my children or have them live in fear of me. I've been waiting to pass this agreement on to you. We need to make this a lifelong agreement that we're never allowed to hit each other for any reason, ever! And you will never hit your children either, if you have them someday. Whenever a father strikes a son or a son strikes a father, something is broken between them that will never heal. I swear I will never do this to you, and we need to swear to each other that we'll never hit each other in anger and that we'll always find a way to talk things through when we disagree. Do you understand what I'm saying?"

"Yes," Danny responded, nodding.

"Just like Glad said to me that someday I would be having this conversation with you, someday you will have a family. I want you to imagine having this conversation with your children someday. Can you imagine that?"

"Yes."

I extended my hand. "You have my promise, Danny. Do I have yours?"

"I promise," Danny replied with a smile, and we shook hands.

A feeling of immense reverence for Glad's wisdom came over me. This was a father-son moment I had yearned to experience for so long. In that instant, Danny knew I loved him and was there for him, and that was what he needed from me. I had delivered a proclamation entrusted to me from Glad that would now transcend my lifetime. Now I was charging Danny to carry this forward to his children someday. Glad's approving presence surrounded us like an armored cocoon, and we were safe and tethered in her wisdom.

This was a seminal moment connecting our separate pasts to the present. I had no idea how to be a parent, but I knew I could learn to be the father Danny needed.

With only seventeen years between us, and because we'd been apart from each other for his entire young life, most of the time, Danny and I felt more like best friends than father and son.

We continued to venture out on weekends for about three years and never had a conflict or even a disagreement between us. Then, one day, unexpectedly, Rich called to tell me that Danny's mother and her now-husband had done something to force Danny to live with them. I could feel the anger and tension in his voice. His tone told me there had been a significant confrontation, but he wouldn't talk about the details.

I had an uneasy sense that, somehow, I was about to be put in the middle of the family's tug-of-war for Danny.

The next day, I spoke with Danny's mom and arranged a time to visit and meet his stepfather, Martin.

I took a few deep breaths in hesitation as I knocked on their front door. When Martin opened the door, I saw he was a giant of a man who was significantly older than I was. He stood at least six-six. He extended his hand to greet me, and I was surprised by his gesture of welcome. At the same time, I felt his own uneasiness lurking just beneath the surface.

He led me to his kitchen table, where we sat across from one another. We sized each other up, and I could instinctively feel he was a possessive, controlling man. For Danny's sake, I stayed calm and friendly.

Martin wanted me to know he would be raising Danny in his home but, at the same time, told me I would always be welcome. What he was really conveying was that I was welcome as long as he approved. Then, Martin launched into a long rant of condescending comments that left me dazed. I sat in silence with a look on my face right out of *Children of the Corn*. He still didn't shut up, and an uneasy tension built between us until he finally noticed I was becoming annoyed with him. He wanted to be the alpha, in control, but I was Danny's real father and an alpha who wouldn't be controlled.

This will never work, I thought.

I glanced around the kitchen, seeking to locate anything I could use as a weapon if Martin became aggressive. Fortunately, Danny rescued me. He interrupted Martin's monologue by informing me we were running late to get to the movie we'd planned to see.

Martin and I shook hands, and fortunately for both of us, that's the last I ever saw of him.

Danny was now eleven, and I could feel a sense of distance emerging. Unfortunately, Martin's effort to drive a wedge between us was succeeding. Within a few weeks, Danny and I began to drift further apart. He shared that Martin was very controlling and was telling him bad things about me. I feared for my son's safety and felt more and more distant from him. Danny would be living just a few miles from where I grew up, and the drug scene, gang violence, and crime had grown even worse since I had left.

I could tell we would soon be completely separated from each other and decided to provide him with some insights Glad had provided me with many years before. Her words of wisdom had helped me grow up and survive in this same neighborhood and in the Marines, and it had probably saved my life more than a few times.

I picked Danny up and went for a long drive to Lake Pleasant, just outside of Phoenix. We pulled over to a lookout point and sat in the cool air conditioning while watching the mirage of heat coming off the surface of the desert ground where it met the water.

I turned to Danny and said, "Go empty."

"Go empty?" he replied. "What do you mean?"

"This will save you from some bad situations," I said. "It's a strategy I learned from Glad that she used when she was in dangerous situations. She would empty her fear and anxiety to remain calm. It really worked for me growing up as well. When I was in the Marines, I learned how to 'go empty,' as I call it, to deal with aggressive people and to avoid a lot of confrontations. Whenever I found myself in a situation where violence was expected, I learned how to lose all expression and rid myself of all emotions. I would show no anger, no fear or aggression whatsoever. I found I could quickly calm myself by breathing slowly and deeply through my nose. The calmer I became, the more the other person would begin to wonder why I was so relaxed and unafraid, and they would start to question themselves."

Danny's eyes were big. He stared back at me as he took in what I was saying.

"Most aggressive people are like barking dogs, especially when they're in groups. They expect to generate a reaction of fear or aggression. When there is no reaction and you remain calm and empty, it creates confusion and doubt in their mind. Give them nothing, stare through them, make no direct eye contact, but do not look away either. Be empty, and breathe slowly and deeply to calm your heart rate. Most often, the other person will begin to question if they should attack because this isn't the reaction they were expecting. They'll usually move away from you, eventually, while throwing insults to save face. Stay empty as they de-escalate, and then go about what you were doing, paying the situation no mind until you can make a calm exit."

"What if they don't move away?" Danny asked anxiously.

"If violence is inevitable, be empty. The element of surprise is to your advantage. They won't know when or where you'll strike. Even if you lose, you'll gain respect for your courage and composure."

That was the last in-person conversation we would have for a few years. I think Danny was under a lot of pressure from his new stepfather to give him his full attention. Eventually, Danny stopped responding to my attempts to reach him. I continued to send birthday and Christmas cards with notes of encouragement, and I always added my phone number, asking him to call whenever he felt like it.

Clearly, this was not the outcome I had envisioned, and now, for the second time, I had no choice in the matter and was prevented from being in Danny's life. Somehow, I knew this wasn't permanent and that I would be back in his life at some point. But with so many people in conflict around his custody and no legal say in the matter, I needed to be patient, step away, and not add to the conflict.

The healthiest thing I could do, I concluded, was to heed the warrant officer's advice: keep working on myself and focus on who I was becoming. When it came time for Danny and me to reconnect, I was determined to be the best version of myself.

CHAPTER 17

Success Strategies

My journey into personal development had come a long way since my exit from the military. The advice of the warrant officer in Okinawa stayed with me: be a learner and focus on who I was becoming.

As I kept building my book collection, I discovered audiobooks. I found them to be much more helpful. For all my interest and dedication, I still had a difficult time reading more than a few pages of any book without falling asleep. However, with audiobooks, I found my mind could stay engaged. I was captivated, listening for hours on end. From then on, whenever I came across a new thought leader, I would search to find any audio content available from them.

Another cosmic hint from Glad appeared when I came across an audiobook series titled *Success Strategies* by Jim Rohn. The title was perfect, and I immediately knew it would be a major influence in my life. I bought my first journal and began to capture his quotes and insights immediately. In total, I listened to the entire audio series of six, one-hour cassettes at least sixty to seventy times over a span of two or three years. Whenever I was driving or exercising, *Success Strategies* was my go-to resource for learning.

The insights provided a philosophical foundation I wish I had from a young age; it would have dramatically altered the course of my life by helping me make better choices. Jim's voice and his timeless messages provided the wise, fatherly advice I never received growing up.

The most remarkable example of this wisdom impacted me so profoundly, I had to stop and sit down while on a run in order to relisten to the following quote, over and over. I committed it to memory: "We must carefully examine the credentials of those who wish to enter the place in our mind where our thoughts are formed."

I shook my head at the simplicity of this powerful statement of truth. It reverberated through my entire being. It was a truth I desperately needed to hear, and I was *ready* to receive it.

"Truer words have never been spoken," I said to myself.

A sudden insight flashed into my mind, and I recalled my conversation with the warrant officer in Okinawa several years prior. It was a buried memory, emerging in perfect synchronicity with this moment.

I remembered asking him how I would know what books to read from the self-help section of the bookstore.

He replied, "It will just feel true for you. Just be open to the right message to come to you." As this sunk in, he paused and then continued. "Do you know when you've heard the truth?"

"The truth, sir? About what?" I said, confused.

"When you hear something that you know is absolutely true, like, *the sun will rise tomorrow*."

"Yes, sir," I responded.

"You know you've heard or seen the truth when it's as if you've always known it. This is what I mean. Just remain open to receiving the right message, and the message you need to receive will appear."

Coming across this great work from Jim Rohn, coupled with my recollection of the warrant officer's wisdom, signified to me that I was entering a new phase in my life. This was a crucial part of my next great adventure and transition.

"Like the great warrior Odysseus, King of Ithaca," the warrant officer had shared, "you are on your journey home from the battle of Troy. In this regard, you are not unique. Warriors have been training for wars, fighting wars, and coming home since the beginning of time, and their friends and families have awaited their eventual return. Within a couple of weeks after getting home, you're going to have a big realization, and here it is: the world is exactly the same, but you've changed." He paused to see if his words had sunk in. "You've changed because of your experiences, but the world is exactly the same as before you left home—that's what I'm getting at."

Suddenly what he had tried to convey to me years before became clear. I would always be a Marine but would no longer be in the military. Without a daily mission assigned to me, I'd need to rediscover what gave me purpose and create a new mission for myself. Holding on to my past identity would cause unnecessary suffering.

As the memory of my conversation with the warrant officer returned to the archives, Jim Rohn's voice echoed again: "We must carefully examine the credentials of those who wish to enter the place in our mind where our thoughts are formed."

Who have I been letting in my head? I thought. *What are their credentials?*

Credentials? This had me stumped until I realized in a flash that there had been no credentials!

For as long as I could remember and throughout my life, I never seemed to fit in. Of course, that was exactly what I desperately wanted: to simply fit in. The only credential I was looking for was acceptance. My only filter was *do you accept me?* I could even convince myself to ask, *With enough effort, will you like me?*

The only people who seemed to accept me naturally were others who didn't fit in or were the worst people I could want to fit in with—troublemakers, non-conformists, ego-driven alpha males, and women I couldn't open up to in order to reveal my true self. I had an impeccable armor exterior, but my deep insecurities and fear of being alone left me craving acceptance from anyone who would give it.

As I continued to listen to the pearls of wisdom Jim shared through his audiobook, the next message cascaded down to the core of my most limiting beliefs.

The Three Types of Association

The first type of association Jim shared was *disassociation*. You must disassociate from anyone who is toxic in your life and stands in the way of who you are becoming.

As these words penetrated my memories, a list of names and faces began to flash across my mind. These were people who had no credibility or credentials to enter the place in my mind where my thoughts were formed but, nevertheless, had been granted full access.

This makes so much sense, I thought, marveling as the truth unfolded before me. *Toxic people are ruining my life!*

"You must continuously weed the garden and rid yourself of toxic people," Jim mentioned through the recording, and I found I couldn't agree more.

The second type of association Jim described really hit me: limited association.

What if the toxic people I now need to get rid of are family members? What if they are essential or necessary to interact with, like a terrible boss or a work associate?

To me, this immediately meant that if the toxic people in my life had a purpose or were inextricably tied to me—like family members—and I had to see them on holidays and so forth, then I needed to choose to limit the time I spent with them. If necessary, I would need to sit them down and tell them why this distance was necessary, and then keep to my commitment.

This was an easy and short list to create.

But when the audiobook reached the third type of association, I felt inspired: expanded association.

Expanded association meant I needed to find people I admired who possessed the traits and qualities I wanted to learn or acquire and get to know them. The message Jim was conveying suggested I take those individuals to lunch and be honest about what I saw in them that I admired and respected.

I began to organize my three lists and considered how I would approach each person. Not long after, I took action. For the people

I would completely disassociate from, in almost all the cases, I chose to simply stop engaging them on every level to see if they would just fade away. For the few people I knew would not tolerate being ignored, I chose to meet with them and tell them I needed to move on with my life. If they chose to move in a similar direction, maybe we could keep in touch, but for the foreseeable future, I really needed to keep my distance from them.

For my short list of limited associations, I sat down with a small number of people to discuss the obviously unhealthy aspects of our relationship. I told them that, effective immediately, I would no longer engage in conversations and activities as we had done in the past.

I remember one person in particular. He was a good friend I had known and respected as a business consultant for many years. Unfortunately for him, he had either terrible luck, or there was simply something about him that left him unsuccessful in relationships. He always wanted a healthy relationship but consistently made poor choices in that area. I needed to limit my communication with him, so we did not discuss those topics.

Not long before discovering the three types of association, I had really blended my perception of his excellence as a business consultant into how he was living his life on all levels. He was well-intentioned, but I shouldn't have listened to the advice he had given me about personal relationships. When I accepted his advice in this area, my relationship in question blew up. I should have used my common sense instead.

When we met to discuss how I would begin limiting our contact, I simply said, "You are a great business associate, but from here on, I don't want to talk with you about relationships. You have not been successful in this area, and I've gotten personally hurt by taking your advice."

He wasn't happy but understood. A couple of weeks later, he tried to reinject his views, and I stopped him mid-sentence. I reminded him, "We talked about this: no more advice in this area. Let's get back to business."

As far as expanding my relationships, this will always be my favorite of the three types of association. This one piece of advice from Jim Rohn has created countless friends and mentors I value greatly.

Until this point in my life, I hadn't been paying attention to the impact of destructive, outside influences. My need for acceptance had clouded my judgment and held me back—until now.

Like the warrant officer in Okinawa, Jim Rohn and his inspirational audiobooks positively interrupted my life trajectory. Life was still confusing and difficult at times, but I could feel my sense of purpose and direction taking hold and growing roots.

As I discovered more about the world of personal development, I began to unearth who I was. Glad's wisdom had proven itself once again. And now I knew with a concrete sense of certainty I had never felt before: the more I chipped away at all that was not me, the more I liked what I discovered underneath.

CHAPTER 18

The Law of Reciprocity

B eing separated from Danny weighed heavily upon me. I shared what had happened with Glad, and as always, she listened patiently before responding.

"He will be an adult in five years, and the time will go by faster than you think," she said matter-of-factly. "But you must also be prepared in the meantime should he choose to reach out to you."

"I agree," I replied, "but how?"

Glad responded, "You will need to learn to set your own needs and expectations as a father aside to remain focused on what Danny needs."

I nodded to myself and listened closely to her wise words. "This can be more difficult than it appears," Glad continued, "simply being of support to Danny without attachments or expectations of him needing to do anything in return. With so many other adults competing for his attention, you will need to earn his trust and relieve any suspicions he may have about your intentions."

Okay, I thought. I could see what she meant.

"You see, John, the law of reciprocity on the surface is really quite simple. We receive in life in direct proportion to what we give and contribute to others. We experience joy in the giving, and our generosity of spirit, in turn, feeds our soul."

I could sense Glad deliberately softening her tone to draw my attention closer.

"To obey the law of reciprocity, John, there are four tenets," Glad shared. "The first tenet: You must be a person who can be relied upon to show up in the world for others. To truly serve others, you must demonstrate you can be counted upon. You have clearly demonstrated this to Danny by seeking him out and finding him a few years ago."

Glad was the embodiment of this tenet. Never once in all of my life had she not been there for me. She didn't simply show up on cue when called upon—she had a sixth sense of knowing when I was in need.

"The second tenet," Glad continued, "is to do what you say you are going to do."

Once again, Glad would not declare this to be crucial if she didn't fully embody it. Aside from her, I had very little evidence of people doing what they said they were going to do.

"The third tenet, John, is to genuinely care about the outcomes for the person you are attempting to help. When you choose to *give* of yourself to help someone, you must do so with their best interests in mind and not your own. If you cannot fully commit to the best of your abilities, then you should refrain or decline to help. Respectfully declining to help is the right response if you cannot invest yourself in their outcome. The assistance we give is either ecological for all involved, or it is not.

"And the fourth tenet: ask for nothing in return."

This last tenet was simple and easy to comprehend, but I could see the conditions and hooks I had been setting in my mind when helping others. This was a moment of transparency and vital self-reflection for me.

How I had been going about helping people wasn't typically ecological. I had good intentions, and I cared about the outcomes for others, but I could see that I did expect some reward or exchange for my help. It was embarrassing to have Glad see right through me, but she loved me enough to help me see this for what it was; I was helping and expecting the experience to fill my emotional emptiness. Just because I could claim I didn't know any better didn't mean I didn't feel the tug of an agenda when helping others.

The honesty of the moment liberated me from my guilt because, now that I knew this tenet, I could not deny it.

"And one last thing to remember, John," Glad said in her soft but determined voice. "The practice of the law of reciprocity and its tenets is a way of being, not simply an act of doing—you must let it become part of you, not just something that you do. As you continue to develop your understanding of this law, so shall you experience the quiet difference you make in the lives of others. You will find that giving of yourself is what brings joy, meaning, and purpose."

CHAPTER 19

Finding Meaning
and Purpose

Not long after Glad shared with me more about the law of reciprocity, I unexpectedly bumped into two messengers, Dana and Ed, who would once again interrupt the upward trajectory of my life. To my surprise, Dana and Ed provided me with the spark that would fuel a lifelong passion in the field of behavioral assessment analysis. They were catalysts for helping me look deep into myself to find what was triggering me and driving my rage.

Aside from Glad's guidance, I count my work in this field of study among the most impactful on my personal hero's journey.

My introduction to Dana and Ed occurred unexpectedly while waiting in line to attend a Tony Robbins "Power to Influence" event in Sacramento. I had been immersing myself into Tony's first book, *Unlimited Power*, and was anxious to experience his in-person work. A funny thing happened: I was close to the entrance, and a giant of a man in a black suit squeezed between our group and up to the closed door. As he opened the door to peer in, he looked back at us and asked, "Have you heard anything about this guy? Is he any good?" We all chuckled back. It was Tony, preparing to launch the event shortly. As he slipped through the door, I noticed two older gentlemen standing near me at a bar table, and it didn't take long before we struck up a conversation and introduced ourselves.

I'd say they were both in their early to mid-sixties. Dana looked like a conservative, engineer-professor type and, though friendly, struck me as something of an introvert. He was reserved but cordial, had dark-framed glasses, and was wearing a brown tweed jacket with matching slacks. I noticed his shirt pocket held a pocket protector complete with several pens bulging out beneath his lapel. Turns out I was right: he was a retired aerospace engineer.

Ed, on the other hand, provided an interesting contrast. He had a big smile and a firm handshake, and he looked to be in pretty good shape. He was sporting a sharp, navy-blue jacket over a light blue, button-down shirt, black slacks, and a red tie that made his presence pop. Ed was the livelier of the two. He readily shared his love for football and explained he was a star quarterback in college.

"You here for the event or just the mixer?" I asked.

"Just the mixer," Dana replied.

"This is a great place to meet business leaders," Ed chimed in. "We're business consultants in the area of team building and leadership development."

Dana said, "We help CEOs and business leaders recruit, hire, and develop high-performing teams."

"That sounds interesting," I responded. "I was in the military and got to work with some great teams."

Ed nodded at me. "I bet you've seen a lot of examples of great leaders and teams as well as poor leaders and teams that struggle."

I chuckled. "Yes, both."

Ed smiled back. "We also teach certification programs to help leaders learn how to use assessments. Once they're certified, we provide performance coaching and conflict resolution training to help individuals and teams who are underperforming."

Just then, the crowd in line started making more noise, and I glanced over to see the doors finally opening. "It's time to head in, but I'd like to learn more about your training," I told them as the long line began slowly shuffling toward the entrance.

Ed smiled. "I can't tell you right, but I can't show you wrong!" he quipped. "Here's my card. Come by our office, and we'll walk you through how this works. You'll be amazed."

We agreed upon a time, and I borrowed a pen from Dana and wrote it on the back of the card I'd been given.

"See you in a few days," I said as we shook hands.

The event with Tony was impressive. He held two thousand people spellbound for the entire day, teaching the power of rapport and how to better connect with people. Back in the early '90s, these concepts were still unfamiliar to most people.

Little did I realize, at the event, Tony would become yet another unexpected messenger put on my path to fuel my passion for learning. After attending the one-day training, my appetite for personal development grew exponentially. I hadn't come across a thought leader like Tony, who was so thoroughly immersed in personal transformation that matched my ethos, drive, and commitment. Tony provided a blueprint of how to construct and organize my personal compendium of knowledge. Toward the end of the day, I registered for his next four-day event, which included a fire walk.

The morning of my appointment with Dana and Ed, I arrived at their office with coffee for the three of us. I entered the office and took in the surroundings. The space was set up as a training area with a large open room and two small offices. Dana and Ed were in one of the offices, and I could faintly hear them having a conversation over their speaker phone.

While I waited, I noticed the stark contrast between the two offices. Dana's was very plain with almost nothing on the walls or desk. It looked very neat and organized. Ed's, on the other hand, was bright and loud, and there was football memorabilia everywhere. Three signed footballs encased in clear plastic shells sat on a shelf beneath framed, corresponding pictures that showed a key play of the game each ball had come from. Another football rested on the front corner of his desk, waiting to be thrown. Along the rest of the wall were pictures of Ed in all his glory as a quarterback from his college days.

The training area had four long tables in the middle of the room pulled together into a square. There were chairs all around and a projector facing a large, pull-down screen. Two sizable whiteboards were placed on each side of the projector screen. The words *Behavioral Assessment Certification Agenda* was written in large letters at the top of the whiteboard on the left.

When they saw me, they motioned me with friendly smiles and stood to greet me.

"Good morning! I brought some coffee," I said eagerly.

We exchanged greetings, and within a few minutes, Ed took the initiative by suggesting we get started.

Dana directed me to have a seat in front of a desk and placed a piece of paper and a pen before me.

"The survey only takes about five minutes to complete," he told me. "When you're finished, come out to the training area, and we'll generate some reports to review. Any questions?"

"No, let's get rolling," I replied.

I settled into the chair and glanced at the survey, then turned it over to see the other side. The entire form, front and back, was simply a double-sided page of adjectives with checkboxes next to them. Not giving it much thought, I blazed through both sides in just a few minutes. As it seemed so simple, I really didn't think much of the survey.

When I was finished, I took the paper, got up, and walked into the large training room area to turn it in. Dana spotted me and reached out to snatch it, then turned to his computer screen and punched keys on his keyboard. Within a few moments, a grin came over his face.

I guess a smile is better than a frown, I thought, watching Dana with curiosity as he turned and pulled a fresh page off the printer. He handed me the new paper, still grinning, and asked me to read it.

As I glanced at the page, I could feel the eager way Dana and Ed were watching me. They looked like a couple of big-eyed, smiling kids looking into the window of a toy store.

As I channeled my focus to the printout, certain words began to jump off the page: *individualistic, convincing, direct communicator, competitive, independent, risk-taking, decisive, non-conformist, forceful.*

I couldn't help but laugh at the accuracy of my results. "Wow, this is amazing. Thanks for telling me what I already knew about myself," I joked. "Freedom from rules and structure! You got all of this from that survey?"

"You bet, and there's more. Lots more," Ed responded eagerly. Both he and Dana were smiling from ear to ear.

Beyond curious, I was hooked. "Show me everything."

The printer came to life again, and Dana pulled off another page. He put it on the desk in front of me to review. On it was a set of graphs. At first glance, they looked clinical and complicated.

"This field of work is called *predictive behavioral analysis*," Ed explained. "These surveys help us understand our behavior and why we do what we do. When we know more about ourselves, we can then better understand others."

Dana chimed in. "These types of tools were initially researched and developed during World War II to determine which recruits would be the best fit to go to bomber school or fighter pilot school."

Ed picked up where Dana left off. "By understanding your own behavior and communication style, you can see more clearly what your strengths are and where you may find yourself getting in your own way."

Ed glanced at the trait measurements on my chart, and a serious frown came over his face. That concerned me. He rubbed his chin as he let out an extended, "Hmm."

I leaned closer to see what he was referring to on my chart and asked, "What is it?"

Ed paused. "Just kidding," he blurted and cracked up. "I just love to see the look on people's faces when I do that. Wow! A six-sigma spread," he said excitedly. "That's rare!"

The budding sensations of anxiety left me. I had no idea what he was saying, but it sounded awesome. Both men sat across from me, leaning forward with interest.

"Is that good?" I asked.

"This means your traits are quite a bit more intense than the vast majority of people."

Dana went into engineer mode and assumed a more serious, technical tone. He pointed to a line he referred to as the *mean line* or midline. Along the graph's sides were marks that looked similar to those on a measuring stick. He pointed out that the long lines were called *sigmas* or standard deviations. There were four dots on the graph, two to the left and two to the right of the mean line.

"The distance between the dots measures the intensity of a person's traits," he explained as he counted off the sigmas between my dots. He got to six. "Seventy-four percent of people fall somewhere inside a three-sigma spread. This is what we meant when we said your traits are much more intense than most other people."

The alpha in me welled up with pride. "So, this is good, right?"

"Well, it's *intense*, that's for sure. Good in some circumstances if directed properly and not so good in others."

I was fascinated. I loved watching Dana process how to explain my results. His head cocked a little to the right, and for a moment, his face held a blank stare that went right through me. Then, he refocused on me. "Let's compare your intensity to a hundred-watt light bulb. It illuminates a room by projecting light in all directions, correct?"

"Correct," I agreed.

"Good. But a hundred-watt laser with the same wattage cuts through steel, right? This is much like the intensity of your traits. If you aren't paying attention, you can dissipate your energy in all directions. But if you're focused on accomplishing objectives, big things will get done. Does this make sense to you?"

"Absolutely! That's a great way to look at this," I responded appreciatively.

Ed jumped in with more pragmatic flair. "Let me put it to you this way: without even looking at your resume, any company looking for sales and business development talent should hire you on the spot. Your traits measure that you have a strong, natural ability to connect with a wide variety of people with minimal effort. Do you agree?"

"Yeah, probably my strongest ability," I replied.

He then pointed to the part of my chart that displayed patience and joked, "You have none."

We all laughed as I shook my head. "Nope."

He then pointed to my measurement of dominance. "Your dominance is extraordinarily high. Basically, it measures that you need to be in control more than you need to take your next breath." I shrugged, and we chuckled as Ed went on. "Next is conformity. This measures that you hate to be managed or controlled."

I laughed. "Yeah, no kidding!"

"Your extroversion is extremely high," Ed continued. "This is what I was referring to about your ability to relate to almost anyone quite easily."

Then, Ed pointed at both my high dominance and my low conformity. "Basically, this means your need for control significantly conflicts with your need to not be controlled."

"Say that again?" I asked, surprised.

Ed repeated, "Your need for control, high dominance, conflicts with your need to not be controlled, low conformity. In other words, you need to be in control but don't like to be told what to do."

The accuracy of what he'd just pointed out rang so true for me it was nearly deafening. The simplicity of it was stunning, and I was floored. "Wow, that's absolutely true! Holy *shit!* That's gotten me into trouble my entire life," I admitted.

"Now you're starting to wake up," Dana responded with a smile. "Once you understand your traits, you see your strengths, and you get a good glimpse of blind spots that trigger you."

Ed continued, "High dominance is also about the need for respect—to be respected, and a preference to work only with people you respect. Is being disrespected a trigger for you?"

"Bingo. My whole life," I replied, shaking my head. "Got me into a whole lot of trouble in the military."

Dana took over. "Low conformity. This measures that you have a significant need for freedom and autonomy—and a need for creativity. Does this resonate with you?"

"For sure," I replied. "I can't operate from inside a box."

Ed said, "What comes along with this need for autonomy is typically a sensitivity to being overmanaged or controlled, especially by people you don't respect. I bet you've seen this movie before."

"Over and over." I rolled my eyes. "How in the hell did this survey pick that up?" I said, astonished that checking some boxes on a piece of paper could produce such accurate and personal results.

Grinning, Ed told me, "Your traits are very similar to mine. When people try to tell me what to do, even in a nice way, I feel an instant sense of resistance."

"I agree completely," I replied. "What I hate about this is when I feel disrespected or controlled, I go off. The words start flowing, and I can't take them back. I'm screaming at myself inside to shut up, but the words are flowing out like projectiles. These are the biggest triggers in my life, and I have no idea how to stop them."

Ed gestured toward my chart again and stated bluntly, "Your need for control is in direct conflict with your need to not be controlled. That's what this is basically measuring. And here's the kicker: if you took your name off of this report and put anyone's name on it with the same traits, they would most likely suffer from these same conflicting triggers as you."

This comment stopped me cold as I repeated what felt like a diagnosis. "My need for control…conflicts with my need to *not* be controlled." The statement echoed in my head, reverberating and penetrating through my armor.

Like Michelangelo with his chisel, I had once again chipped away more that was not me. This was beneath my stony exterior, and it always had been. I marveled at the profundity of this discovery.

Dana and Ed sat silently, knowing the impact of the depth charge they just set off deep within me. I could feel myself welling up as, suddenly, I recalled a flood of people who had dominated me in my youth. All the people I hadn't respected who had tried to tell me what to do flashed across my mind in rapid succession.

For the first time in my life, I understood what I was really up against. It was my first diagnostic look into identifying what had caused me so much pain and grief all of my life. No wonder I was volatile and suffered from chronic dissatisfaction. I was in pain but good at hiding it from others. I could be set off for almost any reason, and nothing of any significance ever felt satisfying. I was numb inside.

The closest thing to a sense of feeling I could relate to was adrenaline from high-risk adventures, like parachuting. That, or rage. I hated being told what to do and would shut people down too hard when I felt backed into a corner.

My survey results were amazing. Having so much of what roiled inside myself laid out before me so clearly—outside of myself—somehow validated and clarified the most significant problems holding me hostage.

It was yet another cosmic two-by-four, meant just for me, placed perfectly by Dana and Ed, upside my oblivious forehead at the exact moment I needed it. I felt sure that, spiritually, Glad had a hand in this too.

My past had been about surviving and continuing to march forward, no matter the pain or hardship. I was chronically dissatisfied with my life and suffered from depression, panic attacks, and never-ending anxiety. But the intensity and dichotomy the survey revealed explained some of what I already knew: no matter the pain, no matter the setback, I couldn't stop moving forward.

Not since my long talks with Glad had anyone understood me or even tried to. Glad's tranquility and patience created a safe place for me to unload my problems and frustrations. In this case, sitting with Ed and Dana, it was a computer-based survey. Just the same, I felt understood.

"How do I get a handle on these triggers?" I asked after I felt confident enough to speak again.

"Ah, now that is the right question," Dana replied, leaning back. "A quote from Confucius: 'He who conquers himself is the mightiest warrior.'"

I nodded. Up until now, all I'd known about myself was that I was volatile and unmanageable—I just didn't know why. At the very least, having it spelled out in front of me without a human trying to counsel or lecture me made the experience much more useful and valuable.

The simplicity of this utterly accurate observation of my need for control conflicting with my need to not be controlled spoke to me as a profound truth. I had always known I wrestled with this volatility, but having it so clearly explained to me blew my mind.

In my head, I once again thanked Glad for preparing me to be open to these kinds of important self-discoveries. I understood these tools and insights had been waiting for me to discover them on my journey and incorporate them into my life. It dawned on me that if I could understand my blocks and learn to overcome them, I could help others to do the same.

I declared to Dana and Ed, "I don't want to learn this; I want to master it! How do I go about doing this?"

Dana and Ed were all enthusiastic and explained the process. Within a few moments, I pulled out my credit card and signed up for an upcoming certification training. It would take place a few weeks later. I was already close to hitting my credit limit, but a quote from Benjamin Franklin I recalled helped me justify the investment: "Empty the coins of your purse into your mind, and your mind will refill your purse with coins."

And it was through this experience I discovered not just a vocation but a deep sense of meaning and purpose that had been missing in my life.

Glad had opened my eyes many years before and provisioned me for my life's journey: to search for and find my purpose. She had assured me I would know when I found it, and once again, she'd been right. Now, *finally*, it was true for me. I was both excited about becoming a behavioral assessment analyst and nervous about what lay ahead. I knew I was on to something special. Just as my printout had so clearly depicted, whenever I became passionate about doing or accomplishing something, I was driven to succeed at what I'd set my mind to achieving.

Special Note:
If you would like to learn more about yourself by taking the
communication survey mentioned in this chapter go to:
harvestingwisdom.com/survey

CHAPTER 20

Discovering Ease
and Growth

I knew I had huge, deep-seated problems and conflicts within me. My initial experience with Dana and Ed exploring my personality traits pegged my inner conflicts so accurately and succinctly that I knew it was an unmistakable message from the universe.

My purpose was being revealed to me.

The universe was saying, "Apply everything to yourself, first." I needed to get a handle on my volatility.

From my years of studying personal development and from all I had absorbed of Glad's wisdom, I understood a great deal about the power of my thoughts. Discovering the nature of what suddenly triggered and hijacked me was a new frontier. It was necessary territory I needed to explore to learn, grow, and secure my sense of well-being.

Now that I knew my need for control conflicted with my need to not be controlled, I began to notice when I was triggered more quickly. When I became triggered, I would find myself ricocheted into a place of choice instead of fear, rage, or anxiety. With a little practice, this opened up a whole new world of possibilities.

Within a few weeks, I attended the certification with Dana and Ed that would cement my convictions. Not only did I understand how to interpret my traits, I also launched into an odyssey of surveying hundreds of business contacts and friends, both individually and in groups.

With each interpretation, I became more competent. Like Dana and Ed, I began to see the deeper patterns inside each person's traits.

As I considered what the future held for me in this field of study, it was as though a superpower had been revealed to me. I knew this to be true because the power my triggers held over me was becoming much easier to overcome, and my ability to anticipate and get ahead of them dramatically lowered my chronic anxiety.

The significant ongoing energy I had been expending to manage my stress was diminishing and available to recycle into further personal transformation. Within a matter of weeks, my friends began to notice a calmer version of me and started asking what was happening.

Just as the interpretation had pinpointed my strengths and triggers, each person I assessed and shared their survey results with was surprised at the accuracy. They were impressed with the way their traits were depicted and how their triggers and blind spots could be clearly identified for discussion.

As my competencies grew, so too did my sense of meaning and purpose. It was just as Glad had predicted: I would someday discover what truly gave my life meaning and purpose, and when it was finally revealed to me, I would know this truth as if I had known it all of my life.

When I felt strong enough in my understanding of the interpretation process, I asked Glad to take the survey.

Of all the people in the world and throughout human *history*, Glad was the person I wanted to understand the most. What drove her? What triggered her, and what internal conflicts might she have had to overcome? Like me, how might she have gotten in her own way?

When I shared with her what I had been learning over the previous year and asked her to take the survey, her response was loving and supportive: "Of course, John."

Upon completion, I mailed her report to her and continually ruminated on it for two weeks until she finally called me to discuss her results.

While I waited, I repeatedly read through her report, reliving our conversations and the stories she shared. But with all my training and what I knew now, I could see her through an entirely different lens. Glad was far more critical in her thinking than she seemed to let on. Underneath her loving and gentle way of being was a deep-thinking, intellectual problem solver with a passion for understanding complex subjects.

Words and phrases jumped off the page at me: *ingenious problem solver, strongly technically oriented, by the book, traditional values, conscientious and self-disciplined, never superficial, needs structure, confidence in own knowledge and opinions, self-expression is direct, factual, and brusque.*

Glad was my polar opposite, yet our love for one another was a powerful, unbreakable bond. I think this is what I instinctively knew already and loved the most about her.

When I answered my phone, I could feel her beaming.

"Hello, John. This is very interesting," she said without hesitation. "You know me pretty well. Did you write this?"

"No, Glad. This is the report generated from the communication survey I sent you," I replied.

"This is impressive. Is this what you've been learning about?"

"Yes," I said proudly. "I completed a certification course about a year ago on how to administer and interpret these reports."

We spoke for almost two hours. It was one of the most revealing and in-depth conversations I have ever had with her. Glad shared with me that during the war, a close friend who was a psychologist had administered an assessment with similar findings.

I waited until the end of our conversation to share that I thought I'd found my purpose, or at least, what was providing meaning and purpose to me.

"Glad, something important has been revealed to me on my journey of self-discovery and transformation and through all of the hardships I have experienced. I have an uncanny ability to relate to the hardships of others, and people really feel heard and understood when I listen to them," I told her. "And this field of behavioral assessment analysis that I was introduced to, not by chance, is providing me with relevant insights to help others on their journey."

Glad was pleased with my maturing understanding of what gave me meaning and purpose. Being of service to others was giving me more than I could have ever dreamed of or acquired by selfish means.

The relentless pursuit of becoming who I was meant to be was now something I could go after more deliberately. The results were more apparent with every passing day.

CHAPTER 21

"Danny's on a Bus to Come Live with You"

It was a hot summer afternoon on the Sacramento River, where I had settled for some years in my mid-thirties. I was enjoying a cold beer and sake with Lou, my favorite chef at Sushi on the River.

My phone rang, and I saw it was Danny's mother. *This can't be good*, I thought. I hadn't heard from her in years.

The instant I answered, she spoke directly. "Danny is on a bus to come live with you. He's out of control, and there's nothing I can do anymore. One of his friends was shot and killed, and he's constantly in trouble. Martin bought him a Harley for his sixteenth birthday and took it away from him until he straightens out."

I quickly walked outside the noisy restaurant, pressing my phone hard to my ear to grasp what I was hearing. "Hold on. *What?* He's on a bus coming *here?*"

I listened in stunned silence as she repeated herself.

Danny was coming to live with me? And he'd be here by nightfall? Though I loved my son deeply, this information was coming to me out of nowhere. My first reaction was shock, followed by panic.

We had never spent more than a day trip together, his stepfather had spent years trying to poison Danny against me, and now he was coming to live with me full-time?

Collecting myself, I quickly realized this was reality. I could want it to be different, but that wouldn't help. The truth was, Danny was spinning out, and he needed me.

This was a call to action, and I needed to answer it.

My panic quickly transformed into a sense of resolve as I imagined Glad guiding my next steps to steady my emotions.

Danny would legally be an adult soon, but that was only society's age marker. What I didn't know was pretty much everything else about him. Nevertheless, I felt the familiar pull of my paternal instincts. I had always yearned to be in his life.

A new chapter was suddenly opening, whether I was ready or not.

I barely remember driving to the bus station to get Danny. My mind was a minefield of confusion and excitement.

The station was in a grimy part of downtown Sacramento, populated with seedy characters. They lurked around the building and the surrounding dark alleyways. I strategically parked to keep a good view of the empty spaces where incoming buses arrived and parked.

I waited for about an hour. My anticipation seemed to slow time itself to a torturous grind. Several buses pulled in as I squeezed and released my steering wheel in an attempt to stay calm. They were emblazoned with city names on the lighted banner above each windshield: Dallas, Albuquerque, Denver. With each arrival, the tension in my chest tightened and then calmed as I realized it wasn't his bus—the suspense protracted time.

Finally, the Phoenix bus rolled in. My anxiety broke over me like an ocean wave, fracturing me into a wide range of manic emotions. I felt everything from the depths of shame and regret to the highs of joy and exhilaration. The wave hit me again and sent me back down to panic. This time, I was ready for it, and I came back up with a powerful sense of resolve.

I walked up to the bus stop's curb just as the door opened. People were beginning to exit, and as I looked up, there was Danny at the top of the steps, staring straight at me with his familiar smile and blond hair. His transformation struck me as he stepped off the bus and walked toward me. He was almost six-one, and he was lean and muscular. My apprehension exploded into exhilaration as we collided into a mutual bear hug.

Danny picked me off my heels with a growl. "I've missed you, Dad."

"I've missed you too, son," I growled back, my eyes tearing.

I put my hand on his head. "What the hell happened to you?" I said in astonishment. "Look at you! You're so tall!"

We beamed in awe of each other.

While we waited for his bags, I sized him up some more. He had a blond ponytail down to his waist and walked with the confident stride of a street-savvy alpha—a stark contrast from the pudgy, nervous boy I'd known four years ago.

"You still like sushi?" I asked.

"Love it," he replied.

"Great, I know just the place."

We arrived back at Sushi on the River and grabbed some seats at the sushi bar.

"Lou, this is my son, Danny. Give us a couple of Block Island Rolls."

We ordered a massive spread of food, way more than we could eat, but I'd counted on having leftovers. We talked for hours. It was late into the evening before we got to what had forced Danny to leave Phoenix.

"So, what's up?" I asked. "What happened that got you on that bus?"

"All kinds of craziness," he said, shaking his head. "The Crips and the Bloods are the two rival gangs in the neighborhood, and I grew up with the younger brothers of the leaders of both. I wasn't part of either gang, but I got along with the leaders. They would pay me to collect drug money from people who were slacking. One night, the younger brother of one gang leader was shot right in front of me. He bled out while I held on to him."

Danny's face betrayed no emotion. Still, I noticed as he recalled the violence, he went from looking at me to staring through me.

Crips? Bloods? I'd heard of these violent criminal gangs, but they had formed after I'd left the neighborhood long ago.

Danny's gaze refocused on me. "My stepdad bought me a Harley for my sixteenth birthday, but when I got in a bunch of trouble, he locked it up and then sold it. And my mom kicked me out. So, here I am."

The Honeymoon Phase

I consider our first couple of weeks together a honeymoon phase; we couldn't have been closer.

Our most memorable experience was visiting Mike, a fireman friend I'd recently met. He was a muscular guy with a big handlebar mustache who looked like a boxer from the early 1900s. Mike was always smiling and had a good sense of humor, but he was the kind of guy you wouldn't want to fight. No doubt he was one of the fittest guys at his fire station. He had our respect immediately.

Mike wanted to show us the speed bag he had set up in his backyard. The large and sturdy wooden structure stood out from the rest of his garden like a shrine, surrounded, as it was, by large plants. Standing about seven feet tall, the base, mounted in the ground like a telephone pole, was made from a twelve-by-twelve wooden beam he had salvaged from a rail yard. Two four-by-four beams were bolted to the sides at the top to form a horizontal overhang, and there were two large, wooden discs about thirty inches in diameter secured to the beams. He'd mounted and hung a medium-sized speed bag in the center.

It looked primitive and incredible.

"Check this out," Mike said with a grin as he pounded out a succession of strikes in an impressive display of power and rhythm. *Ba Bamba! Ba Bamba! Ba Bamba!*

He wailed on the bag at a mesmerizing cadence, incorporating lots of change-up variations for a good two minutes. It was as good as any Mike Tyson exhibition I had ever seen.

What he did next blew our minds. First, he doubled his speed for about five seconds. *Bam! Bam! Bam! Bam! Bam! Bam!* Then, he tripled his speed into a hypnotic rhythm and finally stopped the bag with a forceful, single strike that left the bag pinned against the wood. *Ba bump!*

Danny and I stood speechless and slack-jawed.

Mike glanced at me. "Give it a try."

I stepped up to address the bag and gave it a wallop. My strike was solid, but my next attempt missed by a long shot. The more I tried to hit it twice in a row, the more ridiculous I looked. Compared to Mike, I looked like an infant.

Danny stood by with his hand over his mouth, laughing hysterically.

"Okay, dumbass, your turn," I said, annoyed and embarrassed.

"Step aside," Danny ordered as he took my place.

I couldn't help but grin as Danny experienced the same outcome. After the first strike, his fist only caught air, and he gave me a stern look. Just like me, the more he tried, the more he missed.

Mike chuckled as he grabbed the speed bag. "Your punches are too wild. You gotta keep the circle nice and tight as you hit the bag to set up the second strike."

He proceeded to tap the bag with one fist and the other close behind in a small circular motion. *Bam! Bam!* "You see? One after the other, move your fists in a tight circle. You can do it—just practice hitting the bag twice," he said.

Bam! Bam! Danny smiled. *Bam! Bam!*

"I got it!" he screamed.

After a few minutes of Danny hogging the bag, I gestured for him to step aside and blurted, "Alright, outta my way."

To my astonishment, I immediately caught a double hit, then another, and another. Excited, I went for three. I got it but missed the fourth.

Danny and I traded off for a few minutes, and then we locked eyes as I announced, "We're going to master this!"

"Yeah!" Danny replied with one last slam of the bag.

Mike had the patience of a great coach and beamed with pride.

"Let's build one in my backyard," I declared.

"Hell yeah!" Danny yelled.

I grabbed a pad of paper and started sketching construction plans. Mike helped us create a list of materials. That afternoon, we went to Home Depot and picked up everything but the twelve-by-twelve beam. The next day we salvaged one at the site of an old railroad yard not far from my house. We were in business.

It took us about a day to fully construct everything and mount the pole in concrete. The best part was building it together and feeling the excitement of our coming workouts.

When we finally mounted the bag, Danny and I both stood back in awe and took a ceremonious moment to take in what we had created. It was a sacred shrine of worship to our relationship. The yard area backed up to the river levee, offering a panoramic view of the water. It became our sanctuary.

Mike came over to inspect our creation and blessed our shrine with its first real test: a professional beating.

"Solid," Mike said firmly. "Well done. This will last a lifetime."

The first few days were frustrating, and progress was slow going. But within a few weeks of relentless practice, Danny and I progressed exponentially. We often outdid one another with more bag technique variations.

The workouts broke the ice of the looming conversations we both wanted to have as we slowly delved into our stories and histories.

We picked up where we left off years before and began to catch up. I soon discovered how his life had changed with his stepfather and how he had come to idolize him. I had only met the man once during our brief and uncomfortable encounter four years prior. I appreciated that he forced Danny into a boxing ring to get his bell rung enough for him to find his rage. Up until that point, Danny was too vulnerable and not very tough. And in that neighborhood, not being tough meant you would be preyed upon.

Danny shared how terrified he was to be forced into the ring. His stepdad had taken him to a boxing gym in a bad part of town, and he was in the minority as a white kid. The tough fighters were giddy to take turns peppering him with punches. Danny couldn't defend himself but was forced to stand and take the beatings, day after day. "Bloody noses and busted lips were the norm," he said, and his school teachers were always asking if he was okay. Eventually, Danny found his first win, but more importantly, his confidence. One fight at a time, he earned the other fighters' respect in the ring. This translated into more safety and success on the streets as he now had the skills to fend off the neighborhood bullies.

During one of our bag workouts, Danny asked, "Do you remember the advice you gave me the last time we saw each other? About going empty?"

"Sure," I replied, surprised he had remembered.

"It works—big time!" he said, flashing me a big smile. "A couple of weeks after you told me about it, I was in the cafeteria at school, and this kid and his friends circled me, trying to pick a fight. I took a deep breath in and went empty, just like you said, and everything slowed down. I was scared but calm—it was crazy. The guy walked right up close to me, and I just looked right through him with no emotion. Normally, I would be afraid and would've gotten beat up. But that time, I just went empty and showed no fear.

"After about a minute of him threatening me, with no response from me, I saw his eyes dart toward his friends. I could tell he was confused. When I continued to stare through him, he took a step back with more insults and then turned his shoulder to me and stepped away a few more inches. Right then, I knew he wasn't going to fight, and I just kept calm. Eventually, he picked up his tray of food and walked off, just throwing insults. I calmly took my food and went outside to get away from them. This guy had a reputation for being tough, and people couldn't figure out what just happened. I stayed with it and went empty a lot. After a while, people started leaving me alone."

I smiled, realizing how my suggestion years before had stuck. Going empty, combined with Danny's stepfather's style of tough love, had galvanized my son into a formidable young man. My respect for the man my son was becoming grew immensely.

Tough Decisions

Everything moved smoothly between us until one late evening a few months later when our two planets collided.

I woke to hear the thumping of the speed bag. Danny was pounding away out back. I looked at my watch. *Shit, it's ten o'clock. Our neighbors are probably pissed.*

I walked outside. The backyard was pitch black, but I could see Danny's silhouette in the moonlight. His back was to me, and he was hitting the bag. As I approached, I could make out he had his baseball hat on backward. I could also see the cherry red glow of a lit cigarette hanging out of his mouth. He was pounding away on the speed bag and looked like a kid version of Rocky.

If I hadn't been so annoyed, I would've made fun of him. Instead, I walked up beside him and snatched the speed bag to quiet it.

"Don't you ever put your hands on me!" Danny screamed with his fists up, startled.

"What are you talking about?" I demanded, still holding the bag. I hadn't touched him at all. "Danny, it's ten o'clock—the neighbors are going to complain."

"Come on!" Danny yelled. "You wanna go?"

An image of my enraged father beating me flashed in my mind, and a lightning bolt of rage shot through me, making my fists clench. In a flash, I considered taking Danny up on his immature challenge. Then Glad's voice soothed me, inspiring me to remember the promise Danny and I had made to one another years ago. This internal work created the pause I needed to de-escalate the moment.

That's not me; I'm not him. I am not a monster. I will never become my father, blasted through my mind.

I felt my fists open, and the tension in my arms relaxed. I took a deep breath and filled my lungs with the cool, nighttime air. I gazed through Danny, and my awareness expanded.

My angry son was now only a foot from my face. He had his fists up, and he was yelling and taunting. But I was older and wiser. I stood calmly, keeping my hands down to my sides, relaxed.

My promise to Danny—"We will never strike each other in anger. Ever!"—flashed in my mind like a neon sign. But this wasn't a teachable moment for Danny, and now was not the time to talk about it.

I let him continue his rant for another minute or so, then glanced over his shoulder toward the house. I sidestepped him to walk away from the situation. He continued yelling insults, but I kept walking, paying him no mind.

It took three days for me to muster the willingness and composure to speak with Danny again. When it was time, I chugged almost a full glass of gin with just a splash of tonic. I then poured myself a second in preparation for our talk.

Danny was outside smoking a cigarette, so I opened the door. "Hey, come sit in the living room, so we can talk."

He ground his cigarette into the patio with his boot, marched through the door, and took a seat as I gulped my drink.

"Danny, it's taken me three days to calm down and try to talk to you. There was no reason for you to go off on me the other night," I said in a calm but firm tone.

"Fuck you," Danny replied. "I've kicked bigger dudes' asses than you."

I blew a gasket and fast-pitched my gin and tonic, exploding it into the kitchen wall. The glass shattered in all directions, and Danny flinched backward, shocked. His eyes were wide open, and his mouth hung open momentarily.

"I told you I would never put a hand on you in anger, but this is the *second time* you have threatened me. I've done nothing to provoke you, and this is dangerous. You can't threaten me and then expect to live here. You need to leave right now! You've got ten minutes to pack your shit and get it in the truck, or I will do it for you."

"Screw you," Danny replied.

"Alright, have it your way," I replied. "I'm not going to fight you, but I can sure as hell pack your shit." I walked to the garage to grab some garbage bags.

When I came back, he was still sitting in the living room with his arms crossed, glaring at me in defiance.

"Are you going to do this, or do I need to do it for you?" I asked.

"Where are we going?" Danny snarled.

"You'll find out soon enough. Pack your shit, now!"

Danny finally broke eye contact with me, and as he did, I saw his eyes were tearing up. He slowly stood, took the garbage bags from my hand, and walked into his room in silence.

When we hit the ten-minute mark, I called out to hurry him along. I stood sentry in the doorway to the garage. He moved past me, glassy-eyed and struggling with his emotions. He was wearing his backpack and carrying his duffle bag, packed full with most of his things.

Within a few minutes, we were on the road.

"Where are we going?" he asked again in a concerned tone.

I drove in complete silence until we pulled up in front of the Greyhound bus station.

True to form, I went empty and gave him nothing until I was ready.

"Grab your shit and follow me," I growled, stepping out of the truck. I marched through the doors, and Danny caught up just as I arrived at the ticket window.

"I need a one-way ticket to Phoenix," I told the clerk.

When I grabbed the ticket and stepped away, Danny asked, "What about my car?"

"*Your* car?" I asked him. "The Volkswagen? That's not your car; that's my car. I bought it, remember?"

Danny struggled not to look sheepish. "How am I going to get around?" he muttered.

"I'm confused, Danny," I replied. "You threaten me and then want me to reward you by giving you a car." I stared at my son for a moment. For all his anger, he was a smart kid, and I wanted to give him the chance to process what I was saying. "What's wrong with this picture?"

"I'm sorry for what I did," Danny murmured.

I turned my head as if to better offer him my ear. "What was that?" I asked.

"I'm *sorry*," he said more directly.

"Great, write me a letter when you get back to Phoenix."

He slid down the wall and put his head in his hands. He was crying but didn't want me to see.

I gave him that space and waited for him to speak. Finally, when he looked up, he said, "I'm sorry. I won't do it again, I promise. Don't send me back."

My heart hurt, but I had made up my mind. "Son, you know I love you, right?

"Yes," he replied.

"I am terrified of what will happen if you threaten me again. The game you're playing with me is too dangerous for us." I paused for a moment. "The agreement we made when you were eight years old, do you remember that?"

Danny stared at me in silence.

"Well, son, I vowed I would never hit you, and you made the same agreement with me. Apparently, you forgot about this, but I didn't. Think about it: all I did was reach out and grab the speed bag. I startled you, I get that, but I wasn't attacking you. We could have left it at that. I'm not going to repeat with you what my father did to me—that's never going to happen. You're still my son, and I will always love you, but we have to find another way for me to be in your life. You can't threaten someone's safety when you don't get what you want. This is just too dangerous."

Danny said nothing. Still, I saw my words penetrating his armor, and as his expression softened, I decided to give in a little. "I'll give you the car, and you can drive it back to Phoenix." I grabbed his backpack and started walking back to the truck. Danny leapt to his feet as I called out, "Let's go."

We packed his old brown and tattered Volkswagen up with his bags and some things I wanted him to have. Then, I gave him a few hundred bucks for food and gas.

"I love you, son," I whispered in his ear as we hugged goodbye.

"I love you too, Dad," he said as he squeezed me.

We kept eye contact while he backed down the driveway, and I waved at him as he pulled away and looked ahead.

I hoped I had done the right thing.

CHAPTER 22

"Dad, I Want to Join the Army"

It had been a few months since Danny had driven away in his beat-up Volkswagen, when I received his unexpected call. "Dad, I want to join the Army."

Surprised, I responded, "That's great, son. What can I do to help?"

My support brought more enthusiasm to his voice. "I talked to the recruiter on the phone," he said. "He told me before I can join, I need to get my GED. How do I do that?"

Interesting, I thought. Getting my GED was my ticket out of the neighborhood almost twenty years prior, and now, Danny was in the same situation.

"Break out a phone book," I said, and we found a few companies he could call.

"So, where'd you get this idea of joining the Army?" I asked.

"I've got to get out of here, Dad. The gang situation around here is out of control, and things are getting worse. When I came back a few months ago, all my friends were doing the same thing as before I left, which is pretty much nothing. They're going nowhere, and I'm getting sucked into some bad situations. It's too dangerous—I need to leave."

I was incredibly proud of him for assessing his situation and wanting more for himself. "Why the Army?" I asked.

"My stepdad, Martin, was in the Army, and he thinks it will be good for me," Danny replied.

"Alright, then, get to it, and let me know what it costs. I'll pay for it," I said.

Within a week, Danny was enrolled and began studying to take his GED. Each time I heard from him over the next couple of months, he was cranky and frustrated. By the time he finally received his test date, he was a nervous wreck and thought he probably wouldn't pass.

A week later, Danny called, enraged.

"That recruiter *lied to me!*" he seethed. "Two months ago, he told me I needed to get my GED. So, I get it and go down to sign up, and he smiles and tells me the rules have changed, and now the Army requires a high school diploma to enlist!"

Immediately, I interrupted his meltdown. "Holy shit! Son, wait a minute. Are you telling me *you passed*? You got your GED?" I screamed into the phone.

Danny paused. "Yeah, I got it!"

"Danny, hold on just a second! If you passed your GED, you can definitely pass your high school diploma exam. I know that's not what you want to hear right now, but don't forget: this is your ticket out of that shitty neighborhood. How bad do you want this?" I asked.

Bam! Bam! Bam! Danny slammed the phone onto something and screamed back into the phone, "*I hate this!*" I could hear him hyperventilating in frustration. Then came a long quiet pause. "I get it," he said, hoarse. "This is my only way out of this *shitty* place, Dad. I need this."

"What can I do to help?" I asked. I worried more about Danny being stuck in his dangerous neighborhood than I did about him possibly going to war if he got into the military.

"The recruiter gave me the instructions, and I've got an appointment to get started next week," Danny replied in a defeated tone.

"Well, as I said, you were smart enough to get your GED—turn your anger into action, and let's get your high school diploma knocked out ASAP. You can do this, son. Don't be discouraged."

Another two months went by with minimal contact. Then, suddenly, I got a call.

"Dad, I got my diploma!" Danny screamed into the phone. "I'm going into the Army next month!"

My heart soared. "Congratulations, son! You did it!"

In the weeks leading up to his departure, I obsessed and worried about him getting in trouble. This was a turning point in his life and an opportunity to close this rocky, difficult chapter. He could become his own man, just as I had.

Finally, the day came for his departure, and I breathed a huge sigh of relief. It was really happening: my son was joining the military.

During Danny's time at boot camp, I ruminated day and night on what he must have been going through. I was all too familiar with how much it probably sucked. A couple of weeks went by, and I got a letter from him. I was surprised to read that he was bored to death, on dental hold, and still waiting to start boot camp.

"Can't go through the gas chamber with cavities," he wrote.

A few weeks later, another letter arrived—this one was hilarious.

Dear Dad,

Wow! This is a cool job. I'm sorry I haven't written sooner, but as you know, I'm in a high-speed environment, and I just haven't had any free time to write.

Well, I'm adapting to military life pretty well. I enjoy the physical training of being in the combat infantry. My Drill Sergeant is a mean asshole, but he likes me because I'm tough and a smart ass when it comes to PT (physical training). I always tell him, "More PT, Drill Sergeant, more PT. I like it. I love it. I want more of it. Make it hurt Drill Sergeant, make it hurt." Then, he smiles and smokes my ass until I can't move. I'm always sore and tired, but I feel great.

Danny had found his calling. He loved everything about becoming a soldier, and his new identity was being forged. My son was being galvanized into a professional warfighter.

After boot camp, Danny's first duty station was Fort Drum, New York, with the 10th Mountain Division. I'd always heard of the 10th as the group that had built Colorado's cold weather ski training huts.

During the first couple of years of Danny's enlistment, he got in a few scrapes. Still, he earned the respect of his unit. His third and fourth years were foundational as the Army invested in his leadership development. Boxing was his passion, and he'd developed quite the reputation for winning fights in his company's open matches. He talked a lot about going pro.

Before I knew it, four years had flown by, and here's this kid from Phoenix, spending a good part of the freezing winter out in the snow at Fort Drum.

"You should move out here, Dad," Danny said on a call.

"Are you crazy?" I responded. "I'm watching the news, and the snow dumping on you from the Great Lakes has the whole state paralyzed. No thanks." But his question pierced me in the heart. He had just asked me to move out to be closer to him. I shook my head in disbelief, feeling a deep sense of gratitude.

"Dad, should I reenlist?" Danny asked. "I'm getting pressured hard to sign up for another four-year hitch; I've got four years of combat infantry and leadership development. If I reenlist, I get a promotion and a bonus. If I don't stay in, I'll never be tested in combat." He then punctuated his point with, "Dad, I *need to know*."

"I understand how important this is to you, son. I needed to know when I was in the Marines, but my time never came. For the longest time after I got out, it felt like something was missing, but now that I'm older, looking back, I can live with it."

I chose my words carefully. "If you choose to get out, look at what the military has already given you. It got you out of the 'hood and saved your life. On the other hand, if you choose to re-up, we haven't had any major wars or conflicts in a while, but that can all change in the blink of an eye. When I was in, our country was between conflicts, so we deployed on training missions all the time, and I got to see a lot of the world. Maybe this will be the same for you." I kept my tone encouraging, though no part of me relished the possibility of losing my son to war. He had already fought so hard to become the man he was that day.

9/11

Within a few weeks, Danny called back to tell me he'd reenlisted. It was August of 2001.

When the twin towers fell on September 11, my heart sank.

Danny was going to war.

"We're going to get some payback and deliver some justice," Danny shouted into the phone. We were both enraged. If I could have, I would have reenlisted on the spot to go with him.

Less than a month later, Danny called to let me know he would not be in touch for a while, and we left it at that. What he was really saying was his unit was deploying. With all the talk on the news, it seemed obvious he was heading to Afghanistan. Whoever was behind the attacks of 9/11 unleashed a fury of retribution.

The genie is out of the bottle, and he is pissed, I thought.

As proud as I was of Danny, the stress of his deployment was unrelenting. Every morning, I would wake up on the couch with the news channel still blaring. I scoured the internet and every news station I could find, knowing that Danny was out there somewhere.

I became addicted to binge-watching news channels, killing at least a half bottle of scotch every night, and gorging out on pizza. Within five months of his deployment, I had gained twenty pounds and was suffering from insomnia. I would come in and out of consciousness with the news blaring from dusk to dawn. I closed my eyes periodically but never really fell asleep. I was becoming a fat and paranoid wreck.

I finally heard from the little shit around his eighth month, just as they were staging their equipment for his unit to rotate home.

Not long after his return, I jumped on a plane to Syracuse to visit him at Fort Drum.

Seeing Danny for the first time in uniform was impressive. He had become the professional warfighter he had envisioned, and he carried himself with a confident swagger and a cocky grin as if to say, *Yeah, you think you're tough?*

We went for a three-mile run, keeping it to an airborne shuffle except for a few sprints so Danny could show me how far he could leave me in the dust. Afterward, we went to the boxing gym on base and wailed on speed bags and heavy bags until our arms gave out.

As we sat to catch our breath, he told me about his deployment. The 10th had immediately deployed after 9/11 to Uzbekistan to secure the US airbases in preparation for the coming war in Afghanistan. He was pissed that they didn't deploy directly into combat. For the most part, his unit had stood guard over the airbase, watching the massive deployment of troops and equipment pass through on their way to forward operating bases.

"Not much to write home about," Danny lamented. "But all we could think about was when it would be our turn to inflict some punishment on the enemy."

I remember thinking it was funny that I didn't even know there was an "h" in Afghanistan before 9/11.

As we sat in the car outside, waiting for the heater to warm up, Danny looked at me. "Dad," he said.

"What's up?" I asked.

"When you first came and found me, I'm really thankful we agreed never to hit each other. I get it now."

My heart melted as I reached across and cupped the back of his head. I leaned over to press our foreheads together. "You have no idea how much it means to hear you say this, son."

We sat in silence, taking in the moment. With emotion, I told him, "Glad would be proud of us, son. From the time she first made me promise I would never hit my children or have them live in fear of me, I've waited for this moment. The moment you would acknowledge this agreement back to me. Together, right now, this means you and I have broken the cycle of violence with the men in our family." I was so proud of Danny.

Looking to the sky, I said, "If I died today, I know I would have made a difference in your life, Danny. And now, you will pass this agreement on to your children. Thank you, Glad."

CHAPTER 23

My Conflicting Diagnosis

As I approached the age of forty, my years of evading my inner conflicts had created such immense stress and anxiety that it culminated in a perfect storm of post-traumatic stress, depression, frustration, and paralysis. My critical mind seemed to shut me out—to protect me, I think.

One early morning, I woke up in the throes of a panic attack. My chest was tight, and my pillow was damp from perspiration. I had done a lot of work and development on my own, but I was reaching a boiling point. There was nothing else to try but to seek professional, psychological help. I decided to find a counselor to diagnose what I was facing. I had always known deep down that something wasn't right with me; I wasn't sleeping and was drinking more and more to calm my stress late at night. I was a desperate wreck.

A Veteran friend suggested I see the psych doc he went to for his meds, Dr. Milton, and I jumped at the chance.

My first appointment began by completing a lengthy questionnaire and personal history. I could feel Dr. Milton studying me from behind his desk while he periodically scribbled and shuffled through papers. He was a big man with a huge, gray beard and long hair. Honestly, he bore a striking resemblance to Jerry Garcia from The Grateful Dead.

I handed him my paperwork, and he leaned back in his chair with a smile. "Make yourself comfortable; this will take a bit of time to review."

For the next half hour, he systematically read through each page of the assessment while asking me questions: "Say more about your father. What conflict was he in while serving in the military? The neighborhood violence you mention, how often were you in altercations?"

As I responded, he glanced at me above the top of his glasses. He nodded now and then and seemed to empathize with my horrible explanations and responses. He also took a lot of notes.

Dr. Milton ("Jerry," as I thought of him) finally put his pen down.

"John, there's a lot going on here that we need to manage carefully. You're going to have to face the fact that you will be on medication for the rest of your life," he said unemotionally and with a soft conviction.

My mind stopped as his words reverberated. *On medication for the rest of my life* echoed and echoed until I saw that he was watching me and waiting for me to respond.

"What is it? What did you find?" I finally asked.

He indicated I had a myriad of psychological disorders and began to name them one by one: post-traumatic stress disorder, panic anxiety disorder, bipolar disorder, hypomania, attention deficit hyperactivity disorder, obsessive-compulsive disorder, mild Tourette's, and clinical depression.

His matter-of-fact style of delivery was disturbing. It was as if he was talking about me to a colleague. I just listened in silence, making every attempt to absorb and make meaning of his diagnosis.

"I knew it. I knew there was something wrong with me," I said out loud. The speaking of this out in the open released a flood of emotions I could barely control: relief, guilt, shame. Dr. Milton just leaned back in his chair and allowed me to process the moment.

A deep sense of relief flooded my eyes with tears of validation and vindication. I put my head in my hands, and my tears wet my palms.

"What do I do with this?" I asked, face still buried.

"First thing is, we need to begin to work with some medication to help you get to a more balanced place," he said. He spoke with confidence, which helped to ease the moment.

Relief began to cascade through my body. "Finally, someone understands me," I muttered. This was something no computer-generated personality test could truly reveal. The next step of my journey was now clear.

"It will probably take a few months to get your medications right," cautioned Dr. Milton. "And you will need to see someone while we go through this. I can only diagnose and prescribe your medications."

I found this odd. He was smart enough to diagnose and prescribe my medications but didn't have a clue how to help me through this? I was disappointed, but my emotions quickly moved back to relief and anticipation.

"I'm ready," I stated with a sense of grit. "I can't go on as I have been. When can I pick up my medications?"

The doctor tore a paper off a pad and said, "Here's your first prescription. I want you to follow the instructions very carefully and ease your way to a full dose over the next two weeks. One of the symptoms of taking these meds over time is a feeling of normalcy. Hopefully, you'll begin to feel like your moods and emotions are stable, and your anxiety will be much more manageable. This is our goal, but your mind will eventually begin to question your need for the meds if you feel normal. Don't fall for it. Keep taking your meds. Understood?"

"Yes, understood," I confirmed.

Sure enough, within a month, I began to feel less anxiety. However, I also experienced some drawbacks, like *feeling* medicated, and my sex drive was almost non-existent. I could tell I was less moody, and my racing thoughts had slowed, but I was in an altered state of awareness.

I began to see Dr. Milton once a month to discuss my symptoms, and he would scribble out a new prescription with different dosages.

The emotional roller coaster of managing my symptoms went on day after day and month after month. Every so often, when things seemed to level out, I would start feeling what I would call "normal." After about a month of normal, I'd start to ask myself, *I feel good, so why do I need medication?* Within a week or so of questioning myself, I'd stopped taking the meds without calling Dr. Milton.

And, like clockwork, a week or two after that, I'd be a trainwreck, feeling like the world was collapsing on me once again.

Whenever I got around to contacting Dr. Milton after these episodes, he would say, "We need to go over this again. Feeling a sense of normal *is a symptom of taking these medications*. I know this sounds puzzling, but when the medications are doing their job and working, you are supposed to start feeling normal. Is this making sense now?"

"Yes," I'd reply. "I remember you sharing this with me that first day. I'll get back on my meds today."

I never felt a sense of normal for very long.

Eventually, I became fed up with being on this crazy medicated roller coaster and decided to get a second opinion. Maybe the medications had cured some part of my original diagnosis, but I wondered if another doctor might agree I could safely stop taking at least some of them.

I received a new referral from a counselor who worked with Veterans, and not long after, I was able to meet Dr. Richardson. This appointment would prove to be very different from my experience with Dr. Milton.

I arrived early to my appointment feeling anxious but hopeful. After completing another long questionnaire, I was escorted into the doctor's office.

"Please, call me Mark. Have a seat," he said, taking his chair behind his conference table.

"Okay, Mark. I'm having a rough time with the meds I've been prescribed. Nothing feels right. I feel completely medicated all the time, and I don't know what to do."

Mark began by saying, "Considering what you've described in your intake questionnaire, your diagnosis from the other doctor, and the medications you've been taking, I can see why you would feel medicated."

He stood and gestured for me to come and sit at a table. On it, rested a large, open binder alongside three-dimensional puzzle pieces of all shapes and sizes. There were also some printouts on the table, and they were full of questions.

The doctor seated himself across from me. He gently asked questions and took notes while asking me to perform a series of exercises.

We talked for a few moments between each exercise, then we'd move on to the next. After about an hour, Mark asked me to relax, so he could review our time together. He then shared something I will never forget.

"After reviewing everything we've done today, I am just not seeing most of what you were initially diagnosed with," he said. "What I'm seeing is a completely different picture. You have had a lifetime of severe, traumatic events resulting in complex PTSD. That stands for *post-traumatic stress disorder*. The PTSD you suffer from no doubt has contributed to your anxiety, inability to focus, and your exaggerated startle response."

Mark paused to allow me to digest his words as I leaned back and took a deep breath.

"The first thing I want you to do is to hear me when I say this: your trauma actually happened to you, but your trauma *does not* define who you are." It was like what Glad had told me decades ago: *You are not your fear.* At my shocked expression, he continued, "Let me phrase it differently. You weren't born with the traumatic experiences you've had, were you?"

"No," I replied, confused. I could think of many of them as if they were still happening in real-time, so of course, they'd transpired after I'd been born.

"That's correct," he continued. "Your traumatic experiences are part of your life up until this very moment, and they actually happened. We can't deny this, but your life's journey now is to rediscover who you are underneath and beyond the level of your unresolved experiences. The second thing I want you to do is to let your previous diagnoses go because you don't need to label and burden yourself with them any longer. I work with many Veterans and everyday people who suffer from PTSD. I believe you will need some medications to help you manage your anxiety but nothing to the extent of what you've been taking.

"If you agree to come here and invest some time and effort to work through your unresolved life experiences, eventually, it will feel as though you can let go of some of the heavy burdens you've been carrying. If you do this, I believe the quality of your life will improve. You don't have to believe everything I'm saying, John, but I'm simply asking that you believe this is possible. The majority of the Veterans I've seen who work through their unresolved trauma have eventually come to a couple of realizations: *No matter what you have been through, no matter how traumatic, or even heartbreaking, you deserve to live a fulfilling life.*"

Again, he paused to observe how I was taking this in.

"And when you begin to believe this, through your inner-work, you will eventually come to the second realization: *You deserve to be happy.*"

I stared at him. "Again, John," he repeated. "I am not asking you to believe me, but just to believe these realizations are possible. This is all I would like you to take away from our time today, and I'd like to see you next week. Meanwhile, I'm going to prescribe something to help manage your anxiety as you process through this next stage of your recovery. But this is the key work. You are recovering from some very significant, traumatic events over your lifetime. They will take some time to unpack. I want you to understand this is a *predictable process* we can manage together, and I believe I can help you through this if you will commit to doing the work."

I imagined how Glad must have struggled with the war trauma she endured and the atrocities she witnessed. I wondered if she had ever sought therapy or counseling.

If we don't know any better, or we are unwilling to learn or go through the pain of change, the mental health stigmas and labels we adopt become our story.

In retrospect, I think Dr. Milton, although well intentioned, was projecting some of his own personal baggage onto my original assessment and diagnosis.

The Marine Corps has a saying: *Never take advice from someone who is more fucked up than you are.*

Needless to say, at the time, I wasn't known for giving a lot of advice.

Taking My Power Back from My Father

The more I understood about the roots of my trauma and how I had been carrying the burdens as if I had somehow caused them, it made me angry that my life was being wasted on regret, shame, and suffering as a result of my father's abuse. This all became clear to me through a pivotal experience with a friend who was talking about his father.

After more than a few cocktails, a long-time friend, Roger, would rant incessantly about how angry he was with his father, who had recently passed. He would pound a hammer fist on the table and yell, "That son of a bitch!"

Trying to reason with Roger when he'd been drinking proved useless.

A few days after one of his benders, I bumped into Roger at a Starbucks. As expected, he had returned to his happy-go-lucky self again. As we sat down, I asked how he was doing with the passing of his father.

"I'm fine," he replied, pausing. Then, "I don't feel anything."

I cautiously leaned in and shared the repeated upsets and anger toward his father that came out when he drank. I could see him becoming visibly upset and shaken.

His face went blank as he gazed through me. "Yeah, I'm still pretty messed up about my dad; I hated him," Roger replied. He put his face in his hands and began a two-hour confession of his father's abuse. I sat in silence, empathizing while unavoidably being triggered myself.

"Did you ever confront or talk to him about all this?" I finally asked.

"You didn't know my father," he replied. "I wish I could have, but he would never have allowed it!"

Roger sobbed for a moment and then looked up with a scowl. "If that bastard were still alive, I'd pin him against the wall and sure as hell let him have it!"

Listening to Roger, I thought, *This poor guy will be carrying this burden for the rest of his life.* His father, in his passing, had saddled all of his abusive acts and their history of trauma squarely onto Roger's back, and now he would have to carry this burden forward forever. *He'll never resolve this*, I thought.

My mind wouldn't stop ruminating about Roger, and the thought of my aging father was bringing up all my trauma and everything I hated about him.

Triggered, I determined my father's time had come. *I'm not going to let him saddle me with his abuse when he dies!* Our single conversation in the car years and years ago was not enough. Plus, I'd listened to *him* back then—he hadn't listened to *me*.

It was early evening when I worked up the courage to call him, and he picked up on the third ring.

"Hello? Who's calling?" he asked.

"I need to talk to you. It's important," I stated firmly.

"What is it, son?" my father asked in a concerned tone.

I paused and thought, *This is "The Talk."* Although I knew I was ready to confront my abuser, my throat still tightened, constricting my voice. A light bulb suddenly went off as I rubbed my throat and clenched my jaw. *This is where I hold my fear of him*, I thought. *I can't carry this any longer.*

A lifetime of being forced into submission and forbidden to speak my truth began to boil to an explosion point. I had to get this off my chest.

I forced out the first few words. "You're not getting any younger," I started. I paused, and then: "I need to have a long overdue conversation with you, one that many of my friends wished they would have had the opportunity to have with their fathers before they passed." Without allowing him to respond, I quickly demanded, "I need you to keep quiet and don't interrupt me until I'm through. Can you do that?" This was a voice and tone that he had never heard from me.

"Yeah?" my father replied in a concerned tone.

"You abused, tormented, and fucked up our entire family. I didn't stand a chance at a healthy or even *somewhat* normal childhood. Being born your son was like getting a life sentence. You should have gone to prison for what you did to us! But instead, we all paid the price for your demons."

"Wait a minute," he barked in his typical abusive tone.

"Stay quiet!" I demanded. "I'm not finished. I spent every day of my early childhood hiding in fear under my bed, traumatized, and dreading the moment you would walk through the door. Waiting for you to come home to torment us for no fucking reason was just as damaging to us as the assaults themselves. You should have been our protector, keeping us safe, but instead, you violently abused us. You caused so much pain and suffering. You were a monster!"

I paused to clear my throat and continued to tell him, "I'm no longer carrying this toxic shit for you. Your demons are yours to bear, and your pain is now your problem, not mine. I am not asking your permission. As of now, I am taking my power and my life back from you. I don't care if you own or take responsibility for anything. You know everything I'm saying is accurate, and you get to carry this burden from here. You're damn lucky I didn't slay you a long time ago, and you know I could have. Your abusive childhood did not justify your abuse of us. You know what you did to all of us was cruel and criminal; you should have been locked up for child abuse and domestic violence. Do you have any idea how fucked up everyone is because of you?" I screamed into the phone.

There was a long silence, but I was unwilling to speak before he did.

"I'm sorry, John," he replied in an almost submissive voice. Then, he went silent.

"You're *sorry*," I growled. "Sorry is not good enough. You destroyed my chance of having a normal life. Unless you can start to own what you have done, we will never speak again."

My father sounded like he had a lump in his throat when he spoke next and said, "I do not know what else to say but that I am sorry. I am sorry that I hurt you, John, and I am sorry that I abused our family."

"There's more," I added. "I have lived in fear of confronting you my whole life. The only good thing that came from your abuse was the promise I made to Glad that someday when I had my children, I would never hit or abuse them and have them live in fear of me as I did of you.

"I passed this promise on to Danny; we have kept it and will never break it.

"I am no longer seeking your approval to live my life, and I'm not keeping silent. You're not going to get a pass from me; this is your burden to carry, not mine. It has taken a lot of soul-searching to realize that your abuse was not my fault, and I did not deserve any of it.

"If you want to say something, now is the time. Otherwise, we can leave this right here, and I'm done with you."

"I'm sorry," he repeated.

"Sorry for what?" I pressed, annoyed.

"I'm sorry for how I treated you and the whole family," he replied sheepishly. "You are right, John. I was out of control and abusive."

I wanted him to suffer, and I wanted him to fear me. But I was getting nothing back from him but regret and honesty—not at all what I had expected from him. I thought for sure he would have just hung up and written me off, and I was taken aback by his admission of guilt.

In that instant, I felt that an energetic exchange between us had taken place. I was no longer that scared boy, and he was no longer the monster. The power he once held over me evaporated, and all that remained was my father, nervously trying to find the words to explain himself. Which, of course, he couldn't do.

There was nothing he could say or do to put the genie back in the bottle. The fear and pain that I held onto for so long were suddenly released and given back to him.

My life was mine to live from that moment forward.

CHAPTER 24

Glad's Passing

When I was troubled in my younger years, Glad often reminded me, "Remember, John, you will be an adult for far longer than you will be a child." Looking back, I now see this was her way of focusing my attention on a deep truth: my life situation wasn't permanent.

Her guidance kept pace with my emotional development as I matured into adulthood. Still, she was mindful about delving too deep into touchy subjects, mostly about my father.

One day, Glad called to ask me to come to Ottawa.

Of course, she was quite elderly by this time in my life, and I felt an immediate surge of concern. "Is everything alright, Glad?" I asked.

"Everything is fine," she replied evenly. "I have something I need you to do for me, and it requires you to come for a visit."

I didn't need any convincing. The next day, I had my flight booked, and within a week, I arrived at her home. I couldn't imagine what this was about. During my flight, I obsessed over what Glad might need.

I arrived to see her angelic face beaming with joy. She had aged a bit but was still able to walk and gesture with her hands as she spoke. It was like we had never been apart. After catching up for a bit, I got to the point. "Glad, I'm concerned. What is it that you need to talk with me about?"

"I need you to hang some pictures for me," she responded.

"Sure, Glad, but…" I looked around as if I could find the words on the walls around me. "I'm a bit confused. You wanted me to come from California to Ottawa to hang pictures?"

"I could have had them hung months ago," she responded simply. "But I wanted you to do it, so when I look at them, I will always remember you hanging them."

My heart melted, and I caught my emotions in my throat. "That's sweet, Glad. Thank you. Now I understand."

"There is something I wanted to ask you about," she added, signaling a change in topic. "Have you noticed anything different about your father lately?" Her tone sounded more curious than concerned.

I cocked my head at her. "Is there something wrong?" I asked.

"No, nothing wrong," Glad replied. "But I've noticed something interesting happening with him. Over the last few years, your father has become a full-time caregiver to your mother and grandmother since she moved into their home. Your father has been controlling and abusive to others his entire adult life. But since your mother's Parkinson's has worsened and your grandmother has moved in with them, every day, he gets up, makes and serves them breakfast, and goes to work. He comes home for lunch to feed and care for the two of them. Each evening, he feeds them dinner, monitors their medicines, and sleeps on the couch, waiting for one of them to ring their bell for help."

I listened to her assessment but remained silent, feeling irritable and torn. *What is she asking of me?* I thought.

"I believe for all the years of suffering your father has caused your family, this is his karma, John. And because of your grandmother's constant presence, she tells me he is no longer abusive to your mother. Caregiving has exhausted him. As a result, we are experiencing a gentler, more caring side of your father beginning to emerge. Have you noticed this, John?"

"I'm still pretty angry with him," I admitted. I took a breath and tried to refocus my point of view. "I *have* noticed him being more patient with them and less irritable."

For the most part, after confronting my father a few months prior and clearing the air, I had put him out of my mind; he was aging, vulnerable, and no longer a threat to me.

Glad's Passing

A few years after my visit to see Glad in Ottawa, her health declined considerably, and she was moved to a care home in Regina.

Glad's caregiver placed a call to me on her behalf. When Glad came on the line, her voice was faint and frail.

"I'm afraid I don't have much time, John. Please come see me."

"Yes, Glad. I'll be there as soon as I can." I responded as cheerfully as I could muster. Inside, my heart was breaking.

This was the call I feared the most and always knew would someday come. My beautiful Glad's time of passing was near.

Within a week, I arrived in Regina. Growing up, I had only been to the prairies of Saskatchewan in the summer when everything was alive and blooming. Now, it was gray, and the cold was bone-chilling. I kept a tight grip on the wheel as I drove to the home where Glad resided. A strong crosswind whipped the snow into small flurries all around me, and the roads were icy. I had very little experience driving in such hazardous conditions, but nothing was going to stop me from getting to Glad.

Anxious to reach her, I crept along, keeping a good distance from the faint glow of the brake lights ahead of me.

As I came to a stop in front of the residence, I sat quietly for a few moments trying to collect myself. Would this be my last time seeing her? I wanted to remember her as the Glad of my boyhood, laughing, telling stories, and filling our miserable home with love.

As ready as I could ever be, I cracked the car door open ever so slightly, and a rush of freezing air blew in, startling my senses. Gritting my teeth, I bolted outside and jogged up the snowy drive-way to the porch entrance to ring the doorbell. My thin, California jacket was ridiculously inadequate for the Canadian winter. A caregiver greeted me at the door as I stomped the snow off my shoes.

"Are you here to see Gladys?" she asked.

"Yes, thank you," I replied. My cheeks were red and burning from the cold.

She gestured for me to follow her up a staircase to a small room with a single bed. There, Glad was waiting with a warm smile that lit her eyes like candle flames as she outstretched her hands.

She is so small and frail, I thought, as we embraced. I kissed her cheek with love and reverence. Her eyes were clear and bright as ever, but she was unable to stand or walk.

Glad tried to sit up and winced in pain. "Shingles," she said with her teeth clenched. "I would not wish this upon another human being."

I helped her forward and gingerly placed a pillow behind her. As she laid back, her smile returned, and she lovingly gazed into my eyes, savoring the joy of the moment.

"Thank you so much for coming. I've missed you," she said. A lovely rush of color blushed her cheeks as I smiled back at her.

"I've missed you too, Glad," I replied as I gently stroked the top of her hand. "I'm sorry I've been unable to come to see you. I'm sorry that we only talk by phone. And I'm sorry I've been so terrible at writing letters back to you." I just couldn't imagine my world without Glad, and here I was spending our precious time trying to apologize for my inadequacies.

"John," she replied with firm and sincere love I felt all the way into my bones. "You don't need to apologize. You are fine just the way you are."

I tried to swallow my emotions in order to talk with her. My heart hurt, and I loved her so fiercely. "Glad, I've always wanted to confess to you why I never write letters to anyone. My handwriting has always been too illegible, and it's embarrassing. I can't seem to steady a pen for very long before my nervousness takes over. It started in grade school, and I thought there was something wrong with me, so I've hidden this all my life."

"You were a precocious young boy," she insisted. "I could see you struggled with reading and writing, but you were very advanced artistically. You were in your own little world, and I loved to watch you draw."

"Isn't that interesting," I replied. "You're right. I can't seem to steady my hand to write, but the instant I begin to draw, my hand and mind both immediately relax and steady."

"We are artists, John," she responded with conviction. "Tell me— when you were in high school, I told your mother to be sure to register you for typing classes. She assured me she did. How was that for you?"

I laughed. "At the time, I hated it! When my friends found out, I was made fun of, and I couldn't understand why I was forced to take them." I shook my head and smiled at her. "So, that was your doing? Now I get it."

She smiled at me, and I continued. "After I injured my arm from that broken window and lost the feeling in my hand and three of my fingers, I forgot all about how proficient I had become at typing. I averaged about seventy or eighty words a minute back then. I thought I'd never type again. Then, in the Marines, when I was in Okinawa, a special project came up, and a group of us were asked who knew how to type. Not thinking, I raised my hand, and before I knew it, I was reassigned from my artillery unit—where I was housed with about sixty Marines in a barracks—to sitting in front of a teletype machine, being trained to send coded messages. I had my own private room in some much nicer barracks and thought I had it made.

"I didn't tell anyone about my injury and wasn't sure if I could still type. At first, I was taking too long and making too many mistakes. I was told if I didn't improve quickly, I'd be sent back to my unit. My fingers knew where the keys were, but with very little feeling in them, I couldn't tell if I was only hitting one key or two. But I kept with it! Within a week, I learned how to peck my fingers straight down on the keys, and my accuracy improved. Not long after that, I was keeping up with most of the operators. I eventually became faster than most."

Glad nodded with approval. "What is it like to type your thoughts compared to writing your thoughts by hand?" she asked.

I considered her question carefully. "You know, I never gave it much thought, but there's almost no effort involved when I type. My mind relaxes, and my fingers know what to do on their own. When I write, I immediately get self-conscious—even when I sign my name. It rarely looks the same to me. What's really frustrating is that I'll go from cursive to print several times in the same sentence, often in the same word! I can't stand to write—it makes me look stupid, and I hate it."

"But you see that you are not stupid," she insisted gently.

"No, I'm not stupid," I agreed. "But it feels like something's wrong with me."

"You are an artist, John. If it is easy to type and there is minimal effort, this is an artistic gift you possess, just as I do. You must continue to develop and cultivate this gift, John. Promise me you will do this for me. It is my wish for you." She sent me an encouraging smile.

"I promise," I replied. "I promise I will, Glad. Thank you for helping me see this."

"Now, I want to talk to you about Danny," she said directly. My eyebrows shot up. "When we last spoke, you told me he was in Afghanistan. Is he still there?"

"Yes," I replied. "His unit will be there until mid-winter, I think, but I've heard on the news they may be extended."

Glad frowned as she gazed away from me, deep in thought. "The United States will be in this war for a long time, I'm afraid. I think of Danny constantly. As a father, you must begin preparing for him to return home. He will still be Danny, but his experiences have no doubt already changed him, and I'm afraid not for the better."

Glad's tone was cautious, and I took her warning very seriously, knowing she was right. "John, the Russians had an extremely difficult time in the mountains of Afghanistan, and I'm afraid the US, Canadian, and NATO forces won't fare much better. As a war correspondent, I can tell you, when mountain warfare is conducted, it is the worst kind of fighting. The enemy has the advantage because the terrain is familiar to them; it is their homeland. Danny may find himself in the worst of it. I'm telling you this to prepare you. I'm sorry; there's no time for me to sugarcoat this, John. Your father never recovered from his war trauma—you must not let this happen to Danny."

"I understand, Glad, but what do I do?" I asked, holding her hand.

Her frail fingers slipped between mine. "Trauma, in all its forms, is an assault on the senses that one never forgets. To this day, I cannot unsee what I saw or un-smell the horrendous odors of war and death. It has always been a mystery to me as to why one person responds very differently than the next in the exact same moment of a shared traumatic experience. Danny will come home, and he will never forget his experiences. All we can do is hope that, over time, his trauma from war—and his grief—will fade to allow him to live new experiences to help him heal. Sometimes, having children can be how people recover because they can invest themselves into little souls who are fresh and new in the world. But sometimes, Veterans, like your father, can be violent toward their children, forcing them to live in fear if they cannot resolve their trauma."

I wondered how shutdown Danny would be when he came home and how we would navigate his recovery. My fears were overshadowing my hope.

"John, I knew about your violent father long before I began to come to stay with your family in the winters of your boyhood. I could have stayed with your grandmother on my trips south, but I wanted to put myself between your father and your family. While I could only shield you during my visits, I have been holding an intention of being the dawn of hope in your darkest moments, John."

"Thank you, Glad. I see this now." We locked eyes and stayed that way, entranced. I carefully squeezed her hand. "You *have* been my voice of wisdom, Glad, in every difficult moment I have faced in my life."

Glad's fingers were warm against mine. She nodded and continued. "It was difficult to leave you after my visits, John. You were so afraid. I could only share my thoughts with you to provision you emotionally for your journey ahead with the hope that you would survive and someday create a healthy life for yourself."

I wanted to tell her how she had done exactly that. Glad was my guiding light, a star in the darkness that always enveloped me. The look in her eyes told me she knew.

"When everything is stripped away, and you are seemingly out of choices or options, knowing for certain the sun will surely rise from the darkness may be the only thing you know for sure, John. It is now your time to be the dawn in the darkness for Danny. He will need you to hold this space for him. This is your purpose. This is why you were born. Do you see this, John?" she asked with a smile.

"I do," I responded. Her free hand found mine, and she squeezed them both. "I want to be a better father to Danny than my father was to me. I want this more than anything. I'm just not sure I know how."

"Do you remember our conversation a long time ago that God is love?"

"Yes, absolutely," I replied. "I remember it like it was yesterday. At the time, it was very confusing. I asked you, 'If God is love, why is this happening to me?'"

Glad smiled and, for a moment, seeming much like her younger self, beamed with love. "Good, I remember that too. So, tell me, John, what are we to learn from our suffering?"

"I haven't quite figured that out yet," I admitted.

"I'm going to share with you what I believe to be true about myself and the experiences I have endured in my lifetime," she said. "I want you to understand this to ease your suffering, and I want you to pass these learnings on to Danny. Through my experiences and suffering, I have been given the gift of empathy. Because of my experiences, I can sense and relate to the pain of others. The second gift my experiences and suffering have given me is to find meaning and purpose in my life *from* my suffering. For me, writing my book and sharing the story of the suffering of millions of people provided the meaning and purpose I needed to process what I had endured. I was able to convey my firsthand accounts authentically in significant part because of my suffering.

"To me, God is love because I know *I am not my suffering*. I have joy and hope knowing I have made a difference in your life and in the lives of others. And now, perhaps the wisdom I have shared with you will be passed to Danny and then to his children." She pointed at a small, black velvet jewelry box on her end table. "I want you to have this, John."

I retrieved the case and opened it carefully, revealing a gold ring with a crest engraved on its face.

"When you were a boy," she said, "I had this ring made to give to you someday, and now it is time. This is the family crest of our heritage that spans from England, to Scotland, to Spain and dates back to the eleventh century. I want you to find a way to get it to Danny in Afghanistan and tell him to bring it home safely to you. When you pass, it will belong to him."

The gravity of the moment was immense. I was being prepared for my own passing, and this ring was the mark of our family legacy. I held it in my hand. It was heavy and made of solid gold. The front surface was flat and in the shape of a shield. Etched into the surface was the image of an X in a gothic-looking design. I slid it onto my finger and held my hand out to admire it.

"This is amazing, Glad. Thank you."

"You must be the dawn in his darkness, as I have been for you, John," she repeated.

The ring gleamed in the warm glow of Glad's room. For all its weight, it couldn't compare to the heaviness in my heart.

This visit was the last time I would see Glad.

CHAPTER 25

The Call from Afghanistan

Danny was in the midst of his second deployment in Afghanistan. It was early 2003, and the fighting was intensifying. He got his wish—being tested in combat.

When I finally received an address to send a care package, I packed a large box as full as possible: four large plastic water bottles filled with Absolut Vodka, two dozen Cuban cigars I got from a buddy with a connection, four pounds of mixed nuts, and four pounds of beef jerky.

As Glad had requested, I wrapped the jewelry box containing her golden ring and put it in the package alongside a note that simply said:

"Glad asked that you bring this home to me, son. Someday it will be yours, but for now, I want you to personally return it to me when you come home. Love, Dad."

I didn't hear a peep from Danny for nine months, and I eroded once again into a neurotic mess.

One late evening, in my typical, numb state of mind, I was surfing from news channel to news channel and came across a segment just starting on Peter Jennings World News Tonight about what was happening at the forward operating base close to the Pakistan border. *Finally*, I thought. *Some real news about the actual war fighting.*

Suddenly, there was Danny. I couldn't believe my eyes. He was on the screen, talking to a reporter who held a microphone in his face. He was being interviewed about one of his men, a soldier who had been killed in a ferocious firefight. Danny looked lean, somber, and exhausted as he described the situation to the reporter. His face had aged, and he had the look of a predator with no fear.

"He died for an honorable cause, defending America," Danny said bluntly as his segment ended.

I sat frozen with a lump in my throat. After that suspended moment, I was unable to hold back the river of tears.

A week after the news segment aired, my phone rang.

"Hello?" I answered.

"Dad, it's Danny. I'm calling you from a satellite phone. Can you hear me?"

My heart raced in excitement, and a lump formed suddenly in my throat, "Yes! I can hear you, son. Are you alright?" I asked.

"I'm safe, but Dad…" There was a long pause, and then, "I'm too fucked up to come home," he said in a discouraged tone.

"Where are you?" I snapped back.

"I can't say."

I later discovered he was at one of the most dangerous, remote US firebases in Afghanistan named Shkin, just a few miles from the Pakistan border.

"Dad, I've seen too much and done too much. I'm just too messed up. We lost some guys. I just can't remember what it's like back home. I'm lost."

An image of my father flashed into my mind, and I recalled the stories I'd heard all my life about his terrible homecoming and violent, drunken benders. This was the moment Glad had warned me was coming.

My father sought help only once, and the counselor made the mistake of saying she understood how he felt. He told her she was an idiot and walked out. He never sought help again, and our family suffered the consequences.

As I listened to Danny, a terrible recollection of my father at Christmas when I was very young flashed across my mind. I was flooded with memories of how terrified our family was of him.

One of our trips to Nogales to escape his violence fell just before Christmas. Surprisingly, my mother talked everyone into allowing him to come by for just a couple of hours, so he could be there when we opened our presents. My grandparents were incredibly irritated and uncomfortable.

That year, my grandparents had given me a G.I. Joe, along with a big G.I. Joe Jeep that towed a Howitzer cannon and lots of combat equipment. My father didn't seem happy but sat in silence as I unwrapped all the military gear. I couldn't tell what he was thinking, but his expression and demeanor made me nervous. He had a familiar look that told me he was about to explode.

After many attempts to put G.I. Joe's boots on, I went to the living room and asked my father to help me. He looked down at me furiously, and I thought he was going to kill me. Immediately, he snatched G.I. Joe out of my hands. His hand began to shake as his eyes darted back and forth from me to my grandparents and then back to me. Suddenly, he stood up and shouted ferociously, "Playing with dolls!" and threw G.I. Joe against the wall with such violent force that it broke G.I. Joe's hand off and cracked his elbow loose.

No longer able to contain himself, my father stomped across all of our presents and stormed out the door, slamming it shut.

My grandparents sat in horrified silence with their mouths open. Of course, at the time, I didn't know this, but they had warned my mother something like this was going to happen. For her part, my mother sat sobbing into her hands, totally defeated. I froze, and we all waited for what would come next. I thought, *I hope he never returns.*

Now, on the phone with my tortured son, my mind screamed, *This will not happen to Danny! This isn't happening again! No way.*

"Son, you focus on staying alive, and get home," I said firmly. "I'll be here when you get back, and we'll figure this out together." My heart pounded through my throat, but I had to stay calm. I kept my voice steady and even. "I'll start looking around for what the VA has for counseling and get some things lined up before you get here."

"Gotta go, Dad. I love you," Danny whispered in a crackling voice, and the line went dead.

My heart broke for him, and my panic quickly turned to the resolve of a parent protecting their young. I needed a plan.

I had no idea where to begin, but the only thing I knew for certain was how to learn.

After endless days of scouring all the Veteran resources I could find, I came across the Vet Centers, a network of counseling locations established across the country after Vietnam. I set an appointment to see the site director a few days later. There, I met Mike Miracle, the site director. *What an interesting name*, I thought, because I was looking for just that: a miracle. Mike was a sincere guy who spoke reassuringly about what I was about to go through. However, he dropped a reality check on me with a matter-of-fact tone that ignited my rage.

"I'm going to tell it to you straight: we're overwhelmed with our current caseload of Vietnam and Gulf War vets, and the first wave of Afghanistan vets haven't even rotated back home yet. There is a tsunami coming, and we're just not staffed up to handle it. I hate to have to tell you this, but even if your son Danny is suicidal, with our current caseload, we could only see him maybe once a month."

"*What?*" I yelled as I bolted to my feet in a panic. Dread, fear, and anger poured out of me. My mind spun as I ranted, "Shit! What am I going to do? This is unacceptable! How can this be possible?"

Mike was helpless but sympathetic. He gave me a bag full of brochures, stickers, a list of reading recommendations for myself as a parent, and another list for Danny meant to help him transition. Mike called the Vet Center nearest to Fort Drum in Syracuse and spoke to the site director to introduce me. We parted on good terms, but I was justifiably enraged.

For as long as this country has existed and for as many wars as we've fought, surely we would have gotten homecoming right generations ago. I could not stop my mind from demanding, *Why is this happening?*

Fortunately, when I reached Pat, the site director at the Vet Center in Syracuse, she assured me that she would meet with Danny personally when he returned home in order to see where we'd need to start. She was a good listener, and she was sympathetic to my situation. I finally felt a sense of a plan coming together. I hadn't slept in days, but after speaking with Pat, I was finally able to crash for some needed rest.

When Danny arrived home in January, he was hollow, numb, and volatile. His chiseled jawline and muscular frame were gaunt from daily missions and firefights. Carrying a heavy ruck across the unforgiving mountains of Afghanistan had hardened his body and mind.

I flew out to Syracuse for a visit. When we first locked eyes, I felt as if all the emotion in my heart was about to pour out of my eyes. I said excitedly, "Shit, son! You're ripped," as we collided into a bear hug.

He picked me entirely up off the ground and growled, "I love you, Dad."

"I love you too, son," I sobbed in his ear.

He deflected everything with humor and sarcasm, but just under the surface, I could feel the heat of his anger like magma in an active volcano, ready to explode. He was still "over there," but he was sitting in front of me, pounding down beers and shots of sake.

And there it was, Glad's ring on his little finger. I asked him to let me hold it and squeezed it in my hand for most of dinner, remembering my life with Glad and the wisdom she bestowed on me. At the end of dinner, I handed it back to Danny and asked him to hold on to it for a while longer. He brought himself home with the ring, and this was our hope and wish.

That evening, we had a deep and dark conversation about what he was dealing with. The loss of Evan, one of the men in his squad who had been killed in a firefight, had been haunting him for a few months. Upon arrival back at Fort Drum, he was forced to see a counselor as part of their post-deployment mental health checkup. Like my father, he was offended and enraged by naive counselors who tried to empathize with him. Danny carried Evan's hat with him in his pack, and though the counselors attempted to help him process his loss, they didn't get it. He was unable to be vulnerable and unwilling to open the pressurized compartment of Evan's passing. He had a game with the counselors. He would share a horrific moment with them to see the shock on their faces and then wait for them to well up.

"See, stop telling me you understand," he'd chastise them. "You don't have a fucking clue."

Fortunately, he felt safe enough to share some of his demons with me. It was as though he was able to unpack some heavy emotional rocks from his ruck. I was honored he could still open up to me. It was clear Danny felt responsible for Evan's death.

"He was a good kid," he said, sniffling and holding his head in his hands. For the rest of his life, in the weeks building to late September of each year—the anniversary of Evan's death—Danny's demons would rule his days. Pot and alcohol provided the truth serum and numbing agent he needed to get through the nights.

After about six months of my goading, Danny finally agreed to see the counselors at the Vet Center. There, he met a polytrauma specialist and a counselor—also named Danny—he really connected with, which made all the difference in the initial stages of his recovery.

A few months after my visit, Danny lost Glad's ring, and it was never recovered. He had a habit of dangling the ring on his finger, and one day while driving, the ring slipped off and was lost in the snow. I was initially heartbroken but instantly recovered when I realized Glad's wish—and I believe to be the most useful purpose of sending Danny the ring—had been fulfilled. Danny arriving home alive was all that mattered.

Now it was time to marshal our focus and resources toward unpacking how to get him home mentally and emotionally.

CHAPTER 26

The Study of the Nature of Being

"What is the question to which your life is the answer?"
—MARIA NEMETH

I was obsessed with finding resources to help Danny and other Veterans deal with their trauma. Truth be told, parts of me were still traumatized and broken. I was searching for relief and redemption from my suffering as well.

My journey brought me to know and learn from many thought leaders and healers from every walk of life. And, in what seemed to be a never-ending odyssey on my journey home from Troy, I found purpose in shepherding and befriending a great many numb and traumatized Veterans along the way. I truly related to the underworld of trauma, self-medication, and suffering they were stuck in because I was stuck in purgatory with them, marching along, dazed and self-absorbed.

I was Odysseus—the legendary Greek king of Ithaca from Homer's great works—returning home from the Battle of Troy, jumping from one adventure to the next on my quest to someday return home, healed and recovered.

Mastering Life's Energies

My journey was greatly enriched by the heart-opening work of Maria Nemeth, author of *Mastering Life's Energies*.

I was fortunate enough to speak with Maria by phone while she was traveling abroad. I had reached out to her about how her work would be helpful for transitioning Veterans and their families. She was immediately open to sharing how her work would undoubtedly help. I was encouraged by her compassion and empathy as we talked about the struggles experienced in homecoming and transition. I shared with her the call I had received from Danny in Afghanistan and how traumatized he was when he returned. Maria listened with deep empathy and reassured me that I would find her work helpful.

As she spoke, there was something about her way of being that drew me in. There was a resonance of spaciousness and generosity blended with candor that reminded me of Glad and put me at ease almost immediately. I didn't feel her empathy toward me in a professional sense, as a counselor would; instead, she was holding a space and inviting me to do my work.

"This is the ontological work," she said.

I asked her to help me understand the field of ontology from her perspective.

"Ontology is one of the four domains of metaphysics," Maria explained. "Psychology, the study of the nature of mind; theology, which is the study of the various ways of knowing religion and spirituality; cosmology, which is the study of the nature of the cosmos; and ontology, the study of the nature of being.

"Who we are willing to be in our life is far more rewarding than anything we are willing to do in our life," she explained.

I was captivated by Maria's ability to speak to me in a way that created hope and possibility. For the first time since my conversations with Glad, I felt the presence of unconditional love.

As we concluded our conversation, a familiar twinge emerged within me. It told me to pay attention to this work.

There's Something Right with Me

Drawn to Maria's encouraging hope, I committed to attending her upcoming retreat in Sacramento. On the afternoon of the event, there was some confusion about the venue's location, and I arrived a few minutes late. As I took my seat, I was disappointed I had not arrived early to meet Maria as we had planned. I have a habit of arriving early to secure a front-row seat whenever I attend retreats.

The private event center was curated for Maria's work; it was colorful and inviting. Various parts of the large, open room were already prepared and provisioned to accommodate the group exercises we would experience throughout the weekend. The support staff members worked with a sense of smooth collaboration. Each knew their respective roles, which created a pleasant feeling of being fully supported.

As I sat in the audience, studying Maria's presence, I was immediately reminded of Glad. Maria carried herself with a regal sense of dignity and had an immensely inquisitive nature.

During the first break, I approached Maria while she was making tea, and I apologized for being late. I shared my confusion about the event's address and explained that I went to the corporate office instead of the event location.

"Perhaps, you should have checked your voicemail," Maria responded sharply.

Her tone caught me off guard. I was instantly triggered and took her comment as unnecessary and disrespectful. I responded in kind, "Perhaps you should check yours—I left a message for you as well."

After a tense pause, I blurted dismissively, "Is *this* the voice of wisdom I came to receive?" My mind closed like a vault. "I'm leaving," I grumbled as I turned to walk away.

Maria replied in a more friendly tone, "That's quite a temper you've got there. How's that working for you?" She paused for effect. "I can help you with that if you're open to it."

Immediately, I thought, *Why can she stand here and disrespect me for not checking my voicemail, but I need help because I was triggered and stern in return?*

I was simultaneously pissed and curious but tried not to show it as she set the hook.

"You can go if you want, but if you do, you'll miss an opportunity to work on this."

This was a pivotal moment for me. I could see in Maria's eyes that she was now more sincere. Everything slowed down as I thought, *There must be a reason why I'm here.*

My ego felt threatened and was screaming for me to run, but my pain and suffering called out for help in a louder, more resounding voice.

I was exhausted from the energy it took to conceal the deep rage I kept under pressure from decades of pain. It was destroying any hope I had of living a fulfilling and happy life. In that instant, I knew Maria was right. I needed help.

It wasn't her words that hurt, but the wounds they touched.

In a flash of insight, it occurred to me that I was here, at this moment, at an event called *Mastering Life's Energies* to do exactly that: master life's energies. Once again, Glad had sent a skillful messenger to, as Maria would soon say, "deconstruct my structure of knowing."

I didn't know exactly what to do, but I had a good idea of the first step: I surrendered.

I let out a sigh. "I do need help, and I don't know what to do." A hint of relief came over me as I made my confession.

Maria smiled. "So, you will stay?"

"Yes...I will, thank you," I replied, relieved and impressed with her calm and supportive presence.

"Good, I'll see you in a few minutes." She took a sip of her tea.

As the break came to a close, Maria walked down the aisle and stood in front of the room, gazing slowly across the audience to meet our eyes with a gentle smile. She looked so regal, and her presence conveyed a warm sense of ease; she wasn't just beaming, she was glowing.

"I would like to begin with a question," she started. "Would it be alright with you"—she paused—"if your life got a little easier? Let this sink in. *Would it be alright with you*"—a longer pause—"if your life got a little easier?"

She followed this incredibly potent question with another warm smile as she looked around the room into our eyes. I could feel the entire audience take a long breath in, and we all let out a warm sigh of relief as we agreed, *yes*.

We were like a group of baby birds with our necks outstretched and our mouths open wide, hoping to receive nourishment.

As I pondered her question, I felt a soothing and gentle warmth emanating from beneath my armor.

It was hope.

Until this moment, all I knew for sure was that my life was hard. I couldn't imagine how it could be easier. I think this is why I was caught so off guard by her question.

The entire retreat was an odyssey of emotional epiphanies and heart-opening exercises, each building upon the next in perfect succession. My greatest takeaway was the profound realization that nothing was wrong with me.

For most of my life, *there's something wrong with me* had been a theme I had taken ownership of, and honestly, it had become strangely comfortable. I was used to having low self-esteem and thought it was part of me. This false narrative had allowed me to play small and hide since childhood. It was my deepest secret, and it held me down like a boat anchor.

The traumas I had experienced throughout my life actually happened, just as Dr. Richardson had said. Still, I had wired them up to construct an idealized self that could function in the world. I believed I was my traumas; I thought I was the sum of the pain they had inflicted upon me.

To a great degree, what hurt me had shaped me and influenced what I moved toward and what I moved away from in life. During Maria's retreat, I came to realize that my pain and traumas didn't define or represent who I was.

That realization tethered me to my deepest self. With this new understanding, it felt like my soul was being retrieved back to my innocent self—before my birth, before my life experiences.

Maria shared a mantra that resonated with me so deeply that I will carry it with me always: "I am whole and complete, and I am a hero on a hero's journey."

I knew then beyond a shadow of a doubt that Glad had brought me to Maria. They would have loved each other's gentle directness, sharp wit, and humor.

I have always loved the playful term *monkey mind* to describe that chattering doubt in my head and appreciated how Maria wove this into her work, and I loved her description of it.

"It represents that aspect of the mind," she shared, "that is always chattering at us as it swings from doubt to worry and back to doubt again. Our monkey mind is fearful for our survival. It has no sense of proportion. Everything is big. Everything is a threat, constantly warning us, 'I would turn back if I were you.'"

My monkey mind, swinging from worry to doubt, significantly contributed to my ongoing anxiety, and I was grateful to learn how to minimize and silence its chatter.

Now, each time my monkey mind attempts to present evidence that something is wrong with me, I immediately counter with, *There's something right with me*, which makes me smile.

Mastering Life's Energies has become a life manual I often revisit and constantly recommend and give to others.

One of the things I appreciate most about Maria's work is how my conditioned self, also known as my ego, was revealed to me. The conclusion that something must be wrong with me was constantly reinforced by my mind, which gathered evidence from skewed recollections of the traumas and trainwrecks of my life. Of course, there was a never-ending set of file drawers overflowing with negative evidence my mind felt free to turn to. This, in turn, caused me to have constant internal anxiety and scattered thoughts. No matter how hard I tried or how much I developed myself, the impeccable external image I was curating didn't match the chaos and the magma churning within my inner self.

My internal struggles were very troubling, and I often felt people could sense my incongruence. My lack of internal cohesion prevented my ability to create healthy and lasting relationships on every level of my life, which reinforced the conclusion I held that something must be wrong with me. It was a hamster wheel in a box, and I was the hamster, running as fast as I could in an effort to escape my upbringing and my fear—fear of not being loved, not being worthy of being loved, not being liked, accepted, good enough, smart enough, or successful enough. My life was exhausting, and I wore out everyone around me. Even if I jumped off the hamster wheel, I was still confined to a box of my own making.

I had never considered that instead of being broken, I was whole and complete. And, much like Glad had shared my entire life, I related to the hero's journey. Maria opened my eyes, but more importantly, her wisdom opened my heart to a quality of being that had resided within me all along.

With these tools and realizations, the answer to Maria's question—*Would it be alright with you if your life got a little easier?*—began to manifest. To my surprise, my life began to get easier.

CHAPTER 27

Danny's Passing

"**D**anny's gone. High-speed motorcycle accident."
That's all I recall from a late-night phone call I received July 15, 2009.

"I'll be there tomorrow as soon as I can," I replied, though shock began to hammer me into numbness.

I sat frozen on the bed in my room at the Marriott Irvine in California. Nothing was real. I tried to imagine I had a bad dream and was now awake, but I knew my son was dead. I couldn't cry or scream. All I could do was sit, helplessly gazing into the darkness. My life as I knew it had come to an end.

I realized I had to get to New York and frantically booked a flight. I then walked down the hall to Matt's room, a friend and business associate who had traveled here for an important meeting the following morning.

As Matt opened his door, he immediately noticed my troubled state. "What's up?" he asked, concerned.

"My son is dead," I said bluntly. The words sounded foreign as they came out of my mouth. "I have to go to New York as soon as possible. I won't be coming to the meeting tomorrow. I'm sorry."

He leaned against the door, stunned. "I'm so sorry, John. Is there anything I can do?"

"No," I replied as he gave me a long and sympathetic hug.

"Thank you. I have to go." I turned and slowly shuffled back to my room.

I stared at the ceiling of my hotel room until dawn, waiting to catch the first flight out.

There was no way to process the loss during the somber plane ride. I sat in silence, staring out the window into the clouds.

An old Otis Taylor song, "Live Your Life," rang in my head, so I pulled it up and put it on repeat. Otis was right. Death didn't touch me in my heart; it just walked right up and knocked me down. First, I'd lost Russ—and now Danny—to motorcycles. I vowed never to ride one again.

Tormented and trying to connect with my son, I pulled up another song Danny and I loved and deeply resonated with: "Lay Your World on Me" by Ozzy Osborne.

I choked back tears, thinking I didn't deserve the love Danny gave me. I wanted more than anything for him to lay his world on me, so I could show him I could take the weight and ease his burdens.

Danny was about the only thing I had done in the world that proved I ever existed. He had exceeded far beyond how I measured myself as a man. I had made a habit of reviewing a leadership performance evaluation Danny gave me from his deployment in Afghanistan as a squad leader and brought it with me on the plane. He had proven to be an extraordinary warrior and leader in combat, and he was incredibly proud of his men and their accomplishments. Danny's own leaders were proud to have led men into battle with him.

As I sat, listening to Otis and Ozzy, rereading Danny's evaluation, I visualized who he had become and what he had accomplished.

284 on his last fitness test.

This brought me back to the pride of my own fitness qualifications and the ongoing competition Danny and I had for bragging rights, chasing the perfect fitness score of 300.

Performs superbly under extreme pressure.

The familiar pang of envy struck me each time I read it. "Proud of you, son," I whispered as I continued to read Danny's highlights.

His personal leadership during multiple enemy contacts resulted in zero friendly casualties due to his quick responses and decisiveness.

Through his mentorship, three soldiers were selected for and promoted to sergeant in addition to three soldiers enrolling in eArmyU.

Successfully deployed his platoon to and from Afghanistan during Operation Enduring Freedom.

Keeping him in a rapid deployable unit will increase the readiness of the US Army.

Combatives Instructor.

I tried to imagine how Danny would have trained his men in hand-to-hand combat. I envisioned it to be as real and as violent as he'd fought in real life.

I smiled as I recalled a story Danny once shared with me about how he threw a beating on some guys while on vacation in a lake-front resort town. Crossing an intersection with his battle buddy and their girlfriends, a couple of guys in a car who were stopped at the light made a derogatory remark toward the ladies. Without saying a word, Danny walked right up to the driver's door, grabbed the guy by the hair, and pulled him through his window, slamming him on the pavement. His buddy pulled the other guy out, and they beat the hell out of both of them. To make it even more humiliating, Danny used an open hand to slap the driver, yelling, "Say you're sorry! Apologize! Say you're sorry!"

Danny loved to tell this story, and he roared laughing whenever he told it.

In every area possible on his performance evaluation, he was rated *Excellent, Superior*, and *Promotable ahead of his peers.*

To this day, whenever I need to know he was real, I pull out his eval to reminisce and to feel my pride in him.

The days ahead were miserable. I had never planned a funeral and never want to again. It is a somber yet prideful process of honoring someone you love.

The most memorable moment I will carry with me was placing my hand and a rose on his flag-draped coffin as the uniformed honor guard fired over and over and over.

After leaving Danny's service, I don't recall anything about how I got to the airport or onto the plane, and the ride home was spent in a haze, reflecting on our lives together and what it meant to be his father. I felt a profound loss of identity as a parent.

While Danny served in the military, I was an incredibly proud parent. On all of my vehicle bumpers, I was honored to display a Blue Star with a red border decal signifying I had a child serving in the military.

Blue Star Mothers of America was founded by mothers of active-duty military personnel during WWII to symbolize pride and support on the home front during times of war and hostilities. Blue Star flags are often seen in windows of homes with family members serving. The organization has grown into hundreds of local chapters nationwide with regular support meetings and functions. Though I'm not a big joiner of groups, I attended Blue Star events and found the other parents and families to be a crucial support community I relied upon while Danny was deployed.

It was always uplifting to spot Blue Star decals and magnets on other cars of parents whose children were also serving. Often, we would not just wave and smile but would stop and check in with each other, offering encouragement and support. With repeated deployments to Afghanistan and Iraq, every parent I met had an overpowering sense of optimism and pride, but as our conversations moved past what branch their child served and where they were deployed, we would often deflate for a moment to let down our facades. We were all worried and fretting; some of us masked it better than others. Deep down, we shared the same trepidation of not knowing exactly how our children would return home; hope was our common bond.

But I could no longer identify myself as a Blue Star Father. I remember the painful act of removing the Blue Star decals from my truck, and seeing them on cars while driving instantly triggered me into a painful reminder that Danny was gone.

Mel, a fellow Blue Star parent, tried to comfort me; she pulled up a website about Gold Star Families and asked, "Hey, with Danny's passing, this would mean you're a Gold Star Father now, right?"

"Well, technically, I think yes, but it's complicated," I replied.

Mel continued, "But it says right here, to be accepted as a member, Danny must have been either missing in action or killed while on active duty or as a result of such service.

"Certainly, the high disability rating Danny received from his deployments to Afghanistan would be a factor," she added.

I agreed with Mel and said, "Danny often shared with me that his body needed relief for his PTSD that he could only get it from massive amounts of adrenaline from dangerous, excessive speed on his Harley."

"So, his death could be considered service-related, right?" Mel questioned.

"Yes," I replied, "but I'm conflicted. As I understand it, the purpose of founding the Gold Star organization was to honor the mothers and families of service members who died in times of war while in active service. It doesn't say anything in its charter that indicates its membership is open to the families of Veterans who die after service from suicide or adrenaline-seeking accidents as a qualifying circumstance. This is exactly why I said it's complicated."

Gold Star Families service members who died in battle were fully engaged in a heroic purpose of their choosing, and they died with their honor intact.

Danny's death wasn't about an act of valor; it was about his need to manage his suffering. The fact is that he didn't survive his transition from service.

I explained to Mel, "Over the years at Veteran events, I've met a lot of Gold Star family members whose children were killed in action. When I am around them, personally, I feel humbled and uncomfortable identifying as a Gold Star Father."

A few months after this conversation, I had several discussions with a Gold Star Dad who led a chapter in Southern California. Even though his son was killed in action, he was incredibly open to supporting all the fathers who lost their children, regardless of how they died. Reluctantly, I accepted his invitation to join Gold Star Dads and went through the induction ceremony at the event.

I remain uncomfortable identifying as a member but sincerely appreciate the lengths Gold Star leaders have gone to help families like mine feel accepted and included.

Fortunately, about five years after Danny's death, thanks to a committed VA support person who knew and understood the complexity of his injuries, Danny's death was deemed to be "service-connected."

Someday, maybe there will be an additional "Star" designation created to honor and support the families of Veterans who die from accidents, suicide, and the physical and emotional injuries sustained from war.

As I Sit with You, Son

As I sit with you, son, and gaze upon you
I feel the warmth of your presence,
Your inviting smile,
Your gentle voice assuring me that all is well.
As I sit with you, son,
I feel the pain beneath your gentleness
With a deep breath
And a heavy sigh.
We acknowledge its familiar presence.
It is the pain of your hero's journey,
A pain that only war, trauma, and loss can bring,
A suffering just beneath the surface
Just beyond your smile
Born from surviving
While others did not—
Cringing when called a hero,
Deflecting with a quip and a smile,
Awkward pauses while trying to be nice
A longing to be home,
But rarely being truly home—
Hidden wounds

You would never heal.
As I sit with you, son, and gaze upon you,
I miss you.
I miss our conversations,
Your aspirations,
Your outrageousness,
Your challenges,
Your encouragement.
As I sit with you, son, on the day of your passing,
Rest in peace.
You are the inspiration in my life,
And for so many others,
You have made a difference in this world.

—J.H. PARKER

I am comforted by the thought of Danny and Glad being together in an afterlife without pain and suffering.

CHAPTER 28

The Wounded Healer

G rief and loss are my two greatest teachers. Trauma is a close third.

After Danny's passing, I wandered through my days in a haze, second-guessing myself and unable to put the genie back in the bottle. Why didn't I see this coming? What could I have done to keep him from getting on his bike that night? I could have done a thousand things to change his destiny. I was lost, unable to invest my hopes and dreams in him any longer.

To fill the void, I took solace in losing myself with troubled, at-risk Veterans. Escaping into the darkness with them was sometimes unhealthy and sometimes dangerous, but letting off steam with a bunch of crazies reaffirmed to me that I could hide out and suffer with my tribe and not be judged.

The more I invested myself into the Vets I met, the more I found I could recycle my pain. This gave my suffering a twisted sense of meaning and purpose and prevented me from feeling completely numb.

I couldn't save Danny, but maybe I could be a force for good to save others.

I became the Wounded Healer.

Being close to troubled and traumatized Vets my entire life taught me that it usually took a lot of alcohol before their real demons surfaced. One moment they would be smiling and conveying a sense of love and pride of their military service, then unexpectedly, they would become triggered and sobbing in a fit of rage, grief, shame, or regret.

I also found the Vets who needed the help the most were the ones who couldn't or wouldn't ask for it.

Fortunately, I wasn't bound by the disclosure ethics of professional therapists who are discouraged or unable to disclose their personal stories to their patients. The freedom I found in sharing the troubles I'd had in my life and the mistakes I'd made seemed to create openings for others to share. My journey was so packed with trauma and craziness, I had plenty of material to work with and didn't have to make anything up.

Often, sharing some relevant part of my story conveyed a sense that perhaps I knew some things that may be useful. This neutral, non-judgmental approach seemed to create a friendly rapport that, over time, eventually led to trust.

Even today, the mantra I most often repeat to myself and, more importantly, to the people I choose to help and support is, "I'm not here to teach you because I am in this with you." I specifically share what still triggers me and how I am doing the work to try to transcend my reactive nature.

"If I don't move my pain, it will eat me alive."

Like every traumatized person I have ever met, I could be emotionally hijacked when my critical thinking mind was triggered. It could happen unexpectedly and without warning. Until I got a handle on this, my waking hours were stressful. I would be startled awake at all hours, worrying, doubting myself, and fretting about some concern of impending doom. If I didn't get ahead of it quickly, I would suffer another sleepless night.

People were often surprised when I told them I only needed four hours of sleep a night. "I hate to go to bed, and I can't wait to get up," I would joke. But truthfully, my mind was racing so much from 2:00 a.m. onward that I would frequently check the clock to see if it was time to get up yet. Once my feet hit the floor, I didn't stop moving.

Luckily, I discovered I could recognize when I became triggered almost the instant it occurred instead of jumping on the crazy train for hours or days. I no longer needed to self-medicate with mind-numbing substances or with what used to be my biggest unhealthy distraction: workaholism, a ridiculous strategy I employed for most of my life. No wonder so many Vets were in disastrous pain when they retired. When they came home, they did what they were trained to do: compartmentalize and stow the trauma of what they saw, did, or experienced in order to remain functional and combat ready. I could relate to this. From childhood, I learned to distract myself from dealing with my pain by turning my life into my next mission instead of unpacking and dealing with my troubles.

The Grand Distraction

For most of my life, focusing on anything but my problems became a grand distraction, and my crafty monkey mind was the ringleader of the circus.

If I just had X, whatever X was, I'd be happy. Everything imaginable kept me distracted from knowing myself. My list of qualities the perfect mate "needed" to possess became too ridiculous for anyone to meet. I suffered from chronic dissatisfaction. Nothing really made me happy. I was empty, though I was trying to fill myself up with everything imaginable.

Eventually, I wore out most everything I could think of to distract myself and began to take an honest look into where my life was heading. I quickly realized that nothing would ever satisfy me from outside of myself. I needed to get healthy inside.

The more I began to see the nature of my suffering, the easier it became to examine the places in my mind where my thoughts were formed. For me, the themes of shame and regret occupied the most space in my psyche. Shame itself was a multi-faced monster that needed to be named. I began to write out the forms of shame I experienced and witnessed in others without referencing formal clinical labels and definitions. I was desperately wanting to come to terms with my generational history of shame.

Naming the Faces of Shame

PARENTAL SHAME

A common theme behind my shame was about being a terrible father and how I damaged Danny's life. I found fatherly shame to be a very common theme among the Veterans I knew as well—shame and regret for being hostile or violent toward their children, or because of deployments, for not being there when their kids were born. Worse, they felt shame for not being fully present as a parent when they actually spent time with their children.

RELATIONSHIP SHAME

Being numb to intimacy is a symptom of trauma I lived with for most of my life. Luckily, I discovered a universal truth in this area: the quality and depth of my relationships on all levels could only grow in direct proportion to my ability to accept and love myself first.

I had mastered the art of self-loathing. However, over time, and by doing my inner work, the emptiness that left me feeling an abysmal sense of self-worth slowly filled with self-love. It's funny, the term *self-love* used to be too soft to even say in the privacy of my own mind. Even in my head, I would laugh it off. I learned from this, so I rarely bring self-love up with others until they are in a place to really hear it.

SHAME AND REGRET

The most prevalent theme of my critical mind, the one that's hi-jacked more moments than any other throughout my life, is regret.

Hate is a strong word, but I hate my sense of regret and the hopes and dreams it has stolen from me. Until I learned to drive regret into a corner and take my power back, I could only play small and hide from it. Regret caused me to live the life of an imposter with very little internal cohesion. The successful and healthy exterior I projected to others definitely did not match my unhealthy inner reality of low self-worth.

I once met a Vietnam Vet, nicknamed "Blue," at an American Legion in Sacramento. When he heard about Danny's deployment with the 10th, we instantly became good friends. As Blue was a former Army soldier, he adopted me into his inner circle. During the day, Blue was active and engaged. Helping other vets and their families gave him a purpose. But several nights a week, starting around midnight, my phone would ring. It was Blue, wasted out of his mind.

"Goddamn, John. I love you. Why do you care about me?" His words would slur together, and he would cry uncontrollably. He'd then repeat the same horrific story: an act of taking someone's life that sent him to prison and destroyed his marriage and family. He couldn't drink enough to erase the shame.

IMMORAL SHAME

Immorality is the shame I most often felt and heard from Danny. I lived vicariously through him and was both fascinated and disturbed when he shared his truths with me. These usually came forth when he had consumed enough truth serum.

"Goddamn, Dad. I loved combat," he would blurt. "I can't say this to anyone, but I loved it."

This form of shame wasn't from something he did in combat. Rather, it was from the exhilaration he felt in combat. What he couldn't tell anyone sober was that he loved the supremacy of literally playing God. "Screw that, I was God," Danny said.

He shared detailed accounts of winning on the battlefield and wielding the power to take lives and trophies. "It's primal," he would say. "This has always been true. Since the first caveman pummeled another caveman to take his food and possessions, there is a winner, and there is a loser. One is dead, and the other feasts and drinks on the spoils as the victor."

I've read about heroic battles and of great warriors, but I wasn't a Combat Vet. I trained for it, wanted it, needed it, but never got the chance, and I was sick with envy until the moment Danny called from Afghanistan to tell me he was too messed up to come home.

Until I heard the firsthand accounts of his supremacy in battle and the hypnotic impact it blazes onto a warrior's psyche, I truly didn't fully grasp it.

Some nights, we spent hours on the phone, and Danny shared countless stories of leading his men on missions where they encountered the enemy. When any of his men hesitated or froze in terror, he would calmly move among them, cool and loose, slapping them on the back and focusing their direction of fire. When mortars were landing all around, Danny would calmly walk from man to man, checking on everyone.

"If you're going to get hit in a mortar attack, what does it matter if you are moving or hiding?" he would joke. He did take some shrapnel in his arms from a close hit that proved he should have at least taken cover.

Danny taunted the enemy and took lives when they attacked, and his men loved him for his ferocity in battle. He was addicted to danger and adrenaline.

Leading in combat with other alpha warriors was where Danny found his true calling. They knew he could be counted upon, and he thrived on exceeding their expectations. Inflicting death and justice was what they trained for and lived for, and keeping their men alive, inspired, and moving was what they were born to do.

"One minute, I'm killing this bastard on the side of a mountain, and then a few days later, I'm cooking eggs in my kitchen back home. What the hell?" Danny exclaimed. "I can't get my head around it. Deployed, my weapons were always locked and loaded. We didn't have to speak the language—everything we needed to know was in people's eyes. Sure as shit, we'd be walking by someone, and their eyes would give them away. The instant they flinched to pull a weapon, everything opened up like the wild west. We'd light those bastards up. Now I'm supposed to sit around and watch the fucking grass grow in my yard? I'm bored out of my mind!" he yelled in frustration.

The more I got to know other Vets, the more common I realized this dilemma was. They were more alive in combat than anything else they could do or would ever do again, and nothing else filled the void.

How does a warrior tell their wife or kid, "I love you, but I'd rather be in combat," without ruining those relationships? The short answer is: they can't, and it's not a good idea to try. Civilians can't unhear those words.

The stories I heard from Danny deeply impacted me and provided a window into both his and my father's psyches.

When Veterans trusted me enough to share these same, dark truths, I treated it as a sacred privilege.

LOSS AND SHAME

The shame of feeling responsible for someone's death will haunt a person for life if left unresolved. This is an incredibly destructive form of shame that punishes the survivor.

Danny knew a soldier he'd lost in combat who had died due to decisions he did not personally make. Nevertheless, all he could do was spin out and obsess over the countless choices he could have made that would have changed the man's fate.

Every year, as the anniversary of this tragic event would roll around, Danny's volatility would begin to emerge. For several weeks prior, he would replay the events in his mind. Regret and remorse would take over, and Danny would drink more. It was a vicious cycle that left him with no peace.

I found the only thing that finally began to break things loose and get his attention was the following question: "If you could, would you trade places with him right now? If this were possible, he would be here, and you'd be dead. Would you trade places?"

"In a heartbeat!" Danny would yell into the phone.

"Well, *you can't!*" I shouted back. "You are *here*, and he's not. Would he want you to waste your life?" I wouldn't let Danny answer. "If Evan got a second chance, he wouldn't waste it. *You owe it to him to make something of your life.* You need to wake up! Don't squander the rest of your life and be stuck forever in this shit-fest. Make something of your life and dedicate it to his memory."

"Yeah," Danny would reply. "You're right," and he wept.

SHAME AND HELPLESSNESS

My relationship with Danny was imperfect, and I was absent for a good part of his life, but I was his father, and he was my son. Regardless of our family's hate and dysfunction, no one could ever comprehend the love and the bond between us.

As a parent, I found there wasn't much worse than needing to be needed but helpless to help.

Before Danny passed, every so often, I would get calls from him in the middle of the night. He would be drunk and stoned out of his mind, ranting into the phone, "You asshole! You abandoned me! Why would you *do that to me?*"

Usually, there was angry sounding music playing so loudly in the background, I could barely make out his words. "Why would you kick me out and send me back to that shithole with Mom?"

There was nothing I could say or do in those moments but to be silent and wait until he was finally exhausted. Then, I would tell him I was sorry. Eventually, he'd slam the phone down and hang up.

By noon of the following day, like clockwork, I would get a follow-up call. This time, Danny would be sobbing on the other end of the phone, telling me he was so sorry and that he loved me. He knew his mother ran away from home and left me when she was pregnant, and he was thankful I came to find him. We would then recount the confrontation years prior when he threatened me, and we discussed how it was too dangerous for us to be close to each other.

Our peace accord would hold for six months to a year until the next time he would call, needing to rage. I learned to quietly weather his storms. I loved him through each of them, knowing it would pass.

I can wish that our relationship had been perfect, but it was forever broken and beautiful just the way it was.

Showing Up for Others

Whenever I helped transitioning Veterans and their families, I found a place for my pain and loss. My life experiences greatly served me when holding a space for others. I had numbed and self-medicated my way through a good part of my life, so I understood destructive behaviors and addictions and how to mature through them all too well. I had experienced the pain of grief and loss, so I could relate to their pain on a deep and personal level.

But I always felt the underlying sense that I was hiding out in the eye of my storm. I was calm and willing to come to the aid of someone in need—selflessly, I thought at the time.

But it wasn't selfless. I needed to fill myself with the sense that I was saving lives and keeping families together.

The law of reciprocity had been tucked away from my awareness, during my most painful times but was providing glimpses of where things were heading. I needed something, anything in return from helping others to help me tread water emotionally. It wasn't ecological, as Maria had shared with me, but I knew what I was doing was helping the Veterans I supported.

In my mind, I was desperately imagining Danny was with me in my darkest moments. Being in the shit with a Veteran in crisis gave me meaning and purpose. I can see now how the urgency and adrenaline provided a grand distraction to my psyche, one that kept my demons in their compartments, stowed and pressurized.

I became obsessed with moving around my pain. If I stood still, it ate me alive.

Still, Glad's wisdom gave me the framework for helping others in a way that was clean and useful.

For one thing, *show up*. Veterans are an unforgiving bunch. The way I see it, if I didn't show up, if I couldn't be relied upon, I might as well not come back at all because I'd never fully earn their trust again.

Second, I needed to do what I said I was going to do. If I said I would get back to them, I did. If I said I would be there for them, I was. Most Vets I met didn't trust civilians to do anything they said they were going to do. *If you can't be relied upon, you are worthless* seemed to be the prevailing mentality.

Third, I needed to show I gave a shit! I needed to show I was interested in who they were and what they had been through, so I could understand their model of the world, no matter how catastrophic, heartbreaking, or shameful it was. I was willing to lean into the tough conversations and tell them when they were in their own way. Oftentimes, I had to tell them they were full of shit or call them an idiot to get their attention. I didn't play kissy-face just to make them feel good.

Tony Robbins phrased it perfectly: "Hurt 'em, and heal 'em." Oftentimes, I had to stir up the pain to help heal the pain.

Fourth, I asked for nothing in return. Sure, emotionally I was receiving a lot from helping Vets and their family members, but the bigger reward was leaving them better off than when I found them or when they found me.

I became the dawn in their darkness, just as Glad had been for me, and being that source of light was my reward.

The Journey Home from Troy

As a parent struggling to deal with the loss of a child, I found *The Odyssey*, Homer's epic work, to be incredibly insightful. The lessons and examples it provides are as relevant today as they were when it was written over 2,600 years ago.

Avoiding my pain by being supportive of others did give me a sense of purpose, especially when I was able to generate sparks of hope and possibility. Typically, when I got to know Veterans and began to understand what was troubling them, I'd comment, "You are definitely on your journey home from Troy." If they were familiar with Homer's works, they'd typically smile in acknowledgment. If not, it created an opening to expose them to some ancient teachings that matched their warrior ethos.

Since the beginning of war itself, warriors have gone to battle and families have eagerly awaited their eventual return. Unfortunately, the realities of war and the predictable life and death struggles of making it home are not born into us. We forget the catastrophic lessons learned from past generations that force us to relive them.

When Danny made it home from Afghanistan, I prepared a special movie night for when the time felt right. I showed him an old Kirk Douglas movie titled *Ulysses*. Ulysses is the Latin name for Odysseus. The special effects are corny and dated right out of the '50s, but the story consistently proves to be captivating and thought-provoking. I have watched it with struggling Veterans many times.

What struck me as the most important lesson of the *Odyssey* is the relentless pursuit Veterans must engage in to survive and to one day make it home, all to reclaim their place in the world.

As Viktor Frankl states beautifully in his book *Man's Search for Meaning*, "We must find meaning and purpose to help us survive and endure our struggles. There must be some purpose for surviving our experiences, and it is up to each of us to find it."

Another useful insight I pulled from the *Odyssey* was the predictable nature of how we as humans avoid our pain. It wasn't just me—sex, drugs, adrenaline and danger seeking, and workaholism can rob a lifetime from people who suffer from trauma.

The vast majority of Veterans I have met over the years struggled between the identity they forged in the military and the identity of being just another Joe or Jane in the world when they separated from service.

The most important thing I've tried to convey to transitioning Veterans is the need to re-examine their identity, mission, meaning, and purpose as a military service member to begin reinventing these four critical areas of life as a civilian.

Above all, I try to share with them the value of becoming a learner.

CHAPTER 29

Be What the World Needs

Mindfulness, Non-Duality, and Integrative Restoration (iRest)

I woke to a sunny Sunday morning in Cardiff-by-the-Sea, just a few miles north of San Diego. I had moved to the area just a few months prior to be near the ocean. To clear my mind each morning, I'd developed a ritual of walking near the beach to get coffee.

On this particular morning, I was deep in thought about a talk I would be attending in a few hours. The topic was non-duality, given by Adyashanti, an author and thought leader. I struggled with the term *non-duality*, but a number of friends I spoke with thought highly of Adyashanti's work and found it enlightening. I trusted them and felt encouraged to attend. I was trying to make sense of where I was heading on a spiritual level. Perhaps this was where I was supposed to be. I hoped Adyashanti would be a messenger put on my path, as Glad had taught me to look out for.

When I arrived, the conference room was packed with hundreds of people who were already seated. There were only a few empty seats remaining in the middle section of the room.

I quickly made my way to an open seat just as the room became quiet and soft music began to play. A pale-skinned man in a gray sweater casually strolled down the center aisle and onto the stage. He turned toward us in silence, standing before an oversized chair. Given his name, I had pictured him to be a spiritual man of Asian or Indian descent. To my surprise, he was a middle-aged, clean-shaven, average-looking Caucasian guy with a gentle smile. His presence emanated waves of soothing energy as he quietly gazed around the entire room.

He sat down, made himself comfortable, and began to speak with a calming sense of ease. I opened my journal and prepared to transcribe what I was about to hear.

Adyashanti began by saying, "We do not simply exist within existence, but all of existence exists within us."

I thought this was interesting but a bit esoteric and kept writing. He added, "The most unhappy people are the ones who are always seeking happiness."

True, well put, I thought. My entire life had been about seeking happiness, but here I was, unhappy.

The next concept he shared was confusing for me. "Enlightenment," he explained, "isn't an experience because, in the next breath, you are again looking for the experience." I wasn't quite sure what this meant, but then he dropped a depth charge that rattled my nerves:

"Our awakening will come through the death of the ego."

My attention immediately went inward. My critical mind was the voice of my ego, and its reaction came swiftly. *Don't listen to this. He's an idiot, and he doesn't know what the hell he's talking about.* Then, I observed its attempt to take control. *I'm shutting down*, it seethed.

I spaced out for a good part of Adyashanti's introductory mono-logue, ruminating over how my ego had just hijacked my conscious awareness. I witnessed my ego and its protective nature feeling threatened for the first time as if it were a character that was not me. This was big.

It became abundantly clear that my ego was the duality Adyashanti was referring to. I was beginning to understand what non-duality meant on a deep and personal level, but still, I wondered, *But what about trauma and the intrusive thoughts that rule my life?*

My attention to Adyashanti returned just as he finished his introduction. He asked, "Does anyone have any questions?"

Without thinking, my hand bolted upward, along with hundreds of others. To my surprise, he made eye contact and pointed toward me. "What is your question?"

I must have had a confused look on my face. It was hard to believe he was really calling on me when there were hundreds of other hands in the air. He pointed toward me again, making direct eye contact, and said with a smile, "Yes, you." The hands around me lowered as I stood and began to read some notes from my journal. I could hardly believe I was about to speak my dilemma out loud to him—directly—and in front of an entire room of strangers.

Nervously, I began by reading from my journal. "I think I've heard so far that we are not our thoughts, we are not our ego, and all there is is pure awareness; there is no duality, no separateness. Here's my dilemma: I want this to be true for me, but I suffer from trauma, and I work with a lot of Veterans who suffer from trauma as well. Constant, intrusive thoughts and hyper-vigilance interrupt and strain my concentration. I don't understand how non-duality works when I can't turn off my racing thoughts, especially when trying to sleep. How does non-duality help to deal with this?"

Adyashanti gathered his thoughts briefly before responding. I felt vulnerable with the piercing eyes of the entire room staring at me.

"Thank you for asking such an important question," Adyashanti said with a smile. "The greatest freedom is freedom from self. And the self I am speaking of is also the traumatized self."

I responded, "What do I do with thoughts that are waiting to shake me awake in the middle of the night?"

I was very surprised and honored that our exchange lasted at least twenty minutes. Adyashanti offered many helpful insights that seemed relevant, but he could accurately sense I was still unclear.

Eventually, he leaned back, smiled, and made a suggestion. "There is someone I think who may be helpful to you. His name is Dr. Richard Miller, and he works with Veterans. He has done a lot of research around mindfulness and trauma. Perhaps he is a person you should speak with."

I was immensely grateful. Adyashanti and his words were helpful, but I needed someone who deeply understood trauma. We smiled and nodded in prayer as I thanked him, and I ended the event with a sense of hope and anticipation.

The following day, after some preliminary research on Richard Miller's work and the Integrative Restoration program he created, I left a message for him with his staff. I mentioned that Adyashanti had suggested I reach out to him about his work with Veterans. Within a week, I received a note from Richard. He had agreed to speak with me.

I wish I could say I came to Richard with a beginner's mind, but instead, I rambled on a bit more than I had intended. He graciously listened to my story about the loss of my son and my exploration into many healing modalities and bodies of work relating to trauma.

When Richard spoke, his generous presence created a sense that he was walking with his arm warmly around my shoulders, like he was walking with me in the direction I was heading. I felt that he heard me and understood in the very same way Glad had always made me feel. Richard was yet another messenger who appeared on my path, right on cue.

Our conversation ended with an agreement to learn more about each other's work. I committed to attending an upcoming teacher training Richard would be teaching on iRest, the mindfulness process he had developed. The week-long retreat could not have come at a better time. I was a Wounded Healer in need of relief. I said a silent prayer, thanking Glad for conspiring with the universe on my behalf.

I had always struggled with maintaining *no-mind* when attempting to meditate. Imagining intrusive thoughts as clouds that appeared and faded off into the distance didn't work for more than a few moments. The thoughts I tried to see as clouds kept returning, over and over.

Throughout the retreat with Richard, I discovered how to give my recurrent thoughts a presence and realized that, somehow, in some way, they were returning to get my attention. Perhaps they were messengers, providing lessons I needed to learn. Or they were unresolved experiences needing clarity or closure. I quickly found they may not need to return if I created a space to understand what they wanted and needed from me, and what I could do to satisfy them.

The instant I understood these missing puzzle pieces and how they fit into my psyche, I felt a sense of ease and relief. The more I practiced allowing my repetitive thoughts to have a presence, the more I learned how to address and satisfy their needs. And, just as Richard had promised, most of my troubling thoughts stopped recurring. People and situations would still trigger me, but with iRest, I found I could lessen the intensity and duration of my episodes and self-regulate my emotions more quickly.

Not long after the training, I attended a three-day, silent retreat with Richard in Northern California at a monastic retreat center. Initially, I was very resistant to the thought of being silent for days and didn't understand how it would be helpful. As an extrovert, this was unfamiliar territory. Eating meals, gathering, and quietly finding my way around to meeting rooms with at least a hundred other people also operating in silence didn't sound interesting.

I could not have been more oblivious in my thinking.

During this retreat, we came together several times each day to hear Richard speak about Yoga Nidra, non-duality, and mindfulness, and he would then guide us through visualizations he had developed.

I will never forget my moment of realization during the retreat. It was so profound that I burst into laughter—until belatedly realizing everyone was staring at me. I was embarrassed but relieved and amused. I had opened a gift from the universe, and it was bursting through me.

We had just completed a visualization exercise that had taken us into a state of pure awareness. There, I felt a warm and present feeling of openness. As I stretched and breathed deeply, I whispered to myself, "I am inviting awareness to be more present in my life."

In a blinding flash of the obvious, the universe echoed back, "*I* am inviting *awareness* to be more present in my life."

"I," my ego, the separateness within me created by my thinking mind, was inviting "awareness" to be more present in my life.

In a nanosecond, a cosmic bolt of energy from the universe cracked me open. Then came the giggles, followed by my full-bellied outburst of laughter.

This moment was a testament to Richard's wisdom and insight. I cannot count the number of heavy rocks I took out of my rucksack that morning. I left them all on the metaphorical trail behind me.

Serendipitously, I eventually returned to Adyashanti. It had been a couple of years since my twenty-minute encounter with him at his speaking event. I was in Boulder, Colorado, preparing to go to the airport, when I discovered Adyashanti was speaking at a church in the general direction I would be heading. I took this as a sign from the universe to pay attention.

I arrived just after the event's scheduled lunch break and asked to speak with the person in charge of registration. A young lady approached and asked what she could do to help me, and I shared that I had met Adyashanti several years prior, and he had referred me to Richard Miller. I told her I worked with Veterans and asked if it would be possible for me to sit in on just an hour or so of his event.

I could see she was preoccupied. She told me in a friendly but direct tone, "We can't do that. I'm sorry, you would have to purchase a ticket for the full day." I declined and thanked her as she walked away.

I waited a few minutes to ponder my situation and decided to ask someone else if the person in charge of the event or the promoter was on-site.

"Yes, she is." The person I'd asked pointed to a woman in a suit observing the registration area.

I introduced myself and shared the same information I previously shared with her registration manager. She smiled and said, "Of course. You may stay as long as you like, and there are a good number of open seats. Enjoy yourself."

I thanked her and gave her one of my cards. "If you have an opportunity to give this to Adyashanti, I would appreciate it," I said. As she took it from my hand, she said, "Of course."

I took an aisle seat near the back of the room, so I could make a quiet exit when it came time for me to leave for the airport. Soft music began to play, signaling everyone to return to their seats from the lunch break. Adyashanti walked onto the stage and sat down in silence. He gazed into the eyes of the audience for a few moments before he spoke.

"See through yourself," he said. "It is a consistent mirage."

His spiritual insights and presence grounded the entire room. Just like when I'd attended his event before, he concluded with the same offer: "Would anyone like to ask a question?"

My hand shot up along with a large number of other attendees, and once again, he pointed directly at me and smiled.

I stood confidently this time and said, "In San Diego, a couple of years ago, you referred me to Richard Miller and his work with Veterans. I wanted to thank you. He has been very help—"

Adyashanti interrupted me and held up my business card. "Oh, you're the Veteran guy. I was hoping to have a chance to speak with you."

I was astonished.

We brought our hands together in prayer and exchanged a nod. I thanked him again for introducing me to Richard, and I shared I was collaborating with him to provide scholarships for Veterans through his iRest teacher certification training. It was going well.

I then shared the quote he had offered in our first conversation years before:

"The greatest freedom is freedom from self."

Adyashanti smiled, and I continued, "Through your work and Richard's work, I am very thankful to have found ways to reduce my suffering from trauma since we last spoke. A growing number of Veterans I work with are finding relief as well. Thank you."

I again brought my hands together, and Adyashanti mirrored my gesture of gratitude.

"Thank you," he said. "I look forward to seeing you again. Namaste."

Later, when I told Richard, my now-friend and colleague, about my experience with Adyashanti in Boulder, he was pleased.

We began a conversation about the various forms of breathing that had proven to help the Veterans he worked with relax. I was trying to describe a type of breathing I had experienced all my life when I was in a traumatic situation or when recalling an upsetting event. Richard interjected with a name of a highly researched breathing process he thought I was referring to and began to describe it to me.

"No, that's not it," I replied. "There's something much more intense with my breathing I've experienced when I've been in danger, and it's way more intense than what you're describing."

Richard seemed puzzled I wasn't getting it and felt sure he understood the breathing I was describing.

"Richard," I said bluntly. "Have you ever been hunted? Have you ever been in a life-threatening situation where people are chasing you to hurt you or kill you? What I'm talking about is a type of suspenseful breathing where you are desperately trying to be silent, trying not to be discovered, with people—stalking you just a few feet away—who are trying to sense your presence. It's terrifying, especially if you've been running full out and are trying to catch your breath. your heart is pounding in your ears as you slowly try to breathe in small sips and let the air out super slow like you're trying to fog a window."

Richard listened attentively as I continued. "I'd call it suspenseful breathing. Your heart is pounding so hard in your throat and ears that you are sure you're about to give your position away. Have you ever been in a situation like that, Richard?"

He thought about it and replied, "I have experienced fear but not to that extreme."

He paused to let my energy settle before asking if it would be alright to share a breathing process most Veterans found very helpful when triggered in a similar way.

"Of course," I replied.

"Alright, let's start here," he said. "This is an ancient breathing practice, but for simplicity, in today's terms, I call it square breathing. It's a process of breathing in through your nose for a slow count of five, holding for the slow count of five, releasing for the slow count of five, and holding for the slow count of five, then you begin the process over. Usually, by the third round, you may sense your heart rate begin to slow down and your breathing relax.

"I'm going to take you through the process three times."

I closed my eyes. Richard asked me to relax and instructed me to begin a long inhale through my nose for a slow count of five. "Hold for two, three, four, five. Out for two, three, four, five. Hold, for two, three, four, five." He repeated the process two more times. When we reached the end of the third round, Richard relaxed into a generous silence before asking calmly, "What are you experiencing?"

"My mind is calming, and my body is relaxing; I feel better," I responded. I had always heard of the term "breathwork," but it always sounded so esoteric that it seemed a bit silly to me. But in these precious moments, Richard was revealing to me the depth and wisdom of these ancient practices.

"Very good," Richard said. "This breathing process is yours to use anytime you feel stressed in any way. And, the more often you use this, the more you will begin to experience a sense of relief that you do have the ability to self-regulate at any moment."

It was astonishing to me that a simple breathing process could create such a profound relaxation response. In a masterstroke, Richard had given me the key to unlocking the vault I had pressurized around my heart for so long.

The simple truth Richard had revealed to me? Oxygen was the long sought-after antidote for my anxiety. The more I practiced, the more relief cascaded through my body. More importantly, my sense of ease and well-being was becoming more accessible. Most of my triggering moments became much more manageable and began to diminish, and some vanished entirely.

Intense anxiety persisted in only a few areas of my life, and it had to do with speaking up in meetings and addressing groups of people or when I was caught off guard and triggered. My hands would begin to sweat, and I could feel my chest and throat tightening. My mind created mild panic attacks as it raced and relived my most challenging experiences. The square breathing process diminished the intensity of those episodes, but I was still too much in my head to pull back and gain altitude.

Eventually, I realized I needed to go deeper in the square breathing process to anchor the relaxation response further. I had become an intermediate yoga practitioner over the years and had experienced many guided visualizations using ancient hand gestures called *mudras*. In many cultures, mudras are used in the practice of mediation. After practicing a number of them, I discovered I needed something I could use in real-life moments when interacting with people without bringing unnecessary attention to myself. If I used a typical traditional mudra in a stressful situation or business meeting to calm myself down, the people around me would be more fixated on my hand gesture than what I was trying to convey.

The solution that worked for me was to use my non-dominant hand to create a simple mudra. I put the tip of my thumb, index, and middle fingers together while going through the square breathing process. I took any chance I found to practice the three-finger technique while breathing, whether it was driving in my car, walking, or anywhere else. Eventually, the practice solidified such a relaxation response that if I put my fingers together, my body would instantly be triggered to respond. It was as if pressing my fingers together would automatically result in a deep inhale through my nose. In meetings, I could have my hand in my lap or in my pocket, leaving my dominant hand to gesture while talking, pointing, and writing. It was easy and natural, and my life got easier the more I practiced.

Over the years, I have listened to Adyashanti and Richard while driving, relaxing, and introducing their work to friends.

Had I not seen Adyashanti speak, and had he not picked me from the audience, I would not have met Richard Miller. Thank you, Glad—and the universe—for conspiring on my behalf to bring them into my life.

CHAPTER 30

Vision Quest

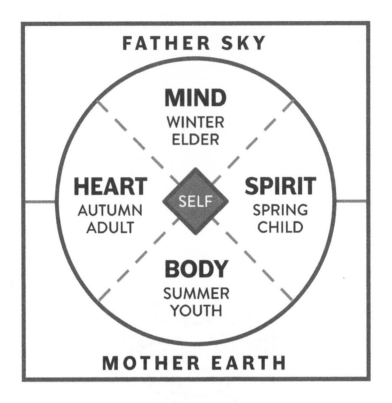

In preparation for the first anniversary of Danny's passing, to honor him and keep him always present, I dedicated myself to doing something meaningful and transformative.

I was fortunate to be invited to participate in a vision quest with a First Nations tribal elder in the foothills of Calgary. Her name was Doreen, and I shall be forever thankful for the contribution the vision quest experience contributed to my life.

The First Nations and Native American tribes throughout North America practice vision quests as a rite-of-passage ceremony. This involves deep spiritual preparation and prolonged fasting. The ceremony typically lasts four to five days and is an individual, practiced isolation experience that takes place in a remote, wilderness area. Traditionally, these rituals are undertaken to mark significant life transitions, such as maturing from adolescence into adulthood and for warriors in their transition home from war to prepare them to rejoin their family and community. The initiate spends time in the wilderness with nature, fasting in total isolation with no food or water and searching for a vision that will serve them in their life.

The elder carried her nation's heritage and ancient wisdom with a stern but caring nature. When she spoke, there was an intention and seriousness that commanded my profound respect and attention.

Day One

Though she had explained what we were about to go through and I understood the process, nothing truly could have prepared me for what would unfold in the days and nights ahead. There was no food for four days and four nights, no water, no talking, no fire, no journaling, no technology whatsoever, and no reading except for the tribal diagram I'd drawn of the Four Directions during the orientation she had given the day prior. It was the only thing we were allowed to view and study during our time in the wilderness. I was to bring the clothes on my back, a blanket, a medicine pouch, a pipe, and tobacco to be offered in gratitude and respect to the elder when she came to check on us each evening.

I had many extended and challenging wilderness experiences in the military but had always been able to stay fed and fully hydrated. The decision to participate in this was an extreme challenge to me, and I felt both anticipation and apprehension as we prepared to depart into the wilderness.

Our guide gathered a party of six initiates together after our orientation and instructed us to speak no further as we departed in silence. I would only see the other initiates one other time at the conclusion of our vision quest. We drove together through the remote foothills of the Canadian Rockies somewhere between Calgary and Bamff. After an hour or so, we arrived at an encampment occupied by a woman tending a large bonfire. As I exited the vehicle, I could feel the warmth of the sun and the crispness of a mountain breeze flowing through the trees. The leaves and grass were dancing with the wind.

Our elder guide asked each of us to find a stone that spoke to us from the dry riverbed and told us to sit around the bonfire. I found an interesting heart-shaped stone. One side was rough and the other was smooth and the color of milky pink. I could lay it flat on the ground, and the shape of the heart seemed fitting for the work I was here to do.

"Place your stone into the fire," the elder stated. "This act signifies that you, like the stone, are entering this experience together. When you return with your vision, I will ask you to find your stone and to take it with you back into the world to remind you of what you have experienced here together."

And with that, she stood and motioned for us to depart in silence and follow her. In single file, we meandered through the beautiful meadows and woods in wonderment of what was to come. The elder walked with a sense of vitality and the agility of a mountain goat. Her presence was reassuring and intentional, with no fear and no hesitation whatsoever. I was impressed and humbled by the way she took in all of her surroundings. As I observed her calm yet powerful way of being, I felt a sincere intention emerge that perhaps this experience would help me harness that same strength and certainty within myself.

Every mile or so, she stopped and took one of us by the arm as she gestured for the rest of us to wait. She walked the chosen initiate into the woods, out of sight, and returned alone after a short time to continue leading us through the wilderness.

As we continued up the hill, we came upon a meadow of beautiful purple, yellow, and white wildflowers. Nestled in the tree line on the far side of the space sat a stitched, animal skin tipi. It was right out of a majestic photograph you would find in a *National Geographic*. As I paused for a moment to take it all in, overwhelmed by the beauty and the scents of the wild, I realized I hadn't been immersed in nature for many years. Our guide gently took me by the hand and pulled my arm up to her side. We smiled at one another as she gestured for me to escort her across the meadow to the tipi.

When we arrived, she put my hands in hers and looked into my eyes. "This is where you will stay for the coming days and nights. I will come to see you each evening for a few moments." She paused and gazed at me, and her eyes probed deeply into my confusion and pensiveness. "There is no place to go and nothing to do but to be still and be with yourself," she added. Her strength and ancient wisdom held my complete attention as I looked into her eyes. I nodded with my hands in prayer to acknowledge her message. With a reassuring smile, she turned and made her way back across the meadow and into the tree line.

I entered the tipi and sat in silence, alone, wondering what I had gotten myself into. A sense of reality came over me: my vision quest had begun. Four days and four nights of this experience suddenly seemed incredibly long.

My mind began to ruminate on the concern that I may die of dehydration after three days. That was, of course, the prevailing belief of countless experts I had found on my internet searches before our trip. I also had many recurring thoughts of hunger and starvation, but I knew that humans had endured periods of famine far longer than this and had survived. Really, hydration was my paramount concern.

How could this ritual have been practiced since ancient times? It then occurred to me the research experts were not of Native American or First Nations heritage. They had no firsthand experience of actually doing a vision quest.

This is a rite of passage, and I trust this ancient wisdom, I said to myself. As I reflected on my elder guide's strength and experience, I found I could tap into a small sense of her resolve and declared, "This must be possible! I'm doing this!"

I made a pillow out of my jacket and lay back to take in the surroundings. The warm sunlight illuminated the tipi's animal skins, and the smell of leather and charcoal from the fire pit just outside of the entrance permeated the air. An awareness came over me that generations of people had been in ceremony in this sacred space before me. In gratitude, I imagined their faces and ways of being.

As the sun began to lower into the late afternoon, I decided to leave the tipi to familiarize myself with the surroundings. We were instructed not to wander far from where we were placed, and the meadow provided an area to walk in a large circle while still in view of the tipi.

Hawks circled above, and the scent of pine, wildflowers, and meadow grass eased my mind. As dusk came, I returned to the tipi and settled into an eerie silence. I looked past the tipi to the meadow and had my first realization that I had wholly entered the ceremony of my vision quest. There were no distractions to provide an escape from the present moment. It felt strangely welcome.

As the sun began to set, I felt the first pangs of hunger.

After a few hours of nervously sitting silently in the darkness, the sound of the elder's voice pierced the night. "Aho."

I came through the door of the tipi to see the elder sitting next to the fire pit. She was waiting for me to sit across from her. There was a chill in the air, but it wasn't cold. Still, I ruminated on how nice a fire would have been all evening.

I offered her my tobacco, and she smiled as she packed it into her pipe. As she lit the tobacco and blew puffs of smoke, she paid her respects to the Four Directions.

"This is your time to be still while you wait for your vision to come to you," she said in a reassuring tone. "Let go of your busy life and all things cluttering your mind." She handed me the pipe, as now it was my turn to repeat the pipe ceremony.

After I was finished, she stood. "I will go now, and I will return tomorrow evening," she said firmly. And with a smile and a nod, she faded into the darkness.

The ancient wisdom I was receiving was humbling. *How many generations of First Nations people have received their vision on this sacred ground?* I wondered.

Day Two

At sunrise, I awoke to a breeze rustling the hides of the tipi. I stretched and let out a groan as my senses filled once again with the smell of leather. I had completed the first night of my vision quest, and this was the beginning of day two.

My food cravings kicked in, but a cup of coffee would have been a meal. Coffee had been my morning ritual as far as I could remember, and I meditated on the rich smell and flavor of espresso and cream with the sweetness of a few drops of maple syrup.

"Mmm, that would be nice," I said out loud.

As my delicious coffee meditation evaporated, my focus turned to a sense of curiosity. I wondered what the day would hold.

Surprisingly, my food cravings were subsiding, and my focus moved from the body sensations of hunger to a question that had been looming since I opened my eyes at dawn. There were three days and three nights remaining. I wondered what I was supposed to do today, tomorrow, and the next day.

Within a few hours, I began to notice more and more of what was happening in my surroundings. I decided to take off my boots and socks to feel the ground under my bare feet. I smiled at the realization that I was a guest in this wild paradise. The chill of dirt under my feet inspired me to stop and feel Mother Earth. I remembered the illustrations I had made from the elder's talk. She had walked us through the Four Directions as a small group to prepare us, and she encouraged us to focus on them during our vision quest.

I understood our vision quest's purpose was, first and foremost, to deepen our relationship with the Creator and the Four Directions. Second, it was to open within ourselves what had been closed from our life's conditioning and experiences. Our journey was to find a way of moving and being in the world with more ease and clarity. The elder had shared that when we are aligned with the natural order of the world around us, our lives take on a deeper sense of meaning and purpose.

As the elder had explained it, the Four Directions are ancient teachings that inform us of the perfect and natural harmony between our inner and outer worlds and our connectedness with all things. These teachings return us to our ancestral voices to heal and reconcile the conflicts within us. They help us understand our relationship with our Creator, plants, animals, and nature and the power they hold for healing the wounds of the heart, mind, and soul.

Standing barefoot in a beautiful meadow of grass and flowers with the sun on my cheeks, bird songs all around, and the wind through the swaying trees was the essence of tranquil solitude. I turned my face upward and held my arms out, hands open and outstretched in gratitude. My eyes softened as I inhaled slowly and deeply to take in all of nature's fragrances. For the first time since I could remember, I felt a sense of peace with myself and the world.

If this is all I'm to do in my time here, I am happy, I thought.

It was the first small awakening of my journey, and it paved the way for things to come.

When I returned to the tipi, my heart was open, and I was curious to learn more about these ancient ways. My eyes circled the simplicity of the mandala illustration I had drawn and marveled at the layers of meaning and symmetry, all in perfect harmony.

The meadow of Mother Earth and the beautiful horizon of Father Sky became very real for me. Surrounded by them, I could see the nature of my growth and development from a child into young adulthood, my maturation into adulthood and, someday, my end-of-life journey as an elder. Considering these phases of growth gave me a sense of ease that a purpose and usefulness awaited me as I continued to mature.

Time passed and my thoughts deepened as I continued to slowly walk the lush, green space. Each time, I arrived in the center to stand with my arms relaxed down to my sides, hands outstretched. The soles of my feet ground into Mother Earth, my eyes gazed into Father Sky, and I repeatedly gave thanks for my existence and opened myself to the vision I came to receive.

After the sun had climbed higher in the sky, I lay spread-eagle in the meadow and remained in awe that way for most of the day. I smelled the flowers, stared into the clouds and felt gratitude for the gifts I was receiving. It was a perfect summer day on the foothills of the Canadian Rockies.

The symmetry and balance of the diagram I had drawn earlier began to connect all around me. From the air I was breathing to the ground I was feeling, everything was in perfect harmony. "Thank you," were the only two words I could conjure and speak, repeatedly, as I awoke to the harmony of all things.

There was no hunger, no thirst; all of the nourishment I needed for my body and soul, I already possessed. My mind was clearing itself of chatter, and I realized the colors of the flowers and trees were becoming more crisp and vivid.

A sense of power and immense fortitude started to build and emanate from within me. Something transformative was beginning, and it was only day two of my time in the wilderness.

In the journey of my lifetime, I had experienced both the severity and comfort of knowing the predictable seasons of spring, summer, autumn, and winter.

The quaternity of spirit, body, heart, and mind was in perfect harmony with the seasons of my life as I envisioned where I was heading. Suddenly, I realized I was envisioning my future with a sense of ease and anticipation instead of the anxiety and apprehension that had discolored it just a few hours before. Something was beginning to settle within me as I smiled and filled my lungs with air. I welcomed its message—*let go*—and I exhaled with a long sigh.

I was in the autumn years of my journey and imagined that I would someday be an elder. This would come with an honor-bound responsibility to pass what I had learned in my lifetime to others as they awakened on their own journey.

The center of the mandala, symbolizing my deepest self, now felt true and aligned at my core with a quality and sensation of warmth and ease.

As I gazed at the beauty of my surroundings and pondered the ancient teachings being imparted to me, the sensations of lying on Mother Earth grounded and tethered my deepest self. I was here to receive my vision, and for the first time since beginning my time in the wilderness, I stopped anticipating what it would be. My thinking mind, otherwise always needing to make meaning, surrendered, and I felt a sense of ease and relief.

A pair of hawks caught my eye, and I watched them circle in a dance together. I've been told by my Native American friends that this was a good omen. I received this sign as an acknowledgment of the respect I found for the Four Directions.

The afternoon sun moved toward the horizon as I prepared for the evening ahead. It was astonishing to me that I had minimal food cravings and no feelings of dehydration. I knew I was here, experiencing this exact moment, to receive wisdom. Though I felt grounded in my relationship with the Four Directions, I was feeling a little anxious to share the day's learnings with the elder when she returned.

As the galaxy opened the heavens, I sat in the moonlit darkness and reflected on the beautiful day I had been gifted. It wasn't long before the elder appeared with a quiet "Aho" to announce her presence.

"How have you been since I last visited?" she asked in a polite tone.

"I'm deeply grateful for today," I replied. As expected, she pulled her pipe from her medicine bag, and I offered her my tobacco. While filling her pipe, she asked, "What did you see?"

"I saw my relationship with the Four Directions and felt a sense of peace I have never felt before," I replied, then I paused in reflection. The gentle sounds of the bugs chirping in the meadow surrounded us. "I'm thankful you shared these ancient teachings with me."

"Share with me what you have learned," she instructed kindly. The elder stared into my eyes, looking for truth or confusion.

"I spent most of the day circling the meadow barefoot, and I felt the energy of Mother Earth," I explained. "I felt the warmth of the sun and looked into the clouds and the stars of Father Sky. I saw my path from a child into young adulthood and how my life is maturing toward someday becoming an elder. I saw the changing seasons as the cycle of life, and I saw my relationship with spirit, body, heart, and mind as my deeper self."

She continued to look into my being. The smoke from her pipe swirled into the sky in pale gray and lavender wisps. Grateful for her time and attention, I continued, "It was a day of deep reflection and awakening for me, and it's fitting that I would be here to learn this wisdom as I honor my son's passing. Thank you."

She puffed her pipe several times and honored the Four Directions. As she handed it to me to repeat the ceremony, she reassured me, "This is good. It is important that you do not fall back asleep, into the dream of your life before today. To remain awake with this wisdom, you must sit with the Four Directions until the sun rises."

And with a firm "Aho!" she placed her pipe in her pouch and stood. "I will visit you again tomorrow." Once again, she turned and faded into the darkness.

I knew this was my time of great awakening. The stars were standing sentinel above me, and I realized they were my companions, there to ensure I would receive the ancient wisdom into my bones.

For many hours, I reflected upon the layers of wisdom and felt a letting go of unwelcome, useless beliefs and conditioned ways of being that no longer served me.

The starry night soon turned into early morning and brought with it a bracing chill. I wrapped myself with the Afghan patoo wool shawl my son had brought me from his deployment to the mountains of Afghanistan. It was a beautifully rich and tightly woven garment that was both cooling in the heat and incredibly warm in the cold. It had been with me on many medicine journeys, sweat lodges, and expeditions, and I always wore it in ceremonies to honor Danny when he lived. Now, I honored his passing. Wearing it brought me closer to him.

As the light of the sun began to show through the trees, I again ventured to the center of the meadow to take in the beauty. The quiet serenity was awe-inspiring. The morning air was cold and crisp, and as I gazed into the sunrise, a calm acknowledgment came over me. My life had transcended into a higher resonance, and I was well provisioned for the spiritual journey ahead.

Day Three

The elder had predicted the third day would bring changes to our awareness. I had returned to the tipi, and as I looked around it and through the entrance to the meadow, the vibrant colors were noticeably more saturated than the day before.

The breeze rustled the swaying trees, and their boughs danced with the waves of flowers that blanketed Mother Earth, and as the wind cascaded across the meadow, she was waking my senses.

I left the tipi again and leaned back against a nearby tree, dozing in and out of a light sleep until I heard the distinct sound of distant giggling. I distinguished there were two people; perhaps they were hikers walking nearby. It could not have been others in our party because we had vowed to remain silent throughout our journey. After a few moments, I slipped back into my solitude only to wake again with more giggling. This time, it was much closer.

I closed my eyes to open my awareness and was surprised to sense the laughter had moved. Now, it was just above me in the trees. I could discern two distinct voices: one of a man and one of a woman.

I looked up to see the likeness of two people. They were sitting with their backs toward me, eight or ten feet above me in the trees.

I knew they weren't real, but yet, they were. I blinked my eyes, but the figures remained. If anything, they were becoming clearer.

They turned toward each other, snickering, and it was immediately obvious they were laughing about me and wanted me to know it. They turned and looked down at me, still snickering, and my mouth dropped open. With a rush of excitement, I recognized Danny's smile and, beside him, Glad's angelic face. They were as real and present as the pine needles and branches all around them.

"We've been here the whole time," they both declared as they broke out in hysterical laughter. Breathless, I looked from one to the other as the sunlight winked off their forms. Every distinguishing feature I loved and missed about both of them was real, and my heart soared. Uncontrollable tears of joy began to flow from my eyes, dripping down my chin and onto the earth.

"We are *fine*. And so are you, John," Glad promised, and they both nodded, smiling in agreement. Birds sang in the background, creating a beautiful symphony punctuated by her crystal-clear voice.

Danny chimed in. "Dad, I *am* fine, and I'm *here*. We are always here; you have never really been alone." My heart beat hard and strong in my chest. Still crying, I nodded at him. Just hearing he was okay provided me with a sense of peace I had been longing for since his passing.

Glad asked, "Do you remember when you were a young boy, I shared with you that God is love?"

"Yes," I replied, drinking in her face and voice.

"Do you believe this to be true?" she asked.

"Because I believe you, it has to be true!" I replied, wiping the tears from my face. "But honestly, this hasn't been my experience. If God is love, why have all the terrible things happened in my life?"

"The answer is in your question, John," she responded with a gentle smile. A rush of wind rustled the trees again and swept across the meadow in great, rolling waves. "There is goodness in you, and you have made this journey here, to this very moment, because deep down you still believe this has to be true. Your life experiences have guided you here and are preparing you for your journey ahead."

That pricked a place of pain within me. I missed them both so much. "How has pain, trauma, and abuse prepared me?" I asked defiantly.

Glad responded calmly, "This is the riddle you have been struggling to solve since you were very young."

I nodded. "That riddle has troubled me my entire life, ever since you first shared it with me," I said. "But in my worst moments, God didn't enter my mind until after I'd survived. *Why is this happening to me?* screamed louder. And then I would think, *God isn't love, and he certainly doesn't love me.*"

"The pain and suffering of your life—do you believe this is all that you are?" she inquired.

I was so tired of hurting. "I know pain. I know suffering, rage, and anxiety," I responded, frustration coloring my voice.

Danny spoke up again. "What about the agreement you asked me to make with you when I was eight years old? You told me how violent and abusive my grandfather had been to you. You said you would never repeat that abuse with me and wanted me to agree that we would never raise a hand to each other in anger. Remember?"

"Of course," I replied quietly. I looked at my son sitting in the tree. "I just wanted to shield you from what I had experienced."

Glad asked, "What emotions were present for you when you wanted to shield Danny? When you asked Danny to make this agreement, were you in pain? Were you suffering? Or enraged? At that moment, what were you feeling?"

"Love," I said immediately. The answer had bubbled out of me unexpectedly and almost automatically.

"Yes," she agreed. "Your love for Danny and desire to keep him safe." More firmly now, she added, "At that moment, was love more powerful than your pain and suffering?"

The blue sky behind Glad and Danny haloed them in brilliance. A new understanding began to rise in my chest. "Yes, it was," I replied more clearly.

"Had you not known pain and suffering, you would not have known the power of love and how it could keep Danny safe," she explained. "The pain and suffering you have experienced is real, and these experiences actually happened. But they have also given you the gift of compassion and empathy rooted in your suffering. Your greatest gift is your ability to serve others because of the life experiences you have endured. Through your suffering, you have been given the gift of empathy. Can you let this into your heart?"

"Yes, I think I can," I said, feeling her wisdom empower me one heartbeat at a time. "It makes sense. Why else would I have been put through all of this?"

At once, the elder's voice echoed loudly in my mind: *When you live in your pain and try to help others, you become the Wounded Healer.*

With a surge of clarity, it hit me: *that* was who I was, the Wounded Healer.

As this realization came over me, a light rain began to fall. It was late in the afternoon, and I hadn't noticed the clouds darkening in the sky. I stood under the pine tree beneath Glad and Danny, feeling the mist on my face while my realization settled.

And then, just as they had appeared, my vision of Danny and Glad began to fade. I knew I would always miss them, but there was no sadness as they echoed, *"We are always here."*

We smiled at each other, and the three of us gently whispered, "I love you."

The rain grew stronger, I felt the need to be cleansed. I stripped naked and walked to the meadow's center. I stood in deep meditation, arms outstretched, and allowed the rainwater to cleanse my face, my being, and my soul of all my suffering. My mind eased into gratitude. The empathy I had for others was because of my life experiences—all of them. Nothing could be excluded, as each had shaped me into the person I was, the person who received this message in this moment.

Through my pain and suffering, I finally found a place of honesty and truth.

This was the profound vision I came to receive: the understanding of empathy.

I returned from the meadow emotionally drained. I slipped under the blanket Danny had given me to warm myself and quickly faded off to a peaceful sleep.

Hours later, I woke to the voice of the elder calling my name. It was dark and still lightly raining, so I invited her into the tipi.

I offered tobacco to fill her pipe, and we sat in silence, patiently lighting and puffing her pipe as we once again honored the Four Directions. With each sharing of my tobacco, my respect for my elder guide grew immensely.

When we concluded, she asked, "What did you see?"

As I gazed at her, she sat, wise and patient, looking into my eyes.

Finally, I found the words to describe my experience. "It was as though a prayer was answered," I said. "*God is love* has been a mystery to me since early childhood. Today, I discovered in my vision that not only is it true, *God is love* provides me with the empathy for other suffering I have been looking past. My pain and suffering wouldn't allow me to see anything else until now.

"Throughout my life, my suffering and emotional numbness left me feeling unworthy of love. From before I could even speak, I thought there was something wrong with me. Why else would such terrible things be happening to me? Until this afternoon, I hadn't understood how my suffering was a catalyst. This wisdom has been revealed to me to keep me from falling back asleep, and I need to share it with the people I love and with a world that is suffering. The purpose of my suffering has been the gift of empathy, my ability to share another's feelings. I empathize with others' pain and suffering because I have deeply suffered."

The elder nodded. Rain pelted the animal hides that sheltered us. "This is good."

Day Four (Integration)

I woke on my fourth day feeling incredibly vibrant. My mind was calm and clear—I felt no stress, no hunger, and no thirst whatsoever. As I lay on the tipi floor, gazing up at the stitching and the sun as it glowed through the hides, I felt I could easily go without food or water for many more days.

Reflecting on my experiences over the last few days, I felt a moment of truth had emerged. I had learned something profound about myself, and it could not have happened in any other way. My narrow view of the path I had been on for my life had expanded. Now I could see there was so much more, and there was a larger plan for me. Instead of viewing my life and circumstances from the prism of victimhood and seeing the world from inside the effects of my trauma, I was outside of my history, drawing wisdom and healing from the suffering I had endured.

I saw that I no longer needed to withdraw and shield my insecurities from the world.

Until just a few days prior, my life had been about fitting in and doing my best to appear healthy on every level. I needed to be seen by others as impeccable, but my inner conflict was consuming massive amounts of my available energy.

Chronic depression had always been lurking just below the surface, and I continuously judged myself harshly for never being good enough, smart enough, or strong enough. The internal fortitude it took to hold this toxic duality together was unsustainable, and I knew this at my core. I referred to my struggles with this conflict of duality as chronic dissatisfaction. No matter how much I accomplished, I could never outrun my low self-worth or the feeling that something was wrong with me.

Now, after starving and dehydrating myself for three days and three nights to enter this heightened spiritual state of clarity, I was overwhelmed with gratitude. I had let go of my pain and embraced the wisdom of empathy. It was a quiet shift that was mine and no one else's.

My newfound spiritual grounding tethered me to a deep sense of knowing that I was transcending the protective armor surrounding my wounds. The boundaries and walls which were, at one time, necessary for my survival were collapsing into wholeness. I no longer saw myself as broken.

This fourth day of integration, reflection, and preparation before returning to the world outside of the bubble I had been visiting was coming to a close.

As darkness came, the elder arrived to visit me for the last time.

As we sat together in ceremony, I enjoyed the gentleness of her presence. We honored the Four Directions and again shared tobacco.

The experience of my vision quest was beyond words, as she knew it would be. She smiled and waved as she disappeared into the darkness as magically as she had appeared.

I gazed into the galaxy of stars and honored the Four Directions and my sacred space. The warmth of the tipi called, and I fell gently into a deep and peaceful sleep.

When I woke the next morning, I was energized with the thought of completion. My vision quest had come to an end, and it was time to circle up with the others.

At the beginning of our experience, we had been told to wake at sunrise and return to the camp where we had arrived days before. Within a short time, all of us had gathered, and we marveled at how each of our appearances had changed since seeing each other last. We were all thinner and a bit grimy, but each of us was pleasantly calm, smiling, and beaming. We were radiant and joyful, grateful for the gifts our guide had helped us open.

The elder guide asked us to join her around the fire and to bring the stone we had selected on our first day of the ceremony. The heart-shaped stone I had chosen had broken into two halves from the fire's heat and fit perfectly back together. I held the pieces in my hands on my lap and felt their healing energy. They represented the parts of me that had become whole. A smile came over me, and I took this as a sign that I had healed my Wounded Healer's broken heart. I gently wrapped the halves in a small piece of animal hide and placed them into my medicine bag.

The elder shared a few final words of wisdom and congratulated us on the completion of our vision quest. She then gestured for us to come to the other side of her camp, where she had prepared a meal for us to enjoy. What I found incredible was that I felt I could have gone many more days without food. But when I saw the massive kettle of buffalo stew alongside a platter of biscuits, that notion completely vanished. The first bowl was finished almost as soon as I sat down. Within a minute or two, we were all lining up for second servings. The large, meaty pieces of buffalo and potatoes soaking in the thick and hearty broth was heaven, and it was one of the absolute best meals I have ever enjoyed.

CHAPTER 31

The Plant Medicine Journeys

"I slept and dreamt that life was joy.
"I awoke and saw that life was service.
"I acted, and behold, service was joy."

—RABINDRANATH TAGORE

My life and who I was becoming were being borne purposefully along deeper currents, regardless of the stress and challenges of everyday life. Although I had found my purpose—being of service to others—and though it provided me with a great sense of satisfaction, the experience of joy still eluded me.

I liken the journey inward into my personal transformation to opening the layers of a Russian matryoshka doll. Cracking open one layer would simply reveal the next. The thick outer shell of each breakthrough or insight would bring a sense of anticipation—*Is this it?*—only to discover the next layer's hard, protective surface.

I began to grow more and more concerned that whatever resided in my deepest, darkest self, once opened, might not fit back in the bottle. As I inched closer, I needed to be mindful of how I opened the container.

As Maria would say, "Nevertheless, I am willing."

No matter what I learned, how far I'd grown, or how much understanding I had gained about myself, the magma deep within my core remained. After all I had learned and experienced, now I was aware *this* was where I needed to drop in.

It was clear to me that what I was moving away from was pain. In the Marines, we looked at pain as weakness leaving the body. I discovered that, if appropriately channeled, pain could be a potent ally and a source of motivation. My pain kept me moving in countless dangerous encounters instead of being stuck and paralyzed.

My heart-opening vision quest experience with Glad and Danny had worked to reinforce Glad's promise that truly *God is love*. But not long after returning to the realities of my existence and lived experiences of the world I lived in—in physical reality—I soon found my realization fading. I now felt two opposite feelings at war within myself: joy and pain.

I looked upon joy and *God is love* as a magic elixir I sought at the end of my hero's journey; it was my "why" that would keep me going as I marched through hell to find it. The layers to be excavated within me needed to be unearthed like an archeological dig, first identifying what I discovered before hopefully transcending it.

At the time, I believed *God is love* and the joy that came with it was the Russian doll's final small chamber, existing just beneath my magma until a stark realization came to me.

Why would molten magma of rage and retribution be guarding my joy?

A quote from Maria came to mind: "That which is defenseless need not be defended."

Joy doesn't require protection or shielding; it is defenseless.

It hit me like a punch in the gut, pulling all of my energy and leaving a sickening feeling in my solar plexus. It was my wounded and wild inner child. I had stumbled upon him peering out at me, and he was threatened by the pressure of my surrounding siege. He was frantically blocking the entrance inward.

It reminded me of a bumper sticker I had seen many years before: *I met my inner child, and he's a mean little fucker!*

That summed it up.

The pressure I was feeling was my mean inner child underneath the armored layer of magma, screaming commands to my monkey mind who nervously chattered away as its interpreter: "He says for you to turn back! He says he will kill you if you come any closer."

This was an insight I had not expected. My wounded inner child was burrowing deeper into hiding as I realized his emissaries, also known as my ego or monkey mind, had been conspiring to take command of my protection since infancy. They were dug in with swords drawn, spears darting through their Spartan shield wall and waiting to destroy any hope my higher self had for change.

Instinctively, I fell back to consider the new insights I gained from my reconnaissance and to assess my choices.

I recalled a large Land Rover freeway sign in the '80s with a split picture. To the left was a Land Rover ascending a rocky mountainside with the slogan, *As Slow as Possible*. To the right was a picture of a Land Rover fording a deep stream at a fast rate of speed with the slogan, *As Fast as Necessary*.

"As slow as possible but as fast as necessary" became my mantra as I prepared and shaped the battlefield for the siege ahead.

I chuckled as I metaphorically slid the sharpening stone down my blade, preparing for the coming assault.

At that moment, another insight came to me: *was it wise to view my mean and wounded inner child as my enemy, as someone needing to be conquered?*

No, I responded with a deep inhale and a sense of relief. *Of course, not.*

The final descent into myself to rescue and heal my mortally wounded inner child was the crucible of my life's quest, but there was no war. I had made this all up as a romantic fantasy of me vanquishing my enemy at the crucible of my quest. I could see this now and smiled as the aggression toward my wounded self subsided.

I will never raise a hand to you in anger.

This would be a mission of peace in uncharted territory, and I would need a guide. When traveling in foreign lands, it is unwise to venture into ancient ruins without a guide who knows the safe paths and the ways of the territory ahead.

My vision quest experience in Calgary brought me back to Glad, and I realized how detached and untethered I'd become since her passing. She helped me discover that my life of pain, trauma, and suffering had to serve a purpose. I was able to feel empathy and vulnerability in a deeper and more meaningful way, and it allowed me to help and serve others. Still, until my days in the wilderness with Glad and Danny, I couldn't get underneath my armor to really feel anything.

Under that armor, I felt a sense of fear, an urgent warning being sounded that I needed to explore deeper inward before my numbness returned.

With Glad as my voice of wisdom, I would find a way.

Another insight emerged. Perhaps I needed to transmute my magma into something more useful. It represented an infinite energy reserve I already possessed; it had simply been misdirected.

If I could transcend the fear and volatility it created within me and recycle this source of power into something purposeful and good, perhaps I could harness it as energy.

Grandmother Ayahuasca

I chose plant medicines and their ancient ceremonies to be my guides.

For decades, I had heard of Ayahuasceros, South American shamans living in the rainforests for thousands of years, using plant medicines for healing physical wounds and trauma while shepherding tribal members through mystical, spiritual journeys.

Used similarly to the way Native Americans use peyote, a Native American plant medicine of North America, ayahuasca is a blend of two plants from the South American rainforest that creates a profound spiritual experience of being with the Creator of All Things. Ayahuasca is referred to with great respect and reverence as *Grandmother*.

Another common aspect of both peyote and ayahuasca is the act of purging the medicine from the body while embarking on the journey. Most people naturally reach a point of vomiting as a physical and symbolic act of cleansing toxins from the body and psyche stored as holograms of our psychological, physical, emotional, and spiritual experiences.

Grandmother's medicine was the next and most profound step on my path to healing and recovery. Glad, once again, illuminated my way forward.

My first ceremony offered itself to me in Vancouver, British Columbia, only a few weeks prior to the second anniversary of Danny's passing. I was told my journey had begun upon my decision to join the ceremony.

What demons would I need to face and let go of?

In preparation for my journey, I was provided a list of foods to avoid to help prepare and cleanse my body and mind in the days prior. I was warned to respect Grandmother's medicine and the spiritual significance of my choice to walk this path. On the day of the journey, I was only to have fruit until noon and then nothing but water for the rest of the day and evening.

I arrived late in the afternoon at the address I was given: a yoga studio with all of the windows blacked out. The studio was in a run-down and grimy industrial area near the waterfront. An experience of this magnitude seemed out of place in this seedy part of Vancouver.

As I entered, I was taken by the welcoming scent of incense and sage. Candles lit the way through a dark entrance area and down a hallway to the studio. A woman approached me in a beautiful flowing robe that caught her figure as she walked. She bowed her head in prayer and whispered, "Namaste," as she gestured for me to follow her.

I was escorted toward a gentleman in the center of the large, wood-floor studio near the wall. He was positioning an array of musical instruments, bird feathers, and singing bowls in front of himself on a large, sheepskin rug. He looked up and reached for my hand.

"Welcome, my friend," he said in a deep, sincere voice. He smiled. "You are the first to arrive. Please find a place against the wall that makes you comfortable. Everyone will be arriving soon."

Over the next thirty minutes, twelve others walked through the entrance, and one by one, they found their places around the large room. We were each given a small blue cleaning bucket to keep with us for when our body would likely purge the medicine. The night was to be shared in total silence, and we were not to leave our yoga mat unless it was to use the restroom.

As evening came, we gathered cross-legged in a circle surrounding the Ayahuascero to prepare for our journey. The Ayahuascero was an interesting fellow who was stoic and disheveled, wearing loose, wrinkled, white cotton pajamas underneath beaded necklaces dripping with pendants and symbols.

We were asked to set an intention for what we would like to change in our lives, and we were advised to remain open to the learnings we were about to receive from Grandmother Ayahuasca.

Our guide knelt before each person and asked about their intentions for the ceremony. As we shared, he smudged us with sage and blew clouds of tobacco smoke onto us and into our being to clear the energetic field of anything we might have brought with us into the sacred space. As each person spoke, I felt unprepared and nervous about what was to come.

The room was completely dark except for the candles surrounding the Ayahuascero and the single candle that marked the entranceway to the hallway and restroom. My monkey mind began to scream, *This is a bad idea!* I was in a dark room with a group of total strangers, which brought up a sense of panic about what had happened to me in the dark years ago, behind Gentleman Jim's.

Our guide poured a dark liquid into a cup a bit larger than a shot glass and gestured to the sky while holding it above his head. He then said a prayer in a language I could not understand and leveled his gaze upon us. In a gentle and reassuring tone, he asked, "Who will be first?"

Instantly, to my right, I sensed the sudden movement of a young man darting across the floor. He resumed a cross-legged position in front of the guide. With his hands in prayer and fingertips touching his forehead, he bowed in respect. He took the small glass from the hands of the Ayahuascero and gestured to the sky as he whispered something. Then, he touched the edge of the glass to his forehead. He then shot the liquid down, whipping his head back to receive every drop.

My nervousness about jumping into the void got the best of me, and I laid back to allow others to go before me. I felt apprehensive and saw this as a possible sign that perhaps I should leave.

One by one, the others nervously ventured through the ritual. When it was finally my turn, I looked at the guide and slowly scooted across the floor and took the glass from his outstretched hands, sensing into the moment with a deep inhale to capture all of the aromas of leather, feathers, tobacco, and sage. As I put the glass to my mouth, my mind raced with the thought that I was crossing a point of no return. When the murky liquid met my lips and tongue, it was so pungent and strong that it made me pause. Steeling myself, I swallowed it in a single gulp, though I almost heaved with the effort of keeping it down. As I winced, I bowed to our guide, whispering, "Namaste," and retreated to my place in the circle. I chugged a large bottle of water to rinse the taste from my mouth.

I sat in contemplation, taking in the sights and aromas of the dimly lit room alongside my fellow journeyers.

Now finished with the first step in our journey, our guide said a prayer to Grandmother Ayahuasca and suggested we relax in silence and wait for what was to come.

I made myself comfortable and thought about what had brought me here.

I imagined the ancestral meaning of this sacred ceremony. It had guided the people of ancient civilizations through their life transitions—growing into manhood, coming home from war, becoming a leader, and eventually, the transition of becoming an elder. I was now crossing the threshold of an entirely new realm of my spiritual journey, perhaps even more profound than my sweat lodge experiences and even the vision quest I'd experienced a year prior.

In my work with transitioning Veterans, I was fascinated with the stories of how ancient cultures brought warriors back into their communities and families. Plant medicines were known to transcend war traumas, allowing the warrior to reconnect not only to themselves but to the source of all things. I began to meditate on the Four Directions taught to me by the elder Cree woman in Calgary.

The diagram I had memorized of the Four Directions appeared in my mind, and I smiled in gratitude, knowing I had been provisioned for this journey.

The gentle sound of a Peruvian shaker began to pulse to a quiet rhythm, and the Ayahuascero began to sing and chant in an ancient language. As he circled the floor at our feet, I could hear the large group of feathers in his hands catching the air. When he drew near, a gentle breeze from his feathers gently flowed over me as he chanted.

In that exact instant, a seismic tremor hit my energetic field, and a sense of disorientation began to well up inside of me. My breathing began to falter slightly, and a light buzzing started to flow through my temples. I was entering the journey.

Within minutes, the experience began to intensify. I was transported back to moments of rapid altitude acceleration during a helicopter takeoff. It was exciting and terrifying, but this time, I had no parachute.

Suddenly, a visual splashed into my mind. It was a guy from an old Bose surround sound system ad, sitting in an armchair with his sunglasses on, hair blowing back from the sound coming straight at him from a large speaker.

Holy shit! I screamed to myself while gripping and stretching the blanket Danny had brought me from Afghanistan. The velocity of the experience took me completely by surprise. Gripping my blanket brought me an image of Danny, smiling and shouting in excitement as we ascended into the heavens. The more I attempted to control it, the faster I accelerated. I imagined Danny and me launching from Cape Canaveral in the space shuttle, strapped in with our faces stretched from the takeoff's velocity and watching the moon grow larger as we drew closer.

I suddenly felt queasy. A convulsion erupted in my stomach, and a small amount of acid purged upward. Still, I wasn't willing to let go and forced myself to swallow instead of surrendering. Eventually, the nausea subsided, and I felt the velocity slowing like a commercial jet popping up above the storm clouds.

And then, almost as quickly as we had been launched from the earth's surface, I found myself entering into the most peaceful silence I have ever known. I took a long, deep inhale through my nose, and a sensation of spaciousness came over me, bringing a pleasant smile to my face. I felt the weight of my human existence leave my shoulders and neck, and my hands fell to the floor outstretched. Every part of my body relaxed and sank into the floor, leaving nothing but a feeling of bliss.

The tension in my temples vanished, and my jaw opened wide as I let out a deep, long groan of relief.

There was no place to go, and no cares to care about. I felt no tension in any way. I was simply *being*, floating on a blissful and loving cloud.

Ever so slightly, my awareness began to observe the surroundings of my mind. As I looked up and around, I could see a circle of blurs of energy in the space around me. There were beautiful, energetic beings all around me with no features or physical bodies. They were just orbs of energy gleaming with a very slight prism of colors, gently floating next to each other in a circle that surrounded me.

I felt myself gently rising up to join them, and as I looked back below me, I could see myself huddled in a ball, rocking back and forth, suffering.

I fully realized something I had never experienced: the absence of conflict, anxiety, and suffering.

I was no longer suffering.

Tears of immense joy flowed from my eyes, and I began to cry aloud, deeply breathing in and wailing on each exhale.

The release was blissful.

The most profound understanding of my existence began to flow through my being like a tuning fork.

There was not just the absence of conflict—there wasn't even the *possibility* of conflict.

My smile returned as I breathed into this realization. It was a reinforcement of a realization so true and so powerfully clear and pure, it was as if I had always known it and never questioned it.

God is love.

All of my searching and seeking throughout my life led me to this moment. I was being consciously tethered to a spiritual awakening that was profound and tangible. I was in the presence of the Source of All Things, and I was no longer bound to my physical existence; I was pure and vibrant energy.

It felt as though my soul had retrieved me.

My Final Encounter with Grandmother Ayahuasca

Over the course of about four years, I participated in a total of nineteen ayahuasca journeys. A few times, I was able to attend two in a single weekend.

I can't speak for other participants, but each experience for me was initially turbulent. Then, I was delivered again to the very same peaceful place where I found myself observing my suffering. And each time, I felt Glad's presence.

On my last journey, I had two profound experiences.

The first had to do with an uncontrollable physical tic I had developed from a violent and traumatic event with my father at a young age. Whenever a recollection of the event triggered me, an electric shock lit up my nervous system like a set of Christmas tree lights. A charge of energy would bolt from the base of my spine up through my neck, causing a mild convulsion that made my head jerk slightly.

It was embarrassing at times, particularly when I was in important business meetings or giving a talk in front of an audience. Whenever it happened, I became adept at dropping my pen and picking it up the instant the tic would pop up. That, or I would put my hand on my neck as if it was stiff. I would keep talking, and most of the time, people would think nothing of it. As I grew older, this nervous tic became so familiar that I surrendered to it as something I couldn't change.

This all changed during my last ayahuasca journey.

As I observed my suffering once again from a clear and disembodied state, I wondered what more I was supposed to be learning from this. More importantly, what was I supposed to do with this repetitive insight?

Deep into the experience, I felt that familiar, energetic twinge spike up my spine. It darted through my neck and right through the top of my head. My head snapped to my left and then whipped to the right. It was so familiar I let it go without a thought.

Then, as I relaxed to let my nervous tic run its course, I noticed it was not dissipating in its intensity. This was new. Usually, I would shake it off and change my focus while doing some deep breathing, and the charge of energy would subside. A steady buzzing in my forehead and temples emerged as the sensation moved down my spine to my tailbone. This made me nervous and caused me to tense up.

My head whipped right and then left. And then again and again. It wasn't a violent action, but I could feel my body surging with energy.

About every eight to ten sets of motions from left to right, a surge of coherent energy shot straight up my spine into my forehead and temples. My neck would relax as my head nodded in a slow and intentional motion, and each time, I let out a long sigh. Something was happening, and all I could do was remain present and at the mercy of this beautiful energy I had never felt before.

I lay in the darkness, thrashing about for a good while. It was then I felt the presence of a palm across my forehead, then another on my chest, over my heart. It was the hands of the female Ayahuascero, Ena, who was co-leading our journey with her significant other, Howard. She began to sing angelically as Howard played a stringed instrument to her beautiful song. The rhythm of her singing was comforting as my relentless, energetic release continued to flow.

Her gentle presence and strength reassured me to stay present. She had entered my energetic field, attending to the incoherence but evoking and nurturing the coherent, healing energy darting through me.

My thrashing gradually subsided, and the coherent ease returned with a nod in the affirmative. Each time, I would let out a slow *"Yes"* as I exhaled. Finally, the thrashing stopped, and the chaotic energy completely transmuted into a profound feeling of oneness and ease.

As I sat up on my elbows, Ena took her hands off my chest and forehead and put them together in prayer, bowing her head to her fingertips.

"Thank you so much," I said emotionally.

"Namaste," she replied, and she sat in silence to allow us to acknowledge the profundity of my experience. Then, she stood and disappeared into the darkness.

I smiled in relief and felt Glad's energy greeting me with joy and love as I honored and connected with her.

The Purge

For eighteen of my nineteen journeys with Grandmother Ayahuasca, I could not surrender to the purge. There was something about surrendering to an infinite intelligence I didn't understand, and it prevented me from submitting. I would not succumb, and I wore it as a sign of my sovereignty.

On my nineteenth journey, I finally let go of virtually all of my resistance and my need for absolute control. This was my breakthrough. And, once again, my need for control conflicted with my need to not be controlled.

I laughed and shook my head as I recalled all of the times I had soldiered through severe convulsions to purge during my previous journeys.

It was clear I needed to let go, but this time, the medicine didn't cooperate. I felt okay with no sense of uneasiness. *Great, I'll force it out*, I thought. I needed to purge all of my toxic thinking and ways of being.

I sat up and pulled my bucket close to my side, noticing that my body felt energized and aligned. There was no way I could purge while feeling like this.

I took my bucket outside into a courtyard, and for the next hour, I tried everything to force my body to purge. Nothing worked, and my body was now resisting. Every so often, I would see someone open the curtain to check on me, and I would motion back that I was okay.

And then I felt a twinge in my stomach. Then another deep in my digestive tract. Within just a few moments, I developed severe discomfort and was forced to move back into the house to find the restroom through the darkness.

My expectations of what constituted a purge were all wrong. What needed to purge was not anything I had ingested in the previous hours. My body and soul needed to purge a lifetime of accumulated toxins, traumatic and somatic memories stored away in my being and throughout my neurology.

Every part of my body surrendered and released for at least a half hour. Walking back into the courtyard, I was lightheaded and completely drained of all tension in my body.

And the tic from my childhood trauma never returned.

As I sat with my experience, Grandmother Ayahuasca conveyed that I need not return for more journeys. I had mended what the medicine had intended to heal, and it was now time to venture further into the world with my newfound realizations.

Healing the Wounded Healer

After my journeys with ayahuasca, I continued exploring ways to heal and transcend my traumas and life experiences.

Ayahuasca had been intense but necessary to pierce my armor. My journeys served their purpose, but now, I felt the need to seek gentler ways of letting go into pure awareness.

I was invited by some friends to attend a retreat on the central coast of California, where I was introduced to kanna, a South African plant medicine. Kanna has been used for thousands of years to relax the body and mind into more tranquil states. I was told it also provides a profound, heart-opening euphoria to ease and transcend anxiety and trauma.

A close group of people welcomed me. They had been journeying together for many years. Our South American guide offered a wonderful mix of ancient knowledge and wisdom combined with a worldly understanding of what our modern society needs and craves: peace and calm.

I arrived at a beautiful home tucked into a rocky forest hillside south of Monterey. The view was breathtaking, and the crisp ocean air made for perfect sweater weather. Our hosts were gentle souls who had been part of a close group of medicine journeyers for several decades. They were welcoming and lovely people, and I trusted them instantly as they helped me find a place in the ample living space for the journey later in the evening.

From my ayahuasca journeys, I had accumulated a travel wrap of journey necessities: a prehistoric stone bowl for burning sage, my Afghan blanket from Danny, yoga mats, incense, loose yoga clothing, and sandals, all rolled and wrapped in a large sheepskin, held together by travel straps. I could easily throw it in my Jeep and travel anywhere along the California coast.

We began with a wonderful talk from our guide about respecting the medicine and the importance of meditating on our intention for being here.

As we each went before him to receive our medicine, he gently smiled and put his hands in prayer, fingertips to forehead. "Namaste."

Being very familiar with each other, most of the group snuggled together into a giant nest of blankets and pillows. Our guide smiled when he saw me sitting across the room alone and gestured with his hands to dive in if I chose to. I smiled as I acknowledged his gesture with my hands in prayer. I decided to stay present yet away from the group in order to enjoy their presence. I wanted to have a good amount of room for meditation and stretching. I settled into a nice area in the corner with a den a few feet away for yoga, just out of sight from the group.

As I came into the medicine, my breathing deepened, and my heart began to gently open. I melted into child's pose and felt my hips and ankles melt into the floor. There was no stiffness, and my joints opened with ease. My spine stretched long, and my elbows bent as my hands came together in prayer above the back of my head. My forehead melted into the floor. I began to breathe into the posture and felt a powerful settling of my energy as my being moved into complete alignment. I repeatedly groaned as I exhaled in a total release of all tension and disharmony.

I had found my place of solitude and wisdom and stayed in this posture for a good part of the evening. I named the modified child's pose *resting warrior*.

Settling further into the sensation of beautiful ease, my muscles relaxed, and my temples and jaw melted open. All I could do was let go, deeply breathe in, and exhale with an outward, "Ahh…"

Throughout the night, I followed the flow of self-care stretches and postures my body desperately needed. From resting warrior, I lay back over my calves with my shoulders to the floor into a sleeping hero posture. I had not been able to access this full posture without a prop for decades. I fused further into gratitude.

I went through a series of twisting and stretching postures; my being was on fire for more. My Afghan blanket became drenched in my sweat, but I kept it wrapped around me, radiating warmth from my core.

What I enjoyed most about my kanna experience was the solitude and tranquility of being with myself. Journeys with kanna helped me access deeper and broader levels of openness and wisdom. Once again, I found I could tether myself easily to deep and lasting states of consciousness.

Ayahuasca was powerful medicine, and Veterans were traveling across North and South America to participate in the journey. Still, I had concerns about suggesting Veterans sit in dark rooms with strangers all around them while in the hands of Grandmother's powerful medicine. It just felt too risky.

Now, having experienced kanna, I could see how this gentle, heart-opening medicine would guide people with trauma through to their soul's retrieval much more safely. I began participating in kanna journeys with small groups of transitioning Combat Veterans I had come to know very well over the years and determined it was a preferable first exposure to plant medicine.

Over a period of about two years, I assisted in five journeys with a core group of men who were civilian friends and Combat Veterans. The experiences were incredibly rewarding, and I was fortunate to witness the personal transformation of every person who participated. The consistency of their ability to access the heart field and transcend their traumas and military bearing provided countless gentle breakthroughs.

The transformation of these hardened, wounded warriors as they returned to boys physically, emotionally, and spiritually have been among the most rewarding experiences of my existence. Each Veteran lost five to ten years off their face, and their wrinkles and frowns relaxed into gentle eyes and warm smiles.

Plant medicines healed my soul, heart, and body. Today, I can honestly say I feel a deep sense of ease and a profound level of joy.

Now, all of my senses are open, and there is nothing left but to be. As sure as the sunrise, Glad's wisdom has always been true. God is love.

Harvesting Wisdom

"Our experiences are here to serve us, not to master us."
—JIM ROHN, Author of *Seasons of Life*

I could say I wish my parents never met on that bus ride from Tulsa to Phoenix, but then again, I would not have been born to write these words.

Reflecting on my journey has allowed me to remove the remaining burdens from my past that have weighed heavily. I now leave them behind, appreciating their lessons and how they have helped me grow—how they have served me.

Reducing and releasing the burdens of regret and shame has brought both a sense of liberation as well as vulnerability.

Whenever I have felt entirely inadequate to write and share this work, I recall a quote from Marianne Williamson:
"Our deepest fear is not that we are inadequate. Our deepest fear is that we are powerful beyond measure."

I am also thankful for Steven Pressfield, author of *The War of Art: Break Through the Blocks and Win Your Inner Creative Battles.* This work helped me understand the many faces of resistance writers and artists experience when bringing their works from a vision into reality. I was not alone in the sleepless nights of doubting myself, despairing over making little progress that often stretched for weeks and months. It was helpful to hear Steven's message over and over, as I listened to his audiobook repeatedly.

Had it not been for my relentless pursuit to become who I was meant to be by harvesting the wisdom from my life experiences, this book would still be a rambling list of hopeful ideas in my head, never to see the light of day.

To you, the reader, the listener: I began this endeavor with only a glimpse of what would pour out onto the pages, and I felt tremendous doubt you would have the fortitude to reach this final chapter.

Perhaps there is a work of art in you as well that you have been resisting until you are old enough, good enough, successful enough—which, of course, is bullshit. Your work could be in the form of writing a bestselling book, painting a masterpiece, living a dream, changing careers, or simply finding what brings you joy.

If you think you can't, *then you must!*

If you had a terrible and challenging upbringing, this means you have the gift of empathy to understand the pain of others.

If you have lived in shame and regret, stop focusing on the images and home movies stuck in your head; stop projecting them into your future. Take your power back from focusing on your pain and limitations, and focus on who you are becoming. If necessary, break off the rearview mirror in the forefront of your mind and throw it in the trash because what is behind you is there to serve you, not master you.

There are countless reasons and rationalizations to keep ourselves small. Thank them for sharing and shift the focus of your attention toward the summit, taking one step at a time toward fulfilling your hopes and dreams.

Be a good example of what you can do with your life, no matter your circumstances or physical or emotional limitations, real or perceived.

Your life matters. You are here for a purpose, and it is up to you to discover this for yourself. Be of service to others, create your masterpiece, and by all means, fulfill your life's purpose.

If I could have provisioned myself early in life with some key insights and wisdom to aid me on my hero's journey, the short list would be as follows:

- Wisdom is the result of good judgment; good judgment is the result of experience; experience is the result of bad judgment (inspired by a quote by Mark Twain).

- The most universally potent and beneficial mantra for self-care and humility I have learned is: progress, not perfection.

- Your greatest teachers will meet you at the end of your rope—don't give up.

- Your most treasured life lessons will take root in your greatest challenges and suffering. The learning is in the struggle.

- Do what you fear most.

- Tame your monkey mind—its only job is to worry, doubt your potential, and keep you small.

- Nurture your rational, reasonable mind—it knows your highest good and what is best for you.

- Do whatever it takes to free your soul.

- Take new snapshots of yourself and others regularly to own and celebrate who you are becoming.

- Be the joy in everything.

- Be the dawn in the darkness.

We Live in the Land of Redemption

As divided as our country may seem,
there is one common thread that unites us still:
failure equals growth.

Because here,
we can reach far beyond our grasp and fall short
or fall on our face in order to learn what is required to succeed.

We don't get a free ticket because we were born here,
but we are born with the freedom and the right
to create our own destiny.

We get as many chances at success and happiness,
however we define this,
as we have the fortitude or stubbornness to attempt.

We don't rest on our shortcomings.
we get up every day
to be more, learn more, and do more to serve others
than the day before.

We learn, we grow, we evolve,
and take new snapshots of ourselves and our growth regularly
and do so with the people around us.

We are not our past.
we are the choices we now make
because of what we have learned along the way.
It is the freedom to engage in the relentless pursuit
of who we are becoming
that makes the journey worth our effort.

—J.H. PARKER

Author's Ending Note

Through pain and suffering, I have learned a simple truth:
bad things actually happened in my life.
But no matter how difficult, traumatizing, or heartbreaking,
nevertheless,
I choose and deserve to live a fulfilling life.
I choose and deserve to be happy.
My day can still go from the heights of exhilaration to the depths of
despair if I let it.
But more and more often, and for longer periods of time,
I am awake; I am aware,
witnessing my thoughts, and the emotions that follow.
Therefore,
I choose healthy, realistic, and joyful thoughts
because of the power they hold for myself and others.
Lastly,
teachers are human and fall from the pedestals we put them on.
I am not here to teach
because I am deep in the journey of life, still,
to this moment, and forever.

I pen this work as a message of hope.
If you have made it this far,
perhaps, after all you've been through in your life,
you too can now believe:
God is love.
You deserve to live a fulfilling life,
and you deserve to be happy.

Glad's promises have been fulfilled:
I have discovered for myself
God is love,
and
I have found meaning and purpose in my life.

The End

About the Author

J.H. Parker has worked in the field of behavioral assessment analysis for more than three decades, helping business leaders and organizations recognize and accept how they get in their own way and what they can do about it. As a writer, John combines his passion for transformational and spiritual growth to convey personal life lessons with a narrative approach. As a survivor of childhood and adult trauma, he brings reality-based insight to the field of recovery and mental health. He is a former Marine and father of a fallen Army Veteran who served two deployments in Afghanistan.